PABLO PICASSO

THE ARTIST BEFORE NATURE

PABLO PICASSO
THE ARTIST BEFORE NATURE

Auckland City Art Gallery

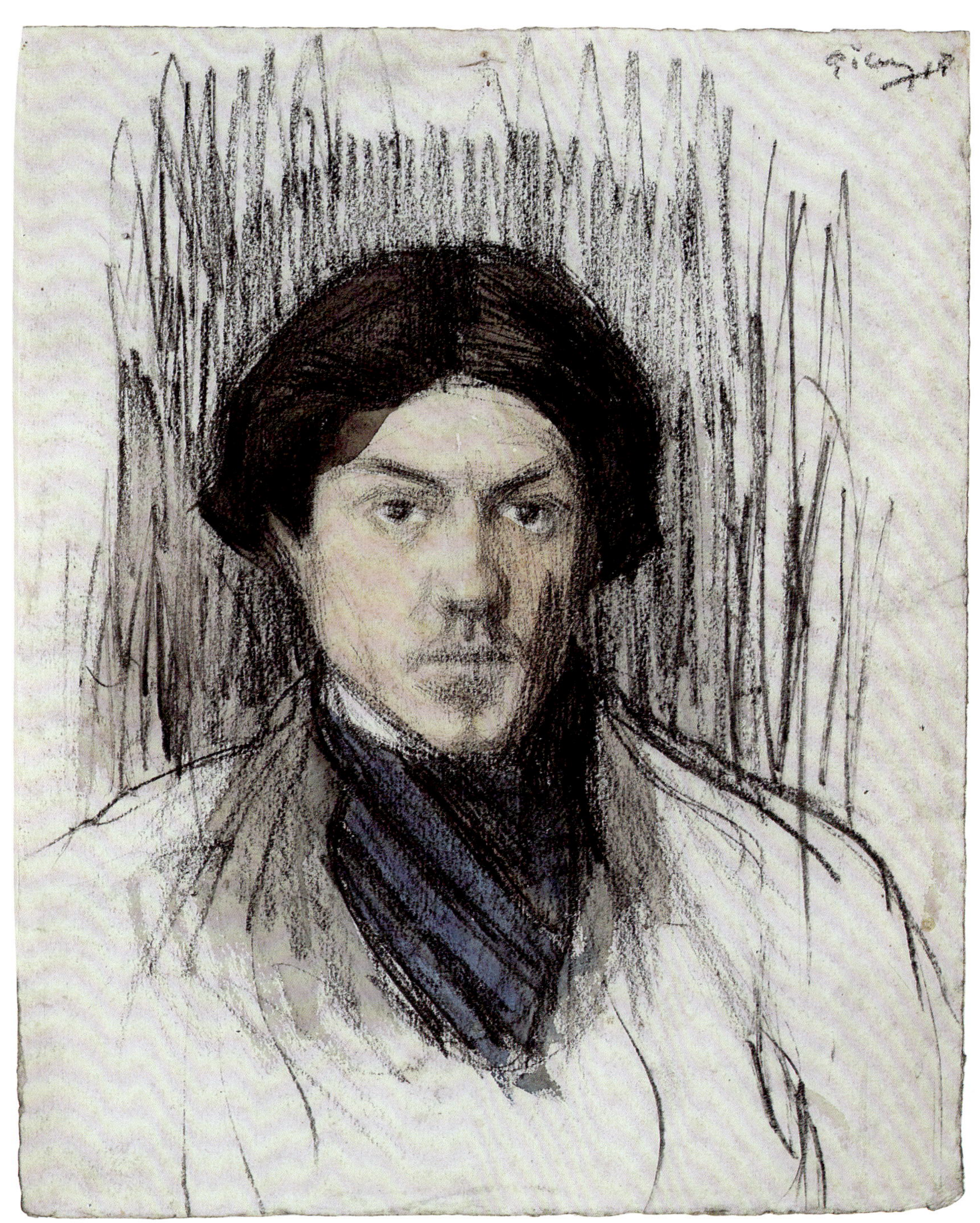

Published on the occasion of the exhibition *Pablo Picasso: The Artist Before Nature* held at the Auckland City Art Gallery 22 September–12 November 1989.

The exhibition is indemnified by the New Zealand Government through the Department of Internal Affairs.

Pablo Picasso: The Artist Before Nature is part of *Picasso: The Life, The Times, The Genius* Organised and presented by the Auckland City Art Gallery.

An **NZI** exhibition.

Exhibition selected by Marilyn McCully.

Cover illustrations: (front) Picasso. *The painter and his model*, 1963. Collection Marina Picasso (no. 58). *(back)* Picasso in his studio in rue Schoelcher, Paris, in 1915. Picasso Archives, Paris.

First published in New Zealand in 1989 by the Auckland City Art Gallery, 5 Kitchener Street, PO Box 5449 Wellesley Street, Auckland

Typeset in Helvetica by KY Books & Art, Hammersmith

Designed, edited & produced by Michael Raeburn, KY Books & Art

Colour and monochrome reproduction by Summerfield Press, Florence

Cartography by ML Design, London

Printed and bound in New Zealand by Academy Press Ltd, Mount Eden, Auckland

ISBN 0 86463 167 7

Contents

Foreword

Christopher Johnstone
Director, Auckland City Art Gallery

This catalogue serves as both a record and an accompaniment to the exhibition *Pablo Picasso: The Artist Before Nature*, the culmination of the Auckland City Art Gallery's long endeavour to give New Zealand a comprehensive introduction to the twentieth century's greatest artist, Pablo Picasso. Despite his enormous production and because of the increasingly high value of individual works by the artist, the difficulties of gathering together representative works covering the whole of his long career have been considerable. Yet the richness and diversity of the present show have been made possible through the extraordinary generosity of our lenders, who are so often called upon to share works from their collections with institutions around the world. Because of these demands, it seems altogether probable that this Picasso exhibition may well be one of the last representative shows of its kind. Nonetheless, New Zealanders now have the opportunity to see and study at first hand important works from every stage of Picasso's development.

This is the first time that an exhibition of paintings, sculpture and drawings by Picasso has been shown in New Zealand, and it follows the fine print exhibitions at the Gallery in 1958 and 1964 (from the Galerie Louise Leiris, Paris), and in 1973 (organised by the International Committee of the Museum of Modern Art, New York); and the *Vollard Suite* exhibition at the Waikato Museum of Art and History in 1988 (from the collection of the Australian National Gallery).

After *Claude Monet* in 1985, Picasso was an obvious choice for the next career survey of an artist of undoubted world significance. *Constable* (1974), *Van Gogh in Auckland* (1975), *Monet* and *Canaletto* (1986) do not in themselves suggest an ineluctable and inevitable progress towards Picasso. But these, among many other international exhibitions, have added significantly to the Gallery's reputation and inspired genuine enthusiasm for what Auckland is doing. They have paved the way for the sympathetic response to our many loan requests around the world and the positive and enthusiastic agreement to lend from those public and private collections listed in this catalogue.

Throughout this time the Auckland City Council, through the Art Gallery Board, has given its unwavering backing to the Gallery's enterprise, and we thank, in particular, Her Worship the Mayor of Auckland, Dame Catherine Tizard; Councillor Elizabeth Currey, Chairman of the Art Gallery Board; Bruce Anderson, Chief Executive; Donne Bagley, Acting Town Clerk; and Vern Warren, former Director of Planning and Community Development. As New Zealand's largest city and, arguably, its artistic capital, only Auckland has the Gallery and population to support the extensive programme of international exhibitions, of which *Picasso* is the most significant. Most of these exhibitions, furthermore, have toured to other museums around the country, and we had always hoped that *Picasso* would do so too. However, the extreme difficulty of borrowing the works that we wanted regrettably precluded a tour if the exhibition was to be achieved at all.

The Gallery could not have contemplated the organisation of *Pablo Picasso: The Artist Before Nature* without the indemnity provided by the New Zealand Government. We are pleased to record our grateful thanks to Dr Michael Bassett, Minister of Arts and Culture, Peter Boag, Secretary of the Department of Internal Affairs, and his staff in the Arts and Cultural Heritage Division for their support and assistance.

Also important in the development of *Picasso* is our sponsor, NZI. NZI and the Gallery have, for several years, joined in partnership to bring major international art exhibitions to New Zealand,and we are extremely fortunate to have the continuing support of NZI for *Picasso* through this country's most significant visual arts sponsorship arrangement. We thank the Chairman, Norman Johnston, and the Board of Directors, Harry Kember, Managing Director, and especially acknowledge Owen Cook, Corporate Affairs Adviser, for his dedicated enthusiasm for the exhibition from the very beginning.

Considerable credit is due to my predecessor, Dr T.L.Rodney Wilson, who initiated the exhibition by inviting Marilyn McCully to be its guest curator. In the earlier stages of the exhibition they worked together, with other members of the Gallery staff, especially Andrew Bogle, Curator of International Art, and established support for the exhibition from many quarters. Since then, building on the groundwork already laid, Dr McCully has worked in close contact with me and my colleagues to realise the present exhibition. Dr McCully's unfailing and enthusiastic commitment to the exhibition is the primary reason for its success, and we owe her a debt of considerable gratitude.

On behalf of the Art Gallery Board and the staff of the Gallery I warmly thank all the lenders, who are listed on the next page, and express our grateful appreciation for their generosity in agreeing to part with their treasures. And I acknowledge, furthermore, our colleagues at the lending museums and galleries, who greatly contributed to the smooth organisation of the exhibition by promptly and patiently responding to requests for information, documents and photographs, sending them speedily from one side of the world to the other.

The Musée Picasso in Paris was one of the first institutions to agree to lend to the exhibition, and we are especially grateful for the sympathetic support of its Chief Curator, Pierre Georgel, and, latterly, his successor, Gérard Régnier, as well as for assistance given by the authorities of the Réunion des Musées Nationaux. Thanks to them, the single most generous loan to our exhibition is of works that were in Picasso's own collection until his death.

In addition, for their substantial loans and help, I have a special need to acknowledge the following: Jean-Hubert Martin, Director of the Musée National d'Art Moderne, Paris; M. Maurice Jardot of the Galerie Louise Leiris, Paris; Mme Marina Picasso and the Galerie Jan Krugier, Geneva and New York; James Demetrion, Director, the Hirshhorn Museum and Sculpture Garden, Washington, D.C.; Ken Hood, Acting Director, National Gallery of Victoria, Melbourne; Anne d'Harnoncourt, The George D.Widener Director, Philadelphia Museum of Art; Dr Vitali Souslov, Deputy Director, State Hermitage Museum, Leningrad; Kirk Varnedoe, Chief Curator, Museum of Modern Art, New York; and Maria Teresa Ocaña, Director, Museu Picasso, Barcelona.

Special thanks are also due to the unnamed private collectors and their agents, especially to a private collector in the United Kingdom, who has supported the exhibition from its inception.

Throughout the development of the exhibition the Gallery has received continuous support and encouragement from the Ministry of External Relations and Trade, the French Embassy, Wellington, and New Zealand's Embassies in Paris and Moscow.

Our thanks are also due to Tony Green, Professor of Art History at the University of Auckland for his stimulating contribution to the catalogue; and to M. Michel Leiris for giving us permission to reprint the essay by D.-H. Kahnweiler, originally written for the first Picasso exhibition to be held in New Zealand.

The editing, design and efficient production of this handsome catalogue is the result of the skill, knowledge and experience of Michael Raeburn of KY Books & Art, London.

My final thanks must go to all my colleagues at the Gallery, in particular my secretary, Julie Koke, for their professional dedication to what, at times, may have seemed an impossible task.

Lenders to the Exhibition

Art Gallery of New South Wales, Sydney
Art Gallery of Ontario, Toronto
Auckland City Art Gallery
Australian National Gallery, Canberra
Cleveland Museum of Art
Hirshhorn Museum and Sculpture Garden, Smithsonian Institution, Washington, D.C.
Musée National d'Art Moderne, Paris
Musée Picasso, Paris
Museu Picasso, Barcelona
The Museum of Modern Art, New York
National Gallery of Art, Washington, D.C.
National Gallery of Victoria, Melbourne
Philadelphia Museum of Art
Queensland Art Gallery, Brisbane
Scottish National Gallery of Modern Art, Edinburgh
Staatsgalerie Stuttgart
State Hermitage Museum, Leningrad
Collection Marina Picasso, Galerie Jan Krugier, Geneva
Ernst Beyeler, Basel
Didier Imbert, Paris
Foundation Prince M., Zurich
Lefevre Gallery, London
Galerie Louise Leiris, Paris
Private Collection, England
Private Collection, Switzerland
Private Collections, Sydney, Courtesy Rex Irwin Art Dealer, Sydney

Acknowledgements

The Auckland City Art Gallery would also like to acknowledge the following people and institutions that have contributed to the creation of the exhibition and to this catalogue. To any whom we have inadvertently omitted from this list we offer our apologies:

H.E. John McArthur, New Zealand Ambassador, Moscow

H.E. Judith Trotter, New Zealand Ambassador, Paris

Jane Kominik, Jonathan Keate, Martin Durrant, Sarah Ingrams, Arts and Cultural Heritage Division, Department of Internal Affairs

Simon Orme, Ministry of External Relations and Trade

Etienne Wermester and, subsequently, Jean-Pierre Jarjanette, Attaché Culturel et Scientifique, French Embassy, Wellington

Valeri Popov, Natalia Myshkova, Department of Foreign Relations, USSR Ministry of Culture, Moscow

Michael Turner, Academy Press, Auckland

Kay Vernon, Catherine Snowden, Art Gallery of New South Wales, Sydney

Catherine Spence, Maia-Mari Sutnik, Art Gallery of Ontario, Toronto

Douglas Druick, Peter Zegers, Paula Pergament, Art Institute of Chicago

Association Française d'Action Artistique

James Mollison, Warwick Reader, Michael Lloyd, Jane Hyden, Darryl Collins, Australian National Gallery, Canberra

Ernst Beyeler, Claudia Neugebauer, Galerie Beyeler, Basel

Max G. Bollag, Galerie Max G. Bollag, Modern Art Centre, Zurich

André Chenue & Fils, Transports Internationaux, Paris

Evan H. Turner, Tom Hinson, Delbert Gutridge, Cleveland Museum of Art

Joan Farras, European Translation and Touring Service, Auckland

Michael Gifkins

Hasenkamp Internationale Transporte, Frankfurt

Phyllis Rosenzweig, Margaret Dong, Douglas J. Robinson, Katherine M. Hopper, Hirshhorn Museum and Sculpture Garden, Smithsonian Institution, Washington, D.C.

Julia Harrison, I.C.I.

Didier Imbert, Gail Brenner, Didier Imbert Fine Art, Paris

Rex Irwin, Sydney

Desmond Corcoran, Penelope Pepper, The Lefevre Gallery, London

M. and Mme Jan Krugier, Simon Studer, Martine Jolibois, Galerie Jan Krugier, Geneva

Gudrun Harms, Kunstsammlung Nordrhein-Westfalen, Düsseldorf

Michel Leiris

Hardie Marks & Associates Ltd

Russell Bell, Marsh & McLennan

Mainstream/FCB

Isabelle Monod-Fontaine, Jean-Paul Améline, Musée National d'Art Moderne, Paris

Danièle Giraudy, Musée Picasso, Antibes

Marie-Laure Bernadac, Paule Mazouet, Musée Picasso, Paris

Julian Castellanos, Museo del Prado, Madrid

Magdalena Gual, Núria Rivero, Museu Picasso, Barcelona

Cora Rosevear, Thomas D. Grischkowsky, Richard L. Tooke, The Museum of Modern Art, New York

John Dick, Jonathan Mason, National Galleries of Scotland, Edinburgh

Andrew Robinson, Ysabel Lighter, Betty Spiro, Ira Bartfield, The National Gallery of Art, Washington, D.C.

Irena Zdanowicz, Phillip Jago, National Gallery of Victoria, Melbourne

Jacques André Wieser, Ofisa, Lausanne

Francesc Parcerisas

Nancy Quaile, Conna Clark, Philadelphia Museum of Art

Caroline Turner, Chris Saines, Douglas Hall, Queensland Art Gallery, Brisbane

Edward Quinn

Isabella Raeburn

Richard Calvocoressi, Keith Hartley, Margaret Mackay, Scottish National Gallery of Modern Art, Edinburgh

Ludovic Ginguay de Beaugendre, Isabelle Volf, Service Photographique de la Réunion des Musées Nationaux, Paris

G. P. Hanna, Simpson, Grierson Butler White

Richard Halstead, South Bank Centre, London

Dr Karin Frank von Maur, Staatsgalerie, Stuttgart

Boris Piotrovsky, State Hermitage Museum, Leningrad

Catrin Lundqvist, Statens Konstmuseer, Stockholm

Thekla Clark, Mara Puccini, Summerfield Press Ltd, Florence

Michael Sweeney

Stephen Trainor

Patrick McCaughey, Wadsworth Atheneum, Hartford

Photographs were, as a rule, supplied by the museums, galleries and owners of the works. We would, in addition, like to thank the following:

Bildarchiv preußischer Kulturbesitz, Berlin – photo Jörg P. Anders (ill. p.32)

Dominguez, Madrid (ill. p.13 *bottom*)

Galerie Louise Leiris, Paris (ill. p.21 top)

Arxiu Mas, Barcelona (ills. p.11 *left*, 22 *top*)

Lee Miller Archives – © 1985 (ills. p.22 *bottom*, 23 *left*, 58 *right*)

The Pace Gallery, New York – photo Al Mozell (ill. p.58 *left*)

Service Photographique de la Réunion des Musées Nationaux, Paris (all photographs of works in the Musée Picasso, Paris, and in the Picasso Archives there, and ill. p.25)

Statens Konstmuseer, Stockholm (ill. p.30)

Picasso Before Nature

Marilyn McCully

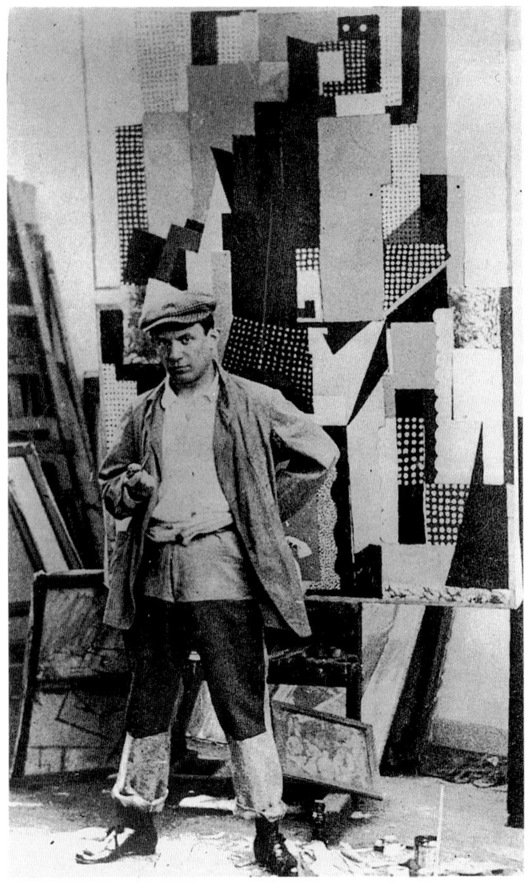

Picasso in his studio in rue Schoelcher, Paris, in 1915. Behind him is the *Man leaning on a table* (Private collection), completed the following year. Picasso Archives, Paris.

Note: Throughout the text works in the exhibition are referred to by catalogue number (no. . .).

In 1932 Picasso responded to a question concerning his approach to art, and in particular towards the traditional definition of art as the imitation of nature, with these words: 'It is not after nature I am painting, but before nature, with it.' Although he had been trained in late nineteenth-century academic methods, which were founded in the practice of copying after nature, from an early age Picasso defied traditional precepts in a search for an art that went beyond imitation without departing from reality. For Picasso imitating nature meant not the imitation of what nature had already created but the imitation of the act of creation itself.

His statement, however, reveals that in defying tradition Picasso was at the same time establishing himself as a part of that tradition. His anticipation of most major twentieth-century art movements and his impact upon them has obscured just how traditional an artist he was, notably in his choice of subject-matter and in his special regard for the history of art. By taking on some of the old masters by 'redoing them' in his late work, Picasso was effectively writing himself into that history as their worthy successor. Moreover, and in spite of the revolutionary implications of his work in the Cubist period, Picasso was never an abstract artist, no matter how deep his probing of the essence of art and its creation.

The works in this exhibition, all in their own ways, lead us deeper into the mystery of creation as Picasso discovered it through the process of making art. The very techniques he used were all rooted in traditional artistic practice, but he carried them to new lengths. The most important and sometimes most provocative of these techniques or artistic devices in Picasso's hands are: distortion, analysis and transformation. Indeed, if all of the works in the show are viewed as a whole and from the point of view of Picasso as an artist in the mainstream of art history – one with unbounded creative energy and with the ability to extend the expressive means of his craft – the conventional presentation of Picasso as an artist with many different styles (whether this is thought to make him a universal genius or just a quick-change artiste) is put into question. At different periods of his life many different influences – ranging from poetry and the history of art to personal or political events – colour and shape Picasso's many works, but in their essence they are still part of that same expressive whole that is the artist himself.

The expressive potential of artistic distortion in Picasso's early work had its roots, as in Picasso's work is generally the case, both in his own origins as a Spanish artist and in the prevailing intellectual and artistic currents of his own time. The

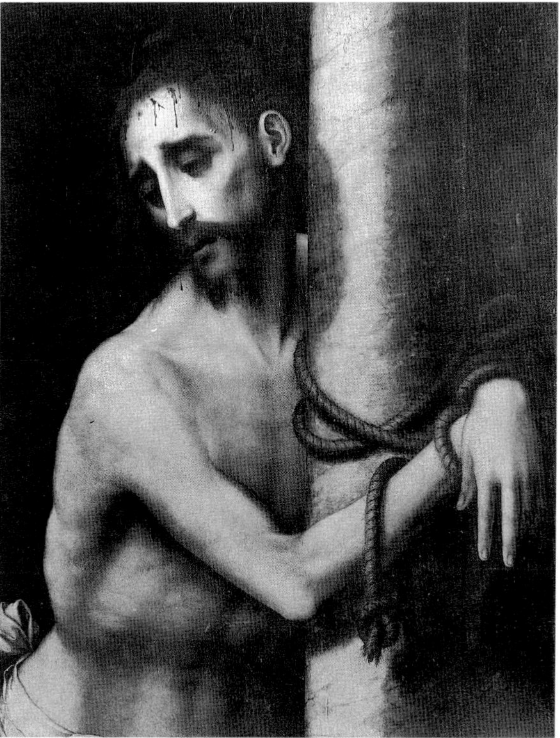

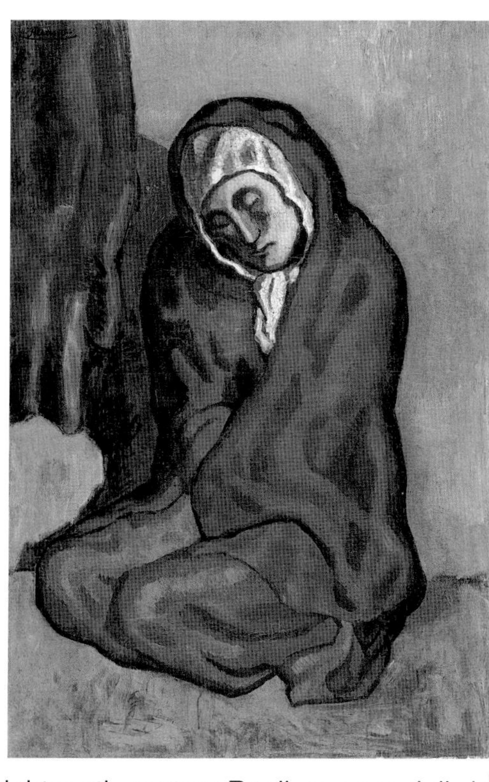

Left: Luís Morales. *Christ at the column*, second half of the sixteenth century. Asensio collection, Madrid.

Right: Picasso. *Crouching woman*, 1902 (no.6).

high-pitched intensity of Spanish sixteenth- to eighteenth-century Realism, especially in religious paintings and sculpture, made their impact on the young artist, whose beginnings in Spain shaped so many of the directions his art and personality would take. The mannerist colours and elongated limbs of El Greco's saints and Madonnas as well as the tenebrist drama of Valdés Leal and Morales underlie the Blue period, in works such as *Crouching woman* (no.6). But his use of distortion to convey psychological mood also reflects his early exposure to fin-de-siècle symbolist painting and literature, initially among the Catalan artists and writers, the 'Modernistes', with whom he associated in Barcelona, in the late 1890s. Later, Picasso's use of distortion develops within new contexts, and he uses it as a kind of personal weapon or magic wand to express on the one hand frustration, anger or horror, and on the other to convey sexuality and love.

Picasso rarely worked closely with other painters – Braque is the great exception – although he lived at different times of his life with women artists (Fernande Olivier, Dora Maar and Françoise Gilot). He preferred instead to surround himself with literary types – poets, writers, dramatists – who stimulated his imagination far more than living artists; the case of the old masters is another story. In the twenties and thirties Picasso's association with the Surrealists, especially writers, fuelled his personal style, and he turned his own technique of distortion into an expressive device to unleash repressed feelings as well as a highly charged eroticism.

Marie-Thérèse Walter, who became Picasso's mistress in 1927, at a time when his marriage to Olga Kokhlova was becoming intolerable, was his principal muse during this 'Surrealist' period of his work. Most of his depictions of her youthful, curvaceous

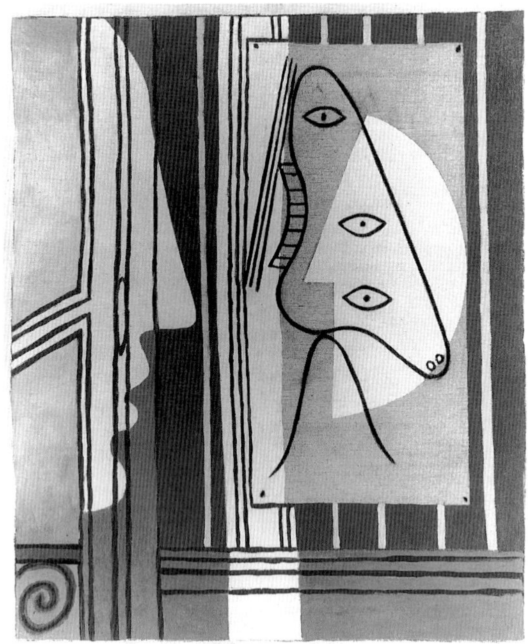

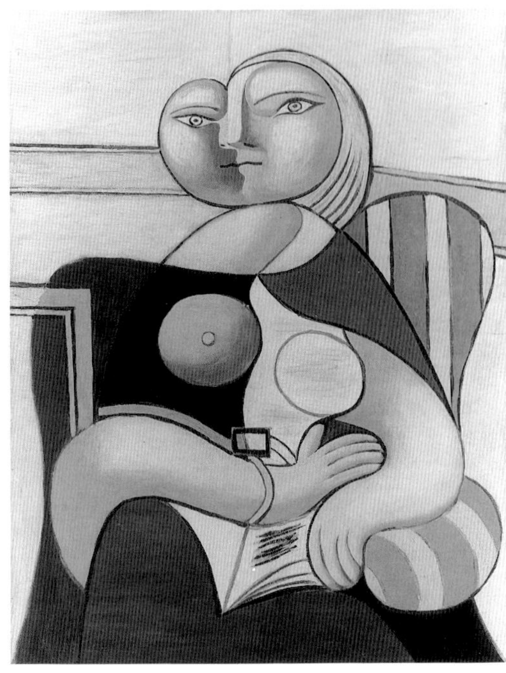

Left: Picasso. *Figure and profile*, 1928 (no.27).
Right: Picasso. *Reading*, 1932 (no.29).

body are lyrical and tender while openly sexual (no.29); they contrast sharply with the protruding teeth, eyes on top of each other, and schematised stringy hair of the angry heads of Olga, which are distorted into screaming monsters – sometimes set against the cool, implacable profile of the artist himself (no.27).

Throughout his work, Picasso remained attached to traditional subject-matter. Following his Spanish heritage, he was primarily a figure painter and occasionally a painter of *bodegones* (still lifes), rarely a landscape painter. While his predecessors of the Golden Age of Spanish art had used the human figure to express mysticism and revelation, Picasso channelled his own emotions, personal experiences and enormous energy into his subjects to express his own as well as universal human experience. In the case of still-life painting, Spanish artists such as Zurbarán or Sánchez Cotán had endowed objects with intellectual or religious meaning, and in a sense this attitude towards the painting of objects can be seen both in Picasso's Cubist works and also in some of the highly emotional, sometimes symbolic still lifes of his later years. But it was the human figure – more often than not the woman who occupied the position as number-one mistress in Picasso's life (like a pasha, he managed to keep most of his women attached to him, partly through money, even when he had found someone to replace them) – that he used not only to act out his fantasies or express his innermost thoughts, but also as the vehicle for the ongoing development of his enormous creative power.

The works that Picasso produced in the decade that starts with the outbreak of the Spanish Civil War in 1936 are some of the most powerful statements of the universal horror of war as well as personal anguish. The fact that his use of distortion reaches its most extreme form in some of these is an indicator of the powerful response he felt to political events in his native land. The *Weeping women* of 1937 (e.g. no.38), whose features are based upon those of Dora Maar, communicate through tears, jarring colours

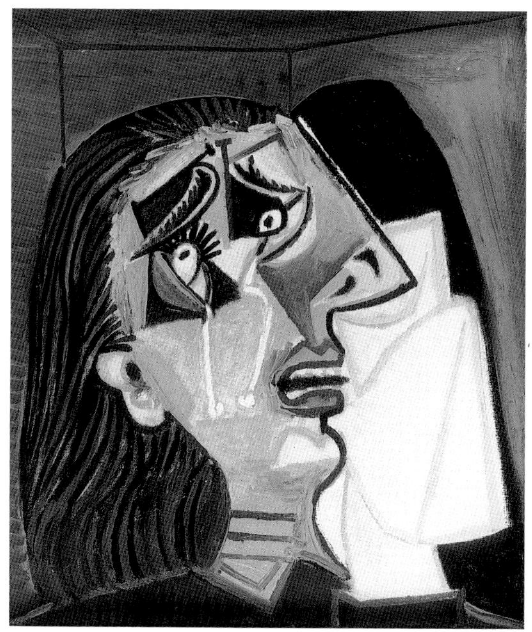

Picasso. *Weeping woman*, 1937 (no.38).

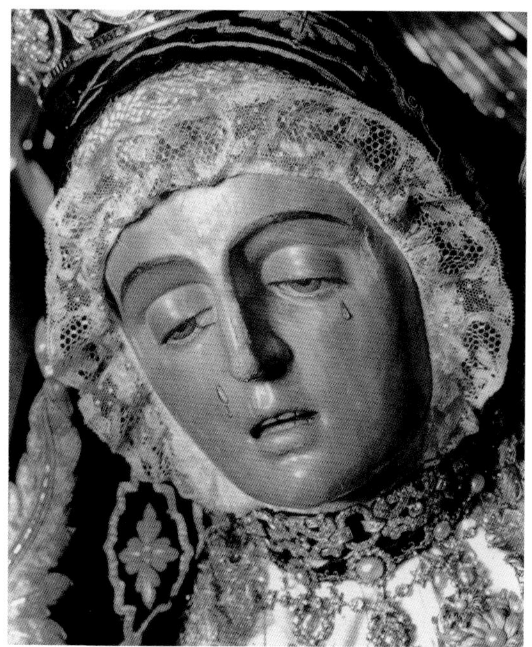

Detail of processional statue of Nuestra Señora de las Angustias, patron saint of Granada, sixteenth century. Church of N.S. de las Angustias, Granada.

and angularity of facial expression the agony of the innocent victims of war. At the same time, they reflect the emotions of the artist himself, whose support for the Republican cause led to his self-imposed exile from Spain for the rest of his life. But these grieving women attain a kind of universality that has few equivalents at any other point in the artist's career. In their essence as images of art, their emotional power lies in their origins among the painted wood, life-sized statues of the Madonna carried in Spain in religious processions, whose tears are jewels that sparkle as they run down their cheeks, and whose garments are real lace, velvets and silver – at once real and other-worldly.

Picasso's search for new ways of expressing the intensity of feeling never let up. Writing in 1945, his lifetime friend Jaime Sabartès saw Picasso, now in his sixties, 'still waging the same struggle with the problem of art, that cryptic language which seeks to summarise impressions, adding fantastic visions and memories of real images distorted by the imagination, for he does not copy from nature, but rather draws upon the resources of his memory.' (Sabartès, *Picasso: An Intimate Portrait*, London 1949, p. 40)

When faced with moments of artistic or personal crisis, Picasso typically exorcised them in his art, and the work done at Royan and Paris during the War communicates the intensity of that period and his need yet again to push his art in a new direction. Boldly executed still lifes (no.44) feature a skull, which both serves its traditional role as *memento mori* – Picasso's old friend Max Jacob, who died in a concentration camp, had once as a young man read Picasso's palm and predicted he would die at the age of 68; in fact, it was Jacob who died at that age – and expresses the state of humanity at a time when emotion is bared to its most profound essence. Equally, everyday still-life objects, fish (no.39) or cockerels, for example, through their vivid, even violent presence in his work, are able to convey the basic needs of man, as well as anger and want.

In his late years, the expressive power of sexuality, which often echoes the great erotic tradition in oriental art before him, is channelled into Picasso's works with uncompromising directness – he is one artist who, through distortion, can show us every orifice, every nuance or curve of both the front and back of his lover's body at the same time (e.g. no.54). In many works great tenderness is communicated through embraces that enclose figures in their erotic worlds and kisses which turn lovers for a moment into a single being (see ill. p.58). The acrobatics of some of the actors in these works – the artist and his model, the old man and his pubescent companion, or the Spanish gentleman serenading his duchess – are inspired in part by wrestlers Picasso watched on television; but their antics are only part of the physical drama which finds ever more daring challenges in feats of artistic invention.

* * * *

Picasso's legendary reputation as an artistic revolutionary came with his role alongside Braque as co-inventor of Cubism at the end of the first decade of this century. But from the purified still lifes done in Saint-Raphaël and Paris in 1919 and 1920 (no.23) or his Neo-classical work (nos.21, 22) right down to the very last paintings, prints and drawings, it is evident that the lessons of Cubism – especially in the rendering of spatial relationships and the possibilities of revealing different aspects of objects or their making – establish the general format and direction of all Picasso's work. No matter how radical the distortions or mysterious the transformations in his art, the analysis of form guides the mind of the painter. Picasso's great mural for the Spanish pavilion in Paris in 1937,

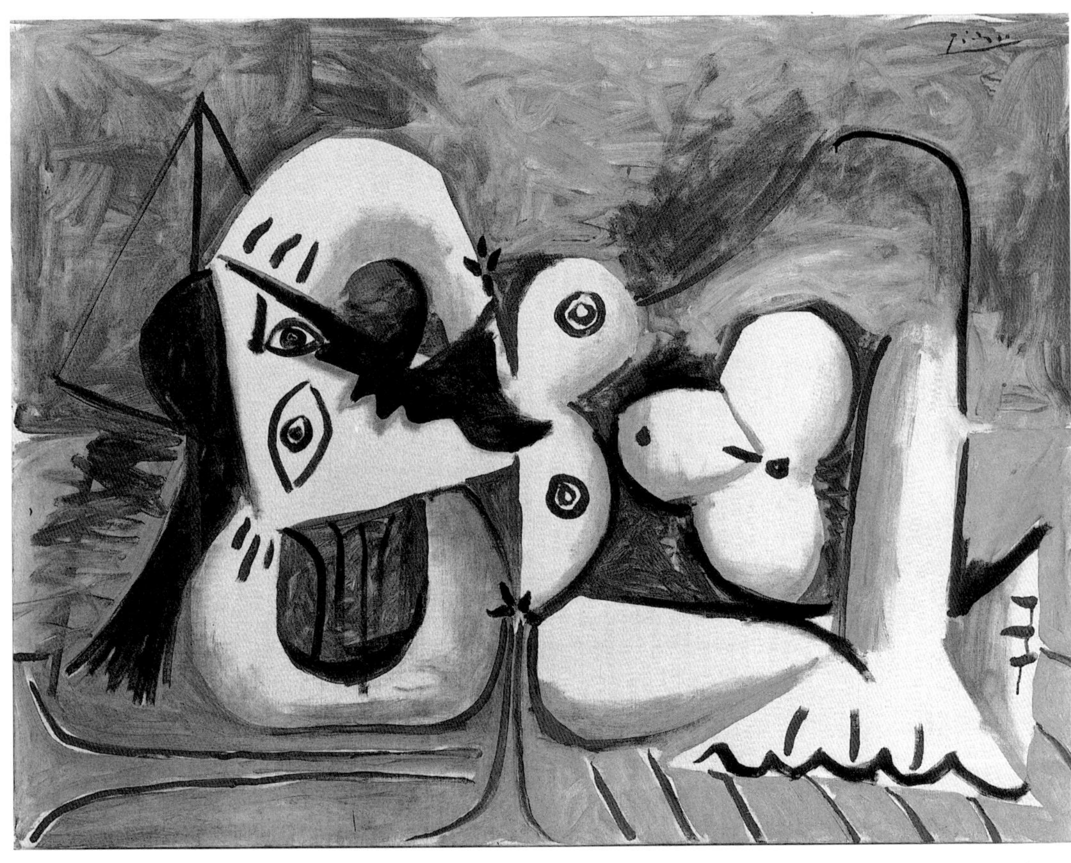

Right: Picasso. *Reclining nude on a blue divan*, 1960 (no.54).

Below: Picasso. *Head of a man*, 1908 (no.15).

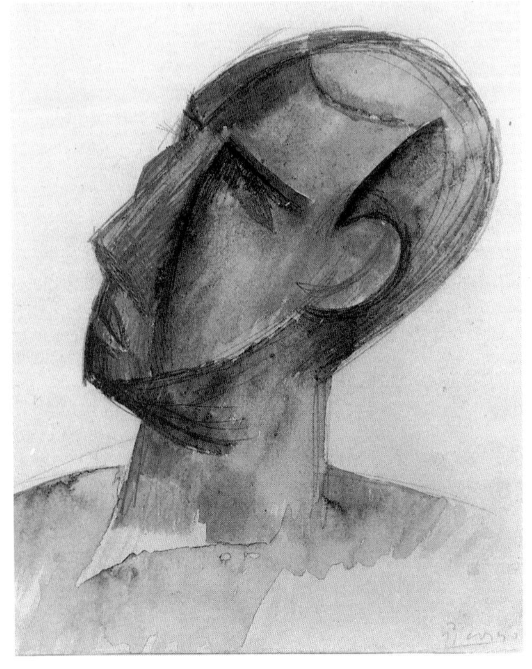

Guernica (see ill. p.50), is essentially a huge cubist space, which can be read as both out of doors (as suggested by a burning house and the lengendary oak tree of the town) and indoors (indicated by corners of a room and a light bulb hanging from a ceiling) at the same time, while the victims, whose gestures are reduced to flattened expressive shapes and outlines, occupy this shallow world in which there is no escape from war.

Soon after his arrival in Paris at the start of the century, Picasso began to explore the techniques of analysis as an approach to painting in the work of artists such as Poussin, Ingres and, closer to his own time, Cézanne, all of whom were questioning the representation and inherent meanings of forms and pictorial space, and whose work implies a level of abstraction as a form of analysis. The harmonious juxtapositions of figures, gestures and objects in the complex compositions of Poussin (see ill. p.25), or the technique of an economical line such as Ingres used to model and at the same time imply space or volume by its absence, appealed to Picasso when he first discovered the traditions of French painting, so different from his own Spanish heritage.

In the example of Cézanne he and Braque found the key to their developing analytic approach, precisely because in his painting they discovered Cézanne moving away from the world of illusion to a view that more closely approximated reality in the pictorial world. In his insistence on the basic processes of painting itself to achieve this, Cézanne was approaching the kind of 'truth' they were seeking in their own work.

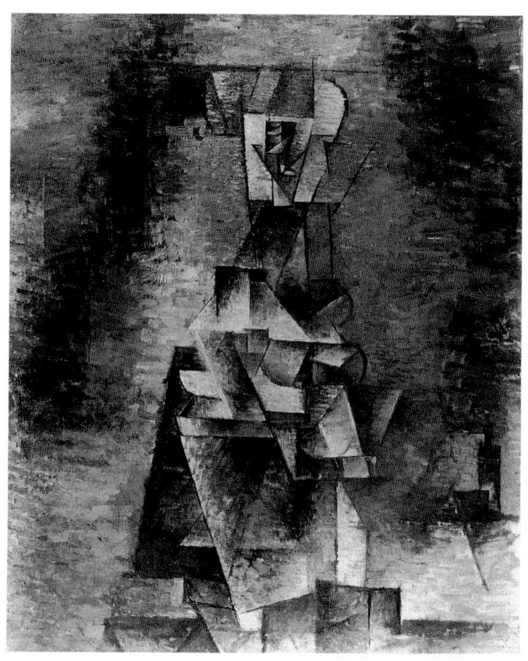

Picasso. *Half-length female nude*, 1910 (no.18).

Picasso once commented on the primary aims that he and Braque shared during the Cubist years: '. . . when we devoted ourselves to our creations we produced "pure truth", without pretentions, without tricks, without malice. What we did then had never been done before: we did it disinterestedly, and if it is worth anything it is because we did it without expecting to profit from it. We sought to express reality with materials we did not know how to handle . . . we surrendered ourselves to it completely, body and soul' (Sabartès, *op. cit.,* p. 212).

In spite of the direction towards abstraction that Picasso appeared to be taking – especially after his trip to Horta de Ebro during the summer of 1909 (no.17) – by reducing forms and space to geometric signs or relationships, his conviction that Cubism was essentially a probing into the essence of real things is at the heart of even the most hermetic works. The idea of analysis is understood on several levels: first, that the object represented has multiple aspects (in time as well as in actuality) and that these are all valid; secondly, that the very process of making art – of representing the object – may be dissociated from traditional method, so that light and shadow, for example, may function independently rather than simply serve their traditional role in painting of suggesting volume or shape; and, thirdly, that aspects of the painterly process can co-exist with the object represented at the same time. For obvious reasons, story-telling is not an aim of the Cubists; presenting the truth is. Using the traditional subject-matter of painting – figure, still life and landscape – Picasso and Braque conveyed information about the objects or their setting in the same way that they represented their form or their position in relation to each other.

Cubism began with this process of analysis, but moved on to synthesis – the depiction of subjects by the assemblage of elements. In Synthetic Cubism the number of informational signs was reduced – only a few aspects of shape or colour or light or even lettering (functioning as yet another two-dimensional element) are indicated – and these have an independent reality as they combine to create a whole. While many of these signs – the various angles of a table or repeated curves, for example, which are used to convey the rim of a glass, an ear or the edge of a violin – are, in a sense, abstracted, they are essentially as close to the truth of the object as Picasso can get without losing reality altogether.

Picasso. *Head*, 1913 (no.20).

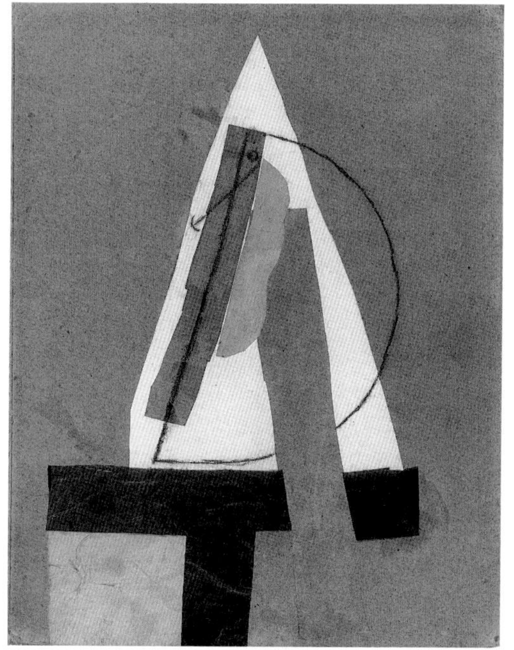

In Picasso's statement above, he mentions the adventure of using non-traditional materials, which in Synthetic Cubism included *papiers collés* (simply pasted-on paper, usually combined with drawing), collage (paper as well as textural ingredients, such as sand or marble dust mixed in paint) or constructions, including metal, wood and actual objects (the sugar spoon, for example, in the *Absinthe glass* series). In these the reality of the material functions on an informational level as well as on an aesthetic one. To free ordinary materials themselves from the world of everyday use and bring them into the realm of art was a radical step taken not only by Picasso and Braque (whose own background acquainted him with techniques of commercial painters) but also by contemporary artists and musicians such as Duchamp and Satie, who similarly appropriated non-traditional materials or things (or sounds, in the case of music) in their work. Today it is difficult to assess the impact of this development, precisely because of the enormous effect it has had, especially in the world of commercial art, on our approach to the visual world, to art and to the language of signs. Nevertheless, the radical implications of this way of working still have the power to provoke responses of incomprehension or dismissal.

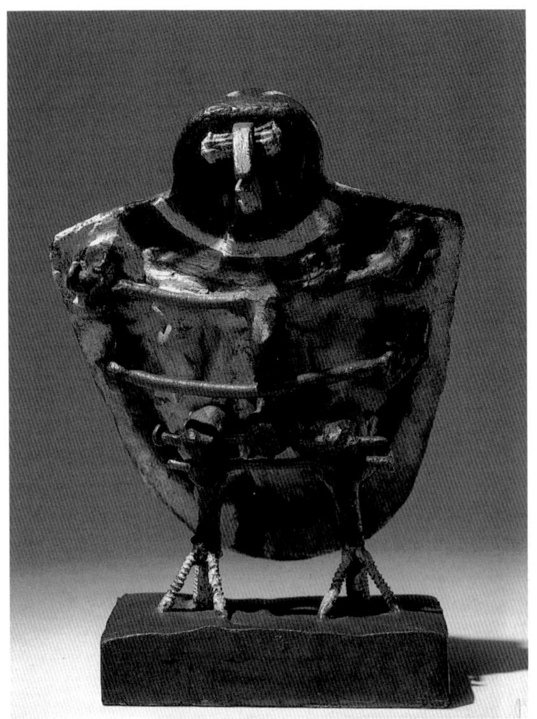

Picasso. *Little owl*, 1951–3 (no.48).

Implicit in Synthetic Cubism are the ideas of transformation: that one thing can stand for another or several other meanings; and that the process of creation also adds to the understanding of the object, or, as the case may be, its ambiguity. Later, in some of Picasso's sculpture, such as in his series of painted bronze owls (no.48), the use of non-traditional materials, including screws and nails (for claws and legs), not only brings humour to the object but conveys the way in which materials themselves are transformed into art.

The notion of transformation is different from distortion in Picasso's work, for rather than heightening the expression of emotion through the manipulation of form or colour, transformation plays the much more ambiguous role of suggesting alternative meanings. In his early work, up to the poetic acrobats of the so-called Rose period (no.11), Picasso's exposure to symbolist literary trends had acquainted him with the notion of suggestion (rather than description) in art and poetry as well as with esoteric thinking, in which objects can signify more than one thing. Gauguin's personal exploration of the inherent symbolic potential of forms and colours themselves – in addition to his use of symbolic imagery – had also stimulated Picasso's own concerns with the power of artistic symbolism; only Picasso wanted to rid his subjects of traditional symbolism or allegory in favour of new meaning – something closer to modern experience.

Picasso's Blue period canvases, such as *La Vie* (see ill. p.41 and no.7) or *The two sisters*, are good examples of the way in which he drew upon associations with Spanish religious allegory as well as fin-de-siècle symbolism. The use of conventional signs derives from formalised gestures or figural confrontations, each with a specific meaning in Christian iconography; in their new context, one in which mood is evoked through the overall blue palette, simplified form and smoothly painted surfaces, the allusion to religion remains, but it is devoid of specific content.

Picasso's formative acquaintance with late nineteenth-century philosophical, literary and artistic symbolism was of enormous importance to him in a larger sense. By 1906–07, at the time when he was developing his first truly revolutionary composition, *Les Demoiselles d'Avignon* (see ill. p.42), he was able to harness both the raw, symbolic power of primitive art and also the formal structure of traditional European art to his own ideas about contemporary life.

Apart from the world of symbols, transformation can also reveal secret affinities. By means of an analysis of the way in which things are made, the relationships between these things and the affinities they possess are made more apparent. A good example, and one to which Picasso turned on many occasions throughout his work, is provided by mythological creatures such as the Minotaur. Because of its hybrid nature (head of a bull, body of a man), it is a creature that typifies the affinities that exist between man and the natural world. For Picasso as for the Surrealists, the Minotaur embodied the sexual drives of man controlled by animal instinct and unfettered by any human intellect.

One of the great mysteries of man's experience in the natural world, which is at the heart of much of mythology as it is of Picasso's art, is the process of creation itself: the idea of metamorphosis. In his sculptural assemblages such as *Baboon with young* (see ill. p.54), Picasso brings life to inert materials by transforming them into art, and the process by which he does it remains an integral aspect of the work itself. We share the artist's visual pun when we discover that the baboon's head is really a toy car, which Picasso

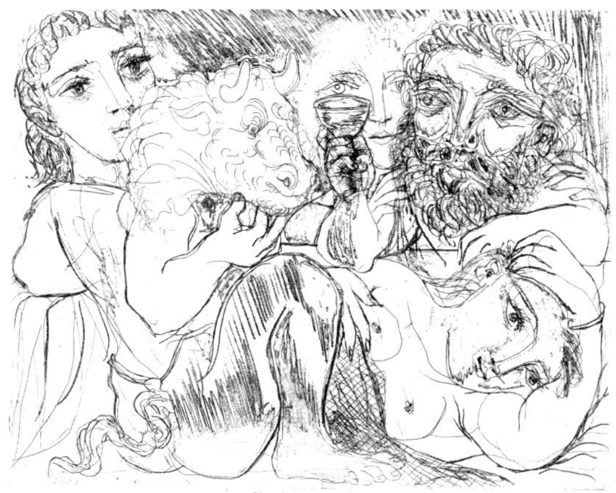

Picasso. *Minotaur, drinking sculptor and three models*, 1933 (no.34).

had appropriated from his son Claude. But it is precisely the undisguised combination of model car, pottery, metal and plaster in the original (Musée Picasso, Paris) before it was cast in bronze that conveys the process of the work of art's making – its own metamorphosis. In this way Picasso communicates not only something of the work of art's material existence, but also its transience – the changing aspect of nature.

From the time of the *Demoiselles d'Avignon*, Picasso started to make the work of art itself more open-ended. He began to approach things in series, so that each painting generates rather than supersedes the next. As he captured the idea of on-going development – something we can see in the overlay of paint or in the regrouping of compositions – Picasso gave life to things by creating them in process. In this sense the artist's use of transformation can be regarded as a still more determined attempt to represent reality, in that everything that is alive is in a state of constant change. For Picasso, with unshakeable belief in his own immortality, change meant not decay or abandonment (what looks unfinished), but, in its endless possibilities of variation, life itself.

After World War II Picasso's personal circumstances – now at the age of 65 with a new, young mistress (Françoise Gilot) – changed, and the joy he felt is reflected in the exuberant re-emergence of mythological themes – cavorting fauns, centaurs and exquisite nymphs in arcadian settings – and in his enormous burst of creativity and vast production. At a time when most of his contemporaries had settled into a tested formula or even retired, Picasso chose instead to probe the limits of his media, including printmaking, sculpture and ceramics, as well as painting and drawing.

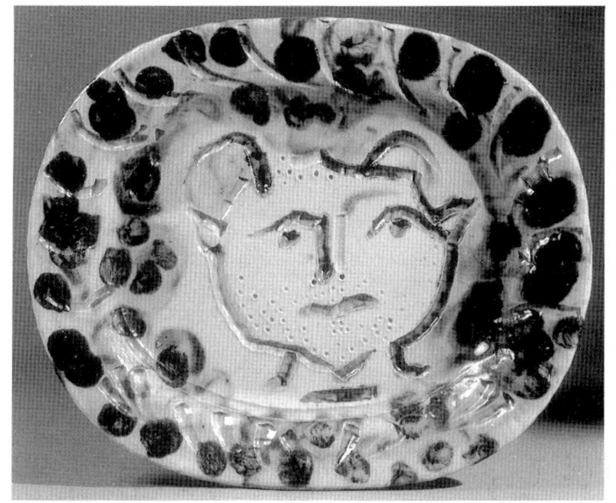

Picasso. *Head of a faun*, 1947 (no.45).

With Françoise Gilot, Picasso returned to the Mediterranean (where he lived for the rest of his life), and there he rediscovered the ancient pottery traditions of Vallauris. Collaborating with local craftsmen at the Madoura factory, the artist began working in ceramics in a way that further stimulated the idea of approaching art in a serial manner.

Before actually modelling ceramic forms, Picasso took the standard, press-moulded, earthenware plates made by Madoura potters as a starting point, and through experimentation (with glazes as well as the handling), he developed themes, such as the head of a faun (no.45) or the bullfight, so that each plate became a part of the developing idea, the process itself, while each one remained a unique work. True to the materials in one sense, they remain plates – not just surfaces imitating a canvas upon which to paint; but Picasso transforms them into art and turns them into fauns or toreros, while the immediate evidence of their making (such as fingerprints and gouges) and his probing of their material existence still evokes the ancient craft traditions of the Mediterranean.

This serial approach can be detected much earlier in Picasso's work, for it began simply as a practice method for the art-student. Carrying a sketchbook with him, he drew life as he saw it; but very quickly the drawings become merely the departure point, and subsequently they begin to arise out of each other, rather than as observations of nature. This practice, which is a constant in Picasso's art, is particularly fascinating in the twenties, when – in the spirit of the Surrealists – he makes use of accident in the development of his sequences: for example, the pressure of his pencil markings might leave an indentation on the following page, and the artist would then use that to start the next image, and so on. Or the head of Marie-Thérèse, so sensual and self-involved – her arms wrapping her head, her double profile looking both inwards and out again – might on the same page evolve into a skull-like, terrifying head of the angry wife, Olga. This

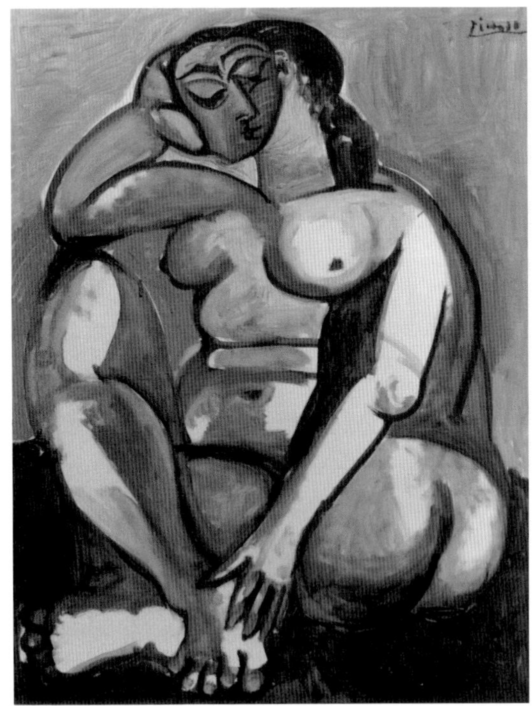

process of creation is what comes to the fore in the late work, the work of the last twenty years, which draws upon the whole of the artist's life for its inspiration.

From the mid-1950s, Picasso found himself yet again in the throes of personal disruption – Françoise had left with their two children, he had broken off his affair with the poet Geneviève Laporte, and a few years of playing the part of the most eligible bachelor on the Côte d'Azur did not really suit him. The entrance of Jacqueline Roque Hutin in the artist's life – they began to live together in 1954 and married in 1961 – coincided with his increasing personal seclusion and his determination to live a long life through work.

The Picasso legend had grown to such proportions by the time the artist turned 75 (in 1956), that in order to protect his privacy and to maintain the pace of work for which he felt an urgent need, the artist, now with Jacqueline as a buffer to his family (much to their increasing dismay) and the world (Picasso was besieged by reporters, old acquaintances, collectors and the like, all demanding a bit of his time, if not a bit of his work), he remained more and more tied to his life in his studio. The fact that so much of the late work is about the female nude (Jacqueline), the artist in his studio (himself), art history and Picasso's own art history, is a reflection both of his artistic preoccupations in old age and also of the way in which he actually lived and worked during those years. But most importantly, by keeping his work open-ended, by constantly reinventing his own art, Picasso believed he could stay alive.

Above: Picasso. *Crouching woman*, 1956 (no.51).

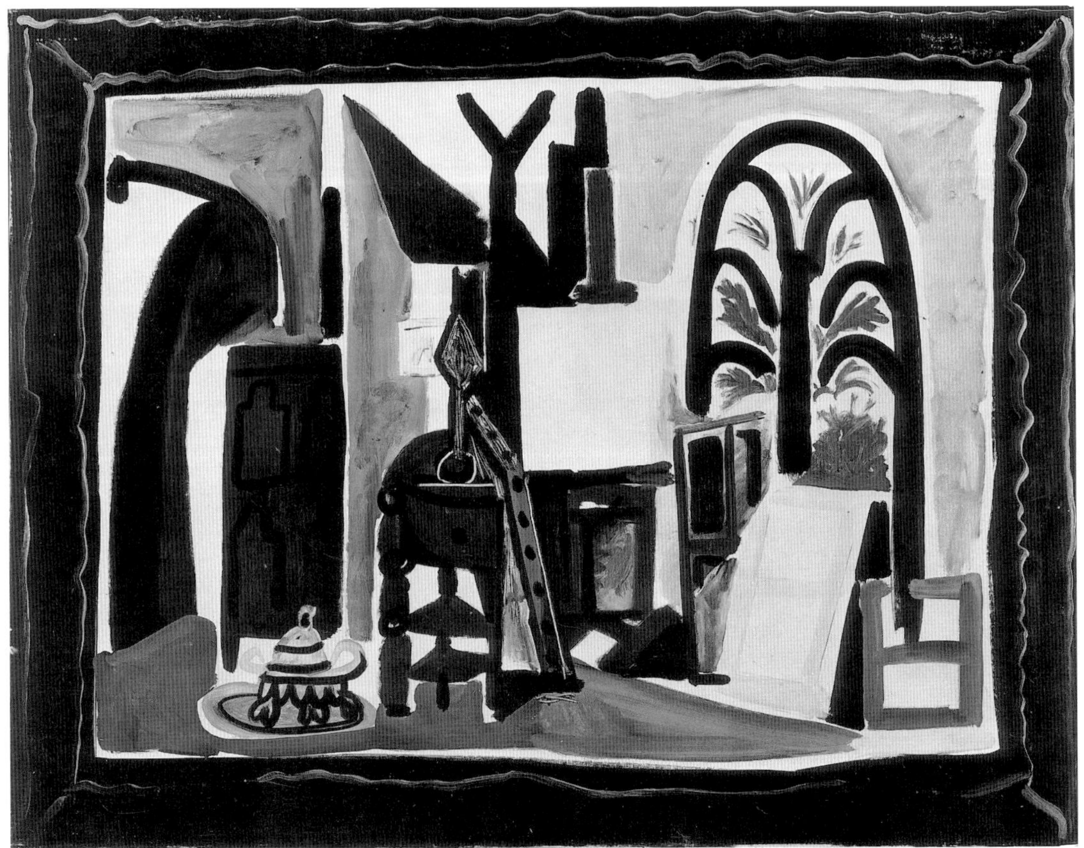

Right: Picasso. *Studio in a painted frame*, Cannes, 2 April 1956. Oil on canvas, 88.8 × 115.8 cm. The Museum of Modern Art, New York. Gift of Mr and Mrs Werner E.Josten.

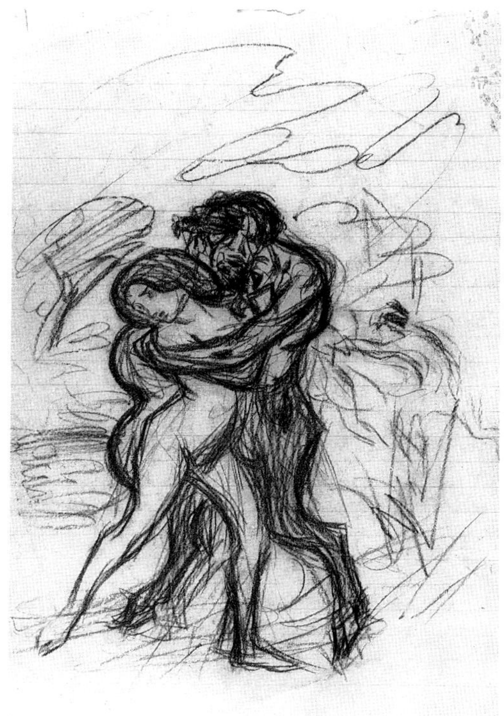

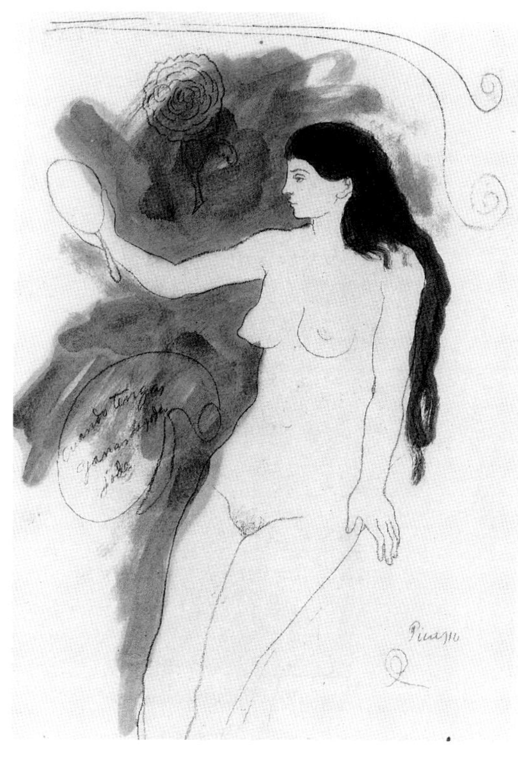

Left: Picasso. *The rape*, 1899 (no.3)

Right: Picasso. *Woman with a mirror*, 1902 (no.5)

Art historians of the last two decades have had the unusual opportunity to examine an enormous body of work by Picasso, beginning with several thousand drawings, paintings and other materials dating from the period before the artist moved to France in 1904 (most of these are now housed, thanks to the Picasso family, in the Museu Picasso in Barcelona), in addition to the vast estate – much of it in the Musée Picasso, Paris, and in the collections of his heirs – that he left at the time of his death in 1973 (not all of which has yet been made available). The scale of the task of studying Picasso's œuvre is dizzying, yet the closer we come to know the work the more we realize that the creative strands that make up the artist are present throughout.

Take, for instance, the way in which youthful drawings of erotic, almost pornographic content predict the obsession with sex of the late years; but what is not evident is that in the late work the process of making art becomes analogous to the act of love. The earliest drawing in the exhibition, the *Rape* (no.3), probably done during the summer of 1899, when the young artist's many sketches reveal an early curiosity about the portrayal of violent sex – here in mythological terms, for in the foreground the woman struggles with a satyr, while a scene of pursuit is hinted at behind them – makes use of a drawing technique typical of the artist's work that year: a loose, flowing line which finds intensity as well as defines the forms in its repetition. Yet the internal struggle and the merging of the figures (aided here by the long, flowing art-nouveau tresses of the girl which enclose them) reappears in full force in the subject of lovers in Picasso's late canvases. There, with great abandon, freely applied strokes of paint interweave the embracing figures, or the artist's brush becomes a metaphor for his sex, piercing not only the palette but his model. Curiously, the genitalia floating in the blue wash alongside the very lovingly drawn *Woman with a mirror* (no.5) are much more of a presentiment of the force of eroticism to come in the late work than the adolescent annotation '*Cuando tengas ganas de joder, jode*' ('When you feel like fucking, fuck').

The arena for sexual encounter in the early work is generally the brothel, the most notable example being *Les Demoiselles d'Avignon* (see ill. p.43). But coincident with Picasso's association with the Surrealists and, more directly, his annual summer holidays on the French coast in the twenties and thirties, the artist found a new world for his nudes to occupy at the beach (nos.30, 31). The depiction of nudity out of doors, released from the allegorical associations in traditional art even as recent as Cézanne's bathers, allowed Picasso to explore uninhibited distortions of the (predominantly female) nude, which in turn express uninhibited sexuality. The beach cabana, the Surrealists' metaphor for illicit sexual encounter, also becomes a personal allusion to his, at first, secret affair with Marie-Thérèse in the late twenties.

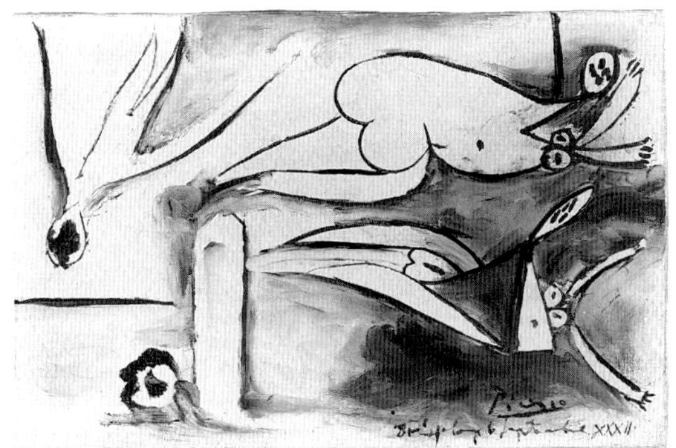

Above: Picasso. *Bathers*, 1932 (no.30).

The outdoor settings of some of the late works retain the allusions to sexual encounter, although in works such as *Lobster and cat on a beach* (no.59), the lovers or rapists are transformed into interlocking animal forms – like the Minotaur, with the sexual urges of man but devoid of conscious motives. One particularly moving work, *The aubade* (no.60), distils the elements of so much of Picasso's preoccupation with the discovery of sex in his earlier work: the dream quality of the painting, that is the unusually amorphous state in which the two figures exist, conveys an atmosphere not unlike the unveiling of the sleeping muse by a faun in the memorable print made in 1936 (no.36); in the painting the curvilinear form of the reclining nude at the right, her breasts, head, arms

Right: Picasso. *Lobster and cat on the beach*, 1965 (no.59).

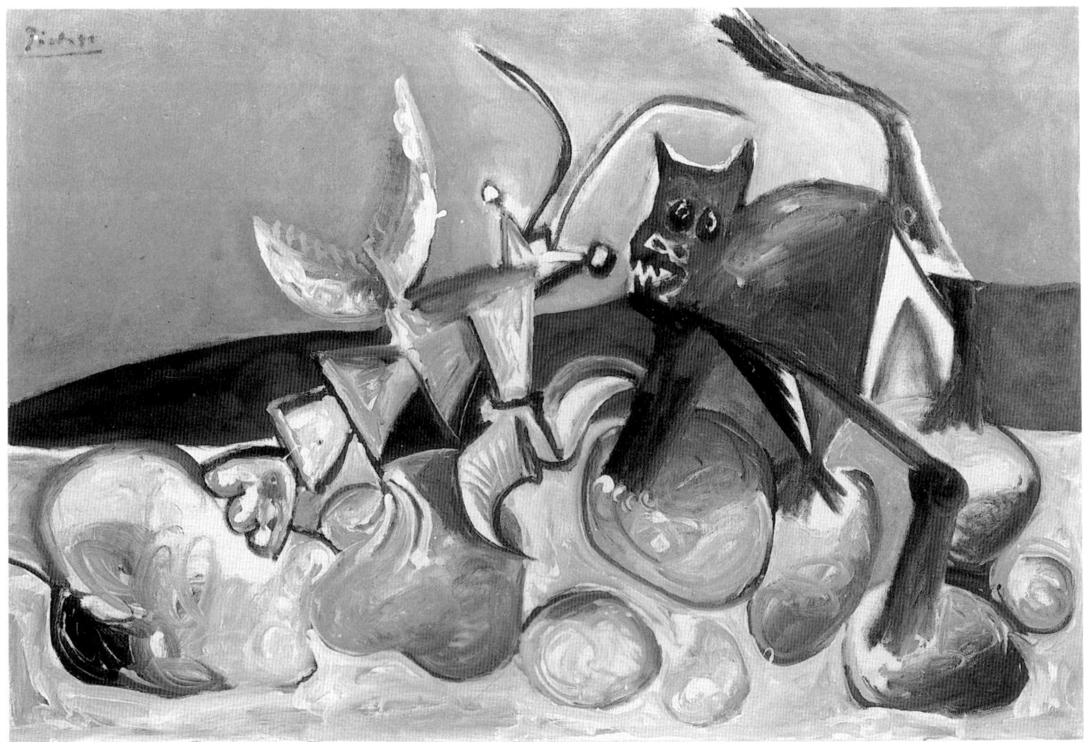

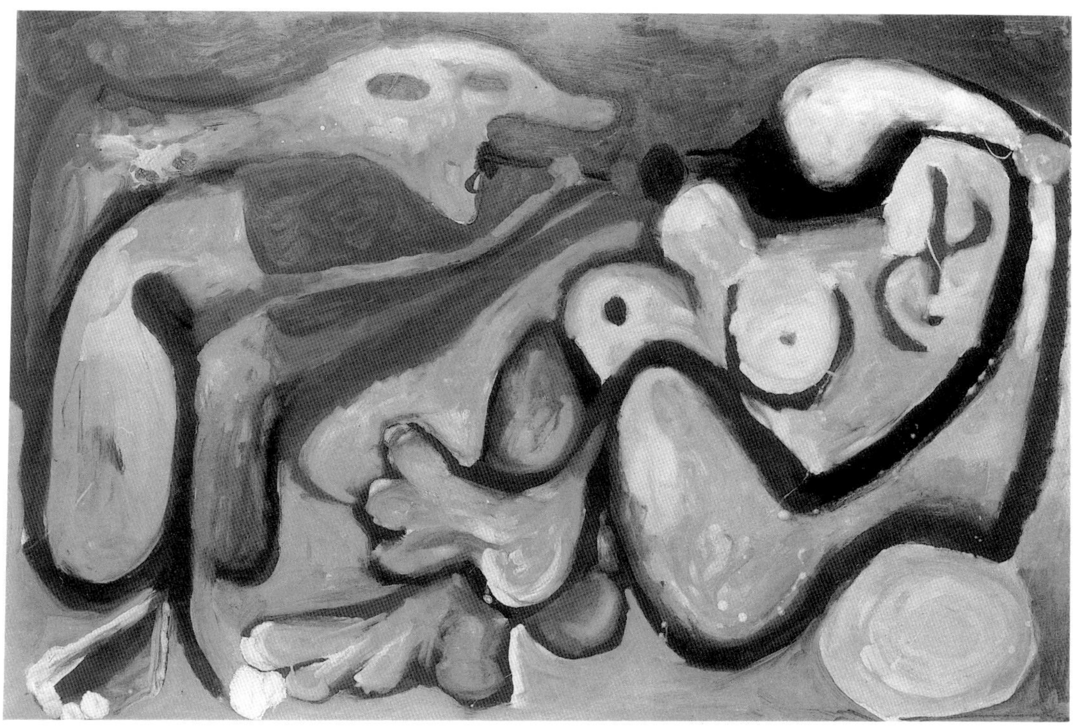

Right: Picasso. *The aubade*, 1965 (no.60).

Below: Picasso. *Faun unveiling a sleeping woman*, 1936 (no.36).

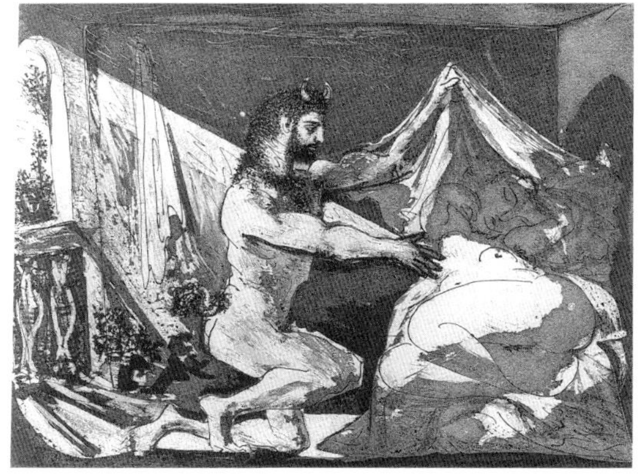

and legs, combine in a manner reminiscent of Picasso's bathers of the twenties and thirties; the quality of music suggested by the pipe played by the faun-figure at the left, evokes the ancient harmonies of Mediterranean mythology – all here in a work painted with the utmost freedom by a man approaching ninety.

The energy conveyed in the late work, even in the sheer quantity of production, reveals that Picasso was determined to find a way to defy nature, to surpass himself in his work, and in this way to defy time itself in order to keep on living. In the realm of printmaking Picasso was able to revitalise his creative process, not only with the technical challenges of the medium, but also to direct his dramas onto a stage, where, as he observed to the photographer Roberto Otero in 1968, '. . . I spend hour after hour while I draw, observing my creatures and thinking about the mad things they're up to, basically, it's my way of writing fiction.' (Otero, *Forever Picasso,* New York 1974, p. 170)

Beginning in 1963, Picasso began a fruitful collaboration with two master-printers, the brothers Aldo and Piero Crommelynck, who had set up an engraving studio in an old bakery in Mougins, not far from Picasso's studio. With them he realised a number of editions of prints, some of them, the *Suite 347* (see ill. p.57), for example, executed with amazing speed and virtuosity over a short period of time. His mastery of even the most difficult of drypoint etching techniques, according to the photographer Edward Quinn, who filmed Picasso at work (see ill. p.57), were proof that the artist's steady hand defied the aging process. Picasso populated these series with a cast of characters drawn from every period of his work, including numerous references to his origins as a Spanish artist: Celestinas, majas, Spanish grandees, even his father, frolic with circus folk, acrobats, Manet, Rembrandt and, above all, the artist himself in his many disguises: as

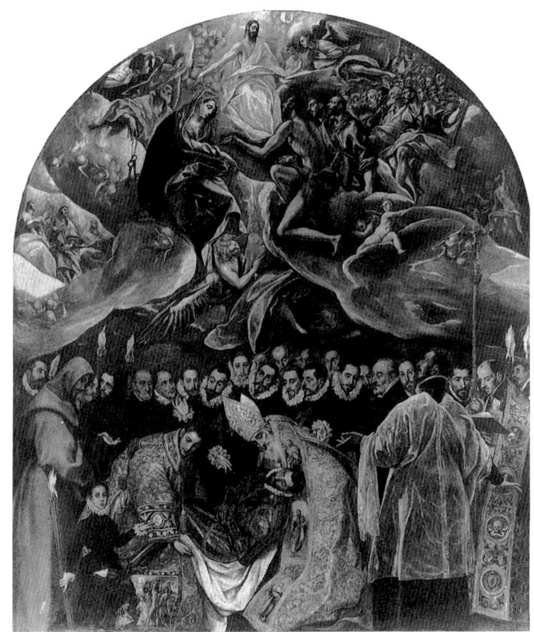

El Greco. *The burial of Count Orgaz*, 1586–8. Church of Santo Tomé, Toledo.

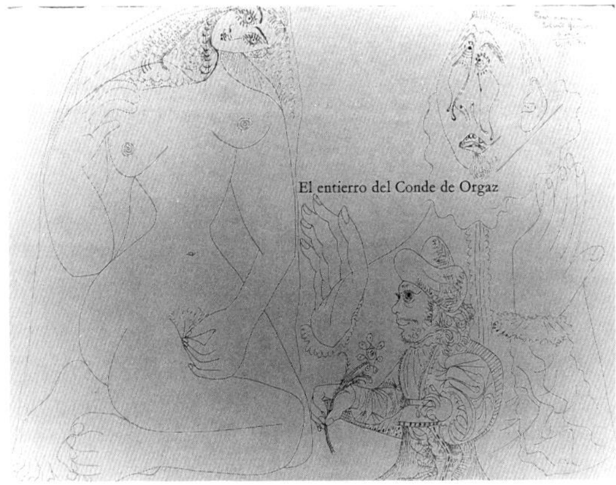

Picasso. Drawing dedicated to Roland Penrose on half-title of *El entierro del Conde de Orgaz*, 1971 (no.63a).

clown, or pope, or sculptor – even as the young painter Raphael making love to his model, the Fornarina.

Picasso himself wrote poetry and several plays during his lifetime, and the association with the Crommelyncks, at the urging of Barcelona publisher and friend Gustau Gili, led to the publication in 1968 of Picasso's play *El entierro del Conde de Orgaz*, with a preface by the Spanish poet Rafael Alberti. Although the text was started in 1957 and underwent several revisions, the prints he selected to accompany it were twelve engravings dating from 1966-67 and one drypoint with a Spanish text dated 9 June 1937 (no.63). Picasso's literary style combines painterly images, especially colours, with a dialogue that finds its model in the anarchistic writing of Alfred Jarry, one of Picasso's early heroes.

El entierro del Conde de Orgaz is the title of El Greco's painting in Toledo (1586) that Picasso had known since he was an art student, and it provided him with a basic cast of characters: the Toledo citizens in their ruff-necked attire in the painting are appropriated for the play. In one scene Velázquez's *Meninas* make an entrance and attempt to bury Count Orgaz in their bed. The verbal patter in Picasso's text at times takes on the rhythms of flamenco, while his quirky use of repetition distantly echoes the style of his old friend Gertrude Stein. All of these stylistic techniques and freely associated images find their parallels in the engravings themselves, in spite of the fact that they are not illustrations. Instead, they embody the spirit of the play, in reality the spirit of Picasso's creativity.

Above all, it is the colossal presence of the artist himself in all the works in this exhibition that ties his work in this selection and, in its enormous quantity, the whole *œuvre* together; for it is his personal energy, experience and distinct and forceful manner of expression that imbues everything he made with something of himself. The attempt to unmask Picasso in his attitude towards nature reveals that he saw himself as a primal creative force, as a force of nature.

His self-portraits, despite the fact that he generally appeared in some form of disguise, are the most direct images he made of himself throughout his long career as an artist. The earliest included in the exhibition, the Washington *Self-portrait* (no.2), presents a self-confident image following his promising reception both in Spain and France, in the guise of dashing bohemian with newly adopted Parisian sophistication. Picasso had, it is true, an unusual beginning: his artistic successes as a teenager (not a child prodigy as some would have it) had secured his family's financial and emotional support in his desire to become a painter (although they had envisioned for him a more conservative future as an academician). Then in Barcelona he was adopted by the local Bohemian circles as their '*petit Goya*', and they promoted and championed him; one of the Catalans he met through them, was responsible for selling his work in Paris and arranging his first exhibitions there.

Yet by 1902 Picasso's own defiance of the easy route – which at that point meant doing pastels of mothers and children or paintings on Hispagnolist themes – was such that his popularity plummeted: critics were upset by the 'lack of individual style' and the raw subject-matter of his prostitutes and beggars. His decision to paint out his own self-portrait in his Blue period masterpiece, *La Vie* (see ill. p.41), probably had as much to do with his uncomfortable relationship with symbolic painting as it did with the autobio-

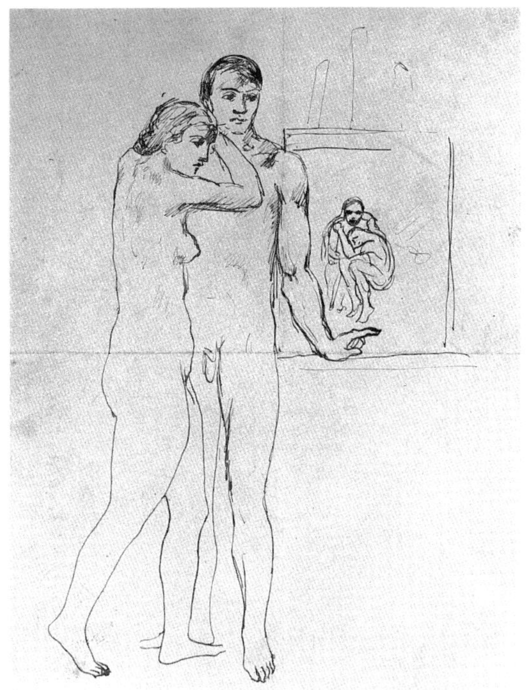

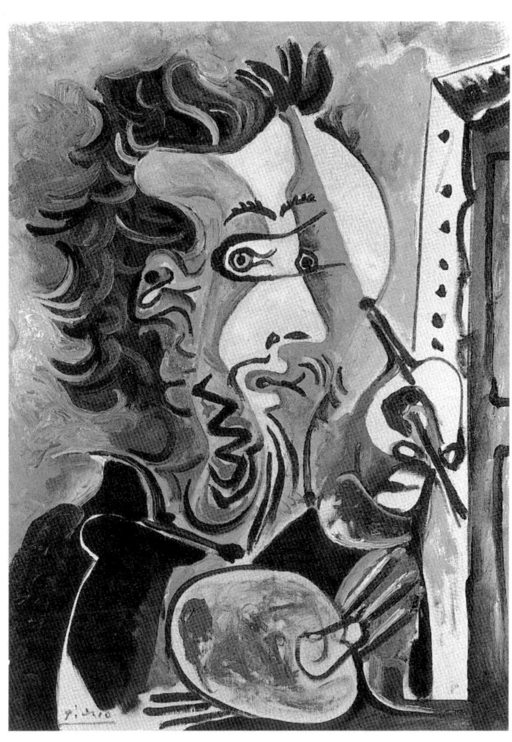

Left: Picasso. Study for *La Vie*, 1903 (no.7).
Right: Picasso. *The painter*, 1963 (no.57).

graphical incidents at the base of the work: he repainted his own head, which can still be seen in a preparatory drawing (no.7), with that of his friend Casagemas, with whom he had first gone to Paris, and who had committed suicide in 1901. The poetic harlequins and circus subjects that followed were (in spite of their popularity among collectors) for Picasso the last gasp of literary symbolism in his work.

Self-portraits appear in the greatest numbers in the last decade of his life. Sometimes he is bearded – expressing a longing for youth as well as a tribute to his first art-teacher, his father – sometimes he is the Minotaur or a cavorting faun. But in many of his finest and most vigorous paintings of men, he is an El Greco saint or a Spanish grandee, the painter of the era of Velázquez or of Goya. And in all of these canvases of enormous richness in palette and brushwork, it is Picasso's all-seeing eye, the eye of the artist that stares out at us and leads us into his world.

As has been stated before, art for Picasso in his late years is often equated with the act of love, and in this sense too all the lovers in the late paintings, some shown with great tenderness, others with acrobatic humour, others with violence, are all Picasso as well. The bald old acrobats, clowns and even the pope in his prints remind us that in Picasso's world he is the principal character in his plays. The most poignant of all the self-portraits, the most noble and the clearest acceptance of truth, are Picasso's last drawings of his head as a skull (see ill. p.58) – here the artist continues to probe for the essence of things, to defy death by work, but in the end to come as close as he can to it in his art. By transforming himself and by keeping open the possibility of yet another unrealised transformation, Picasso seeks to ensure his own immortality.

How Picasso Figures in Time

Tony Green

If, at least, time enough were allotted to me to accomplish my work, I would not fail to mark it with the seal of Time . . . and I would therein describe men, if need be, as monsters occupying a place in Time infinitely more important than the restricted one reserved for them in space. . . .

Marcel Proust

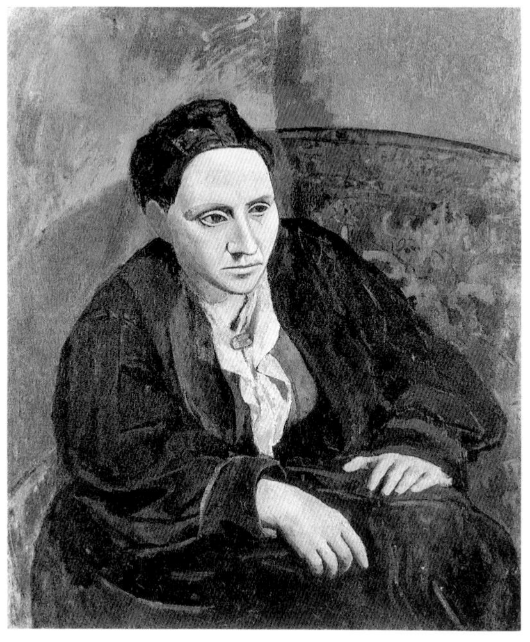

Picasso. *Gertrude Stein*, Paris, 1906.
Oil on canvas, 99.6 × 81.3 cm.
The Metropolitan Museum of Art, New York.
Bequest of Gertrude Stein, 1946.

The Picasso legend ensures that we go on looking in his direction. The noise is such it is impossible not to have heard that name, even very distantly, like mist sighing in the bush. Picasso, Picasso, Picasso: the name is a pipe, snare drum and cymbal combination, ending with a maenad's moan. Just listen to it! You can't beat Fame's Trumpet!

Well, yes you can, by being indefinable, keep switching appearances. Pablo Picasso baffled the art critics by changing his style all the time, so the legend has it.

Furthermore, the legend says that Picasso, as a boy, pleased his art teacher father, and the academy of art; when he grew up he pleased only a few artists and writers; but by the time he was fifty he was the leader of all the modernists, and by the time he was eighty people queued for hours to see exhibitions of his work. Like Constable, Monet and Van Gogh, his name is inscribed in our histories of art, as an old master.

His fame coincides with the conception of an art for public museums, and his art is its most triumphant success. He personifies the modern genius that the modern public hated for its impudence and loved for its challenge to worn out values. The symbols of success are: money, and the luxuries it brings, and entry into the halls of fame, the galleries and museums where the old masters repose.

Picasso's right to be in the museum is still contested by people who think they know what is what because they like Monet circa 1880. Nothing more recent shall get past them. My father's version of the legend is that Picasso was a clever businessman who knew how to take advantage of the public. So he deserved the money, though his carryings on with women might disqualify him from fame.

Even one of his best friends and colleagues, Gertrude Stein, had trouble explaining to her brother what had happened to painting since Cézanne. At first she objected to Picasso's drawing, but later became an ardent defender of Picasso's Cubism, which he regarded as 'tommy-rot'.

In 1906 both her brothers said no when they saw Picasso's portrait of her. He painted her with one eye nearer than the other, the far cheek turning very much quicker than you would expect, the body looming forward, the mouth a curious tight dark line across, dark lines around the eyes and bright lids. Picasso told them that she would come to look like it. And of course she does, more and more. Since she has passed away, it remains as a memorial, and it holds an honoured place in everyone's anthology of Picasso's paintings.

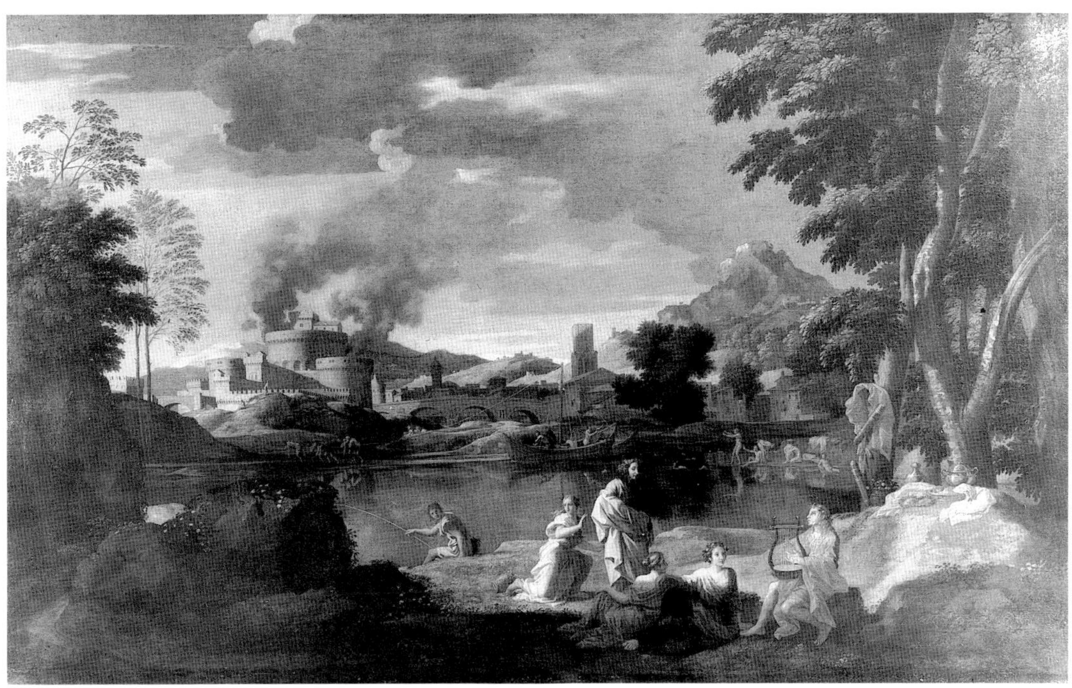

Nicolas Poussin. *Landscape with Orpheus and Eurydice*, *c.*1650. Musée du Louvre, Paris.

Gertrude Stein, in return, wrote his portrait, in which he became Napoleon, as he is now, forever. She is as well loved as he is by lovers of the arts, but among the public at large she is almost unknown, so her portrait of him is not yet as famous as his of her.

* * * *

When I was young, *Orpheus and Eurydice* by Nicolas Poussin in the Louvre was one of my favourite paintings. I always thought the castle with the billowing smoke coming out of it must be Hades. The singer Orpheus who could charm the birds out of the trees is so preoccupied with his song that he does not see the snake in the grass that kills Eurydice. He goes on singing, and she is always about to die.

Unfortunately, it is the fate of most of the figures in the paintings of the Renaissance to the end of the nineteenth century to be stuck in one position. There are exceptions, but only when the painter dares to contradict the prevailing rule that painting should show one action in one time, that the light should seem to come from one direction, and that everything should be painted bigger or smaller according to laws of proportion and perspective.

Once enclosed in a story, as Picasso is in a legend, you are stuck there, as long as anyone remembers it. Legends and stories, too, like essays, obeyed rules that ensured smooth continuity from one sentence to another, from one paragraph to another, from chapter to chapter. Those rules are the most evident truth they displayed, whatever the moral or the argument propounded. The figure in the legend is constructed within that system, the figure in the painting within another. You need always to understand the rules to tell the figure from the ground.

The ruling systems of the arts began to lose their power in the later nineteenth century along with positivism, and by the early twentieth new possibilities began to overtake them. The representations of thought and of feeling by figures in painting, or characters in stories in novels, altered, mainly because of the problem of time. Time is only divided with great difficulty and resists treatment in scientific fashion. In the arts, conceived of as if they all tended towards the condition of music, every work was a performance, in time.

Thought, feeling, action, creation, are encountered as processes, and these could not be accommodated within the supposedly static systems of the Renaissance. Braque, Picasso's co-worker in Cubism before World War I, declared the whole of the older art redundant: it was the 'false tradition'.

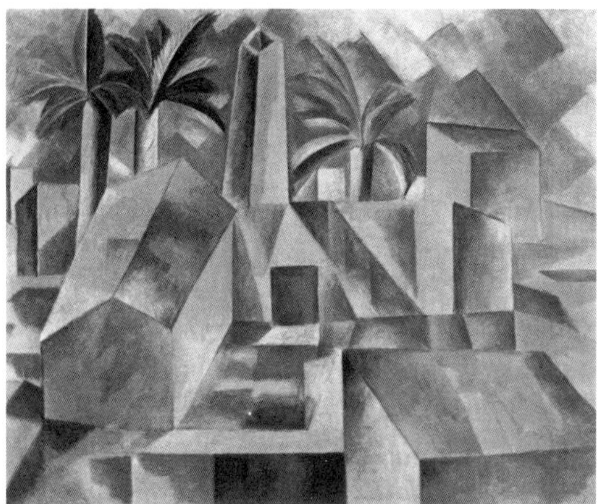

Picasso. *Factory at Horta*, 1909 (no.17).

What he and Picasso then did – Cubist art – radically altered the arts for the Futurists and the Vorticists and the Expressionists, and for all their modernist successors. And it is still so radical that it has not yet been fully encountered and understood nearly eighty years later.

To begin with, Cubism is wrongly named. Cubism has almost nothing to do with painting things as if they are made out of cubes. Like the caption to a photo, the story about little cubes has been so insistently attached to Cubism that it cannot simply be disregarded. But actually Cubism works with new principles: arrangement and improvisation.

Picasso's art undoes the bonds of the conventions of the Renaissance and contradicts the classical diction of painting. But he had so well understood the grounds of the Renaissance system that he could make a strong brew disrupting it. The possibilities of a great disorder opened up. By changing the syntax a new and perhaps better world could be made to appear. But like all new worlds so created, it could be better only for a while. As soon as it grew to be familiar it would fade: a continuous revolution was needed.

Hence the appearance of so many time-themes in the work. Apollinaire claimed that the fourth dimension, time, was opened up by the forms of the new painting. Although arrangement and improvisation are terms most common in music, they also belong with all the other twentieth-century arts, all of them deeply concerned with the problem of time. This common interest unifies them, beyond anything inherent in different media.

As P. Ricœur has shown in a recent book, *Temps et Récit* (Editions du Seuil, Paris, 1983-85), the problem is at least as old as Aristotle. To understand time is to understand the narrative arts, including the writing of history, and even painting. The self, the subject, in which the feeling of change undermines the old assumption of a centred single identity, is in dynamic relation with its objects, and their separation is none too clear. It means that the performance of a painting, stroke by stroke, is an operation in which the painter is not necessarily of the same mind from moment to moment, though the semblance of a purpose, like painting a predetermined personage, may still just hold out completely open slather.

This keeps Picasso in that area of painting where the appearance of images of persons and things is still very interesting. He rejects the possibility of making 'abstract' figures in which people and things cannot readily be seen. Even though painting could be freed that way for a kind of diagramming of forces as their subject-matter, he remains fascinated by the problem of how the picture yields up images.

The earlier Analytic Cubist years are taken up with painted improvisations. Each painting begins from one painted mark and spreads outwards and around in any direction,

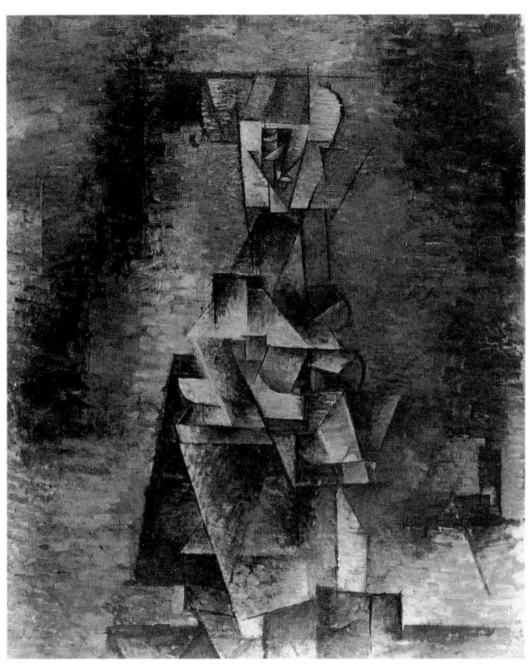

Picasso. *Half-length female nude*, 1910 (no.18).

until the canvas is finished with. This phase could be seen as an investigation into what happens as the thought and feeling change direction at each stroke. It is as if each stroke furthers the form that began to emerge in the one before, but this is left incomplete. Each stroke is also seen as the first stroke of another form that might be permitted to emerge, to be furthered by a few more. But it too is abandoned.

The painter deposits enough clues, however, to make you go on thinking that if you puzzle away at the *mélange* you will finally get an answer to what the image is. Surely, a single clear definite figure will emerge from these partial and discontinuous fragments? There are conventional signs for a guitar-neck, an ear, an eye, and so on, to invite you to see the rest emerge from the blur. But these are not much more than labels, like name-tags.

During the most intense hypnotic day-dreaming in front of a Renaissance picture of seeming presences, the reminder interrupts the reverie, always: this is only paint on canvas. The paintwork always shows, in spite of all attempts to hide it, in the so-called illusionist art of the baroque in Italy, or in the miniaturist precisions of painters like Elsheimer. In illusionist painting, even when everything possible is done to hide the frame, which divides the media-world from actuality, the surface always gives it away.

The substitution of signs that were obviously conventional for figures and objects whose conventionality was not obvious meant that the day-dream or reverie of persons and places was no longer possible. The new painting gave you items from a semiotic system, which is not a system of absolute meanings but of meanings produced by understanding the relations of signs to one another. The painting surface no longer contained the effect of an optical coherence, but a collection of fragmentary and variously conventional signs. It was even theoretically possible to make a painting entirely out of graphic words at that moment.

This kind of painting put the reader into a position where all that are to be seen are signs from various codes other than picturing, so that their conventionality is obvious inserted into what used to be a place for pictures. In Analytical Cubist painting, the reader wanders in reverie enjoying the polymorphous imagery, which shifts and alters under the gaze. Armed with insights from this experience, the new reader could turn back to the Renaissance, and realise that its painting was never natural, but always a production of systems, conventions and rules. Its style showed, and it was no longer possible to maintain the fiction that this was the only absolutely correct way to paint.

The nineteenth-century academic version of the Renaissance was now exposed, by contrast, as a desire to achieve immediacy of presence in art, in which the barrier between style and medium and reader would disappear. A very powerful controlling magic would then be possible, which we know as propaganda, for an ideology. The possibility of ever higher resolution and more sensuous immediacy was promised by including more and more signifying elements. First there was motion, and then sound, then digital coding. Only the fact of its beginning and ending and the filmic cut gives the show away in these arts, that they are artificial.

* * * *

Having found that Cubist paintings are made up of incomplete significations, there is yet another problem. Cubism alters the way in which paintings can be read and understood.

The first guess that most of the paintings are pictures of people is challenged too. It may be alarming to realise that these are not after all pictures of people, but some might be brick buildings and alley-ways, hundreds of them, to run down and get lost in. And then perhaps they may not be that either, but simply a big triangle or a grid and a series of ratios being defined.

These shifts in reading come as you stand at different distances from the picture. The triangles and the grid-like scaffolding from a distance, the face closer still, and the alley-ways closer still. The three interlock, as shifting planes of reference pointing to what the picture is 'of'. The painting is a kind of pleasure instrument, where the pleasure is in feeling the shock of the shifts one makes while trying endlessly to read it, but never succeeding.

The trouble in this reading process is trying to detach it from the Renaissance way of reading pictures. That habit of reading them is deeply ingrained, still wanting pictures that carry one away into dreams of an ideal.

The end of that comes when it is admitted that with Cubism some other way of reading is necessary. Learning to read it means finding out that the more dispersed and incomplete the cues, and the less the certainty about what is represented, the more the process of projection is stimulated. The reader is no longer passive but active.

For Picasso, disordering the older system of smooth consistent painting of figure scenes, or landscapes, or still life, by allowing one stroke to suggest the next, representing the shifting dynamic of a mind in process, shows the artist's mind is not inflexibly made up. These shifts of perspective, of attitude and view-point bring to attention the reader's own variability with time.

This conflict of a new method with a widely held belief system is the one thing that most commonly prevents people from beginning to look at all. It is an unfounded assumption that pictures are read as if by nature when they seem to offer to deliver a presence in the Renaissance, as if by courier. This is not nature, but a culturally determined way of reading.

The older painting, the moderns assumed, had the painter keep his thoughts frozen between the time the image was completed in the mind and the time when the execution of the painting was completed. According to the theory propounded in the influential French Academy of the later seventeenth century, painting begins with a drawing of figures in a scene, in which the outcome is specified before the brush is picked up. The desired image in the mind of the intellectual artist is supposed to commission a mere executant, a workman.

Apart from that period of about five hundred years in Europe, painting has never been read that way. The museums of the nineteenth century opened out to the world of the distant past and the world of the distant continents and cultural modes. Since the seventeenth century in Europe, the suspicion that European manners, language, and religion were relative, and not absolute, had arisen from such an influx of information from the new world coming into the closed old world.

Another appropriate example of attempting to control the image in advance would be the client commissioning an advertising campaign. What the client wants to have people believe is translated into text and image presentations, designed to deliver the right message. The problem is that text and image also deliver a host of messages beside the one wanted, and these must be kept in line or else eliminated. Such messages are encoded in style, and in every aspect of detailed accompaniment to the main feature.

The condition of all reading and understanding of painting obstinately remains multiple, because the thinking that we do, stemming from the alternations of picture and its artifice, joins with our thoughts of mythology, literature, psychology, politics, ritual and so on. Image escapes from predetermined intentions, and thus eludes singular and final reading.

In this sense, there is no final meaning to a Poussin or a Rubens, a David or a Delacroix. The painting is only an occasion for a reverie or meditation for the reader. It is literally a mediation, a working with a medium, something between painter and reader.

In the new painting the outcome is left to the unfolding of a process during the actual execution. There are new options at every stroke, to add to and further the figures that have begun to appear, or to alter them out of all recognition. The resulting figures and their ambiguities are not foreseen initially, as far as one can tell, but improvised as the paint strokes suggest their possibilities. Because options for continuation are left open, and no single goal is specified, images may be fleetingly toyed with, contradicted, reworked, cancelled.

The traces of this process remain visible, and what the reader then finds is a wild range of possibilities opening up, none of which seems to be final. The painting appears to represent a process of thinking going on from initial stroke to final stroke. In this process several angles on one thing are actively canvassed and brought into co-operation. Ideological pre-conception has virtually been dismissed as a project, and a multitude of views is brought into the picture, in an idealistic anarchy.

* * * *

Having practised Cubism for about two years Braque and Picasso set out on a new adventure, involving collage and constructions of old pieces of wood and such. Arrangement and improvisation come to the fore, and composition with a grid or scaffolding of simple geometrical figures fades from view. It is a matter of altering things, and sticking things in that really belong in the world outside the picture or, in the broadest possible sense, the framework, the interface between the work and the world which is its context.

In the collages the image-making potentialities of various signifying materials are combined. There is cut-out and altered newsprint, wallpaper sometimes, black chalk and pen drawing, stencilled letters. A mysterious figure emerging painfully from strange paint is no longer the object. Instead of painterly representation reworked as improvisation, the synthetic phase of Cubism is concerned with constituting signs by all possible graphic treatments, in combination, contradiction and overlap. In this kind of work the type of graphics itself becomes significant, meaningful. A line is a soft smudgy thing, a repeated pencil stroke, the cut edge of a piece of stuck-on newsprint, peculiar shapes made by printed or stencilled letters or numbers, or the pattern printed on wallpaper. Each of these notably material edges tells as outline, replacing the pure line of the classical tradition, which is meant as a dematerialised and ideal description of form.

In a well-known collage that used to belong to the Dada poet Tristan Tzara, there's a bottle, on the left, made of the small ad pages. It has a spout like a soda-water syphon

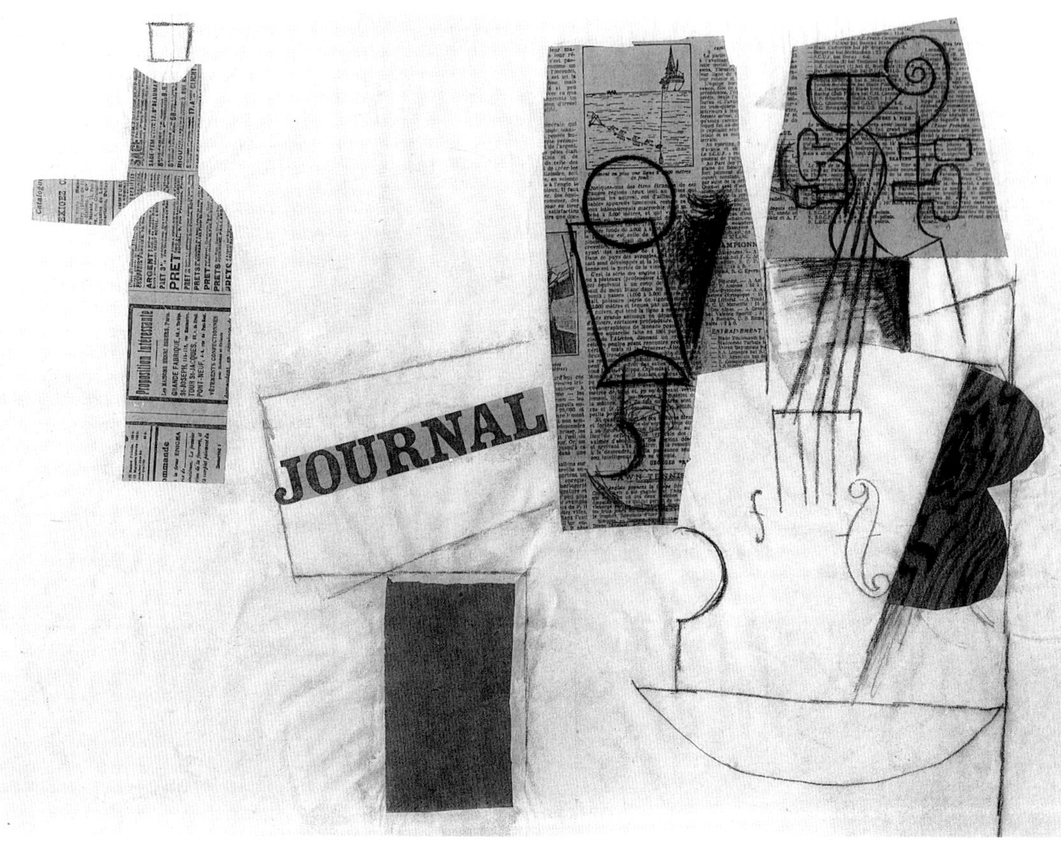

Picasso. *Siphon, glass, newspaper, violin*, winter 1912–13. Papier collé, 47 × 62 cm. Moderna Museet, Stockholm.

on one side. The shine on its shoulder, 'inside' the bottle-shape, also serves as the outline of the shoulder of a smaller bottle-shape inside the first. The newspaper bottle has a drawn cork. On the right there is a texture made from newsprint, drawn on, doodled over, more like. There is a violin emergent in outline.

This bottle is not a bottle, it is the *gendarme* on the point duty directing the traffic. That is his arm, not a soda-water syphon spout, and that cork is his hat. Perhaps he is out in the middle of the street while the music goes on in the café, gypsy violinists collecting a few francs. . . . 'Perhaps' is the word. It is evident that a collage like this is no more tightly held to a plan than the paintings. One could make a reasonable guess at the sequence of operations, and they seem to begin and stop, with as little sense of the older coherence principles as possible.

A piece of the newspaper, *le journal*, says JOURNAL. Here is a piece of the picture doing several things, naming its own material, newspaper, its source in *Le Journal*, and announcing a relation with the diurnal round, the café, etc. The 'J' is cut as if it is not a letter, but an outline for the shape of the piece of paper, so that there is a 'visual language' game going on beside the naming ones.

Trying to describe this picture is difficult because it is impossible ever to pin it down to a single unambiguous reading of objects. It is inconsistent and loosely put together and liberally made up of bits and pieces so that the reading of the picture is fascinating and a train in thought can heave anchor and blast off.

Tristan Tzara's own poetic practice makes use of outrageous conjunctions of words and strange metaphors. He did write a jocular piece about cutting up words from the newspaper and pulling them out of a hat in any order to make a poem, but whether he actually did such a thing more than once or twice is doubtful. The seemingly chance method of composition is one which here assumes that items of vocabulary always produce a readable text when they are juxtaposed, the syntax has to be invented by the reader. Picasso's collages, by isolating the stuck-on materials and making their cuts (contours) ambiguous, also strain the resources of the reader to make sense of them. The syntax is the problem, and in the light of our habitual uses of it we can project onto even these scraps attempts at scenarios to account for it.

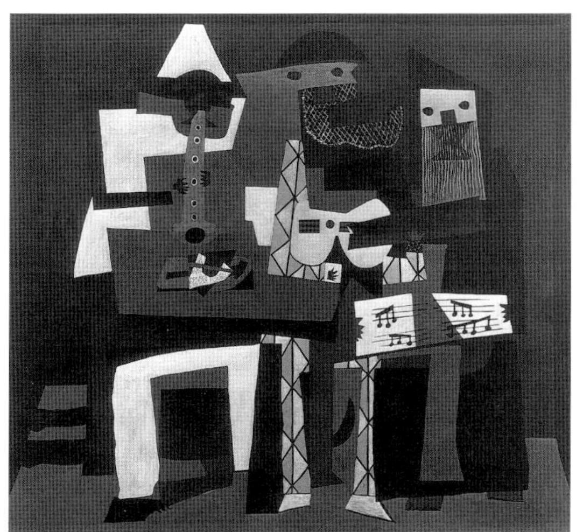

Picasso. *Three musicians*, summer 1921.
Oil on canvas, 200.7 × 222.9 cm.
The Museum of Modern Art, New York.
Mrs Simon Guggenheim Fund.

* * * *

Later, by the 1920s, and with these techniques of disassociation, improvisation of form and an ambiguous representation, the picture returns in full force. In Picasso's painting it comes first in the guise of pastiches of Pompeian painting, then in fantastic painted versions of collage, like the paintings of *Three musicians* or *Three dancers* (see ill. p.47).

This brings us back to painting, and to Picasso and his notion of figure painting. In the Museum of Modern Art version of *Three musicians* there is a dog. What is the dog doing there? Does the dog sing along or does he look after the cash, or is he like the faithful watchdogs in the old master pictures of Venus?

Dogs in pictures have meaning from at least two angles. They may be part of a complex of signs which all relate to a hidden order, of transcendental meaning. With Picasso the symbol system is more likely to be the one that goes with the figures of love and the arts. But as we have already seen, for Picasso there is an issue of how the dog is formed in the picture, so that you can see both it and its formation as part of a process of thinking. The dog is constructed out of improbable rectangles and other slabs of colour within this painting conceived of in those terms.

The dog disappears behind and then reappears again, one of the instances of overlap that partly masks continuity and that therefore asks this question: where is the rest of the dog? The answer is in terms of the method of representation on the canvas: there is no rest to the dog. In terms of the imagination taking hold of the painting as a picture, it is hidden. There is a dog you see, and yet there is no dog, only coloured planes to look at. The paintings of the twenties and thirties are particularly rich in the play off between the materials and the forms and the imagined things and the imagined scene.

But one cannot discount this latter kind of meaning in the old masters. What is peculiar is that it is masked, by the tradition of reading which focuses attention only on eliciting a single meaning, a meaning of the picture as a moral discourse, in which figures are regarded as instruments only, with no power of their own. This is to interpret pictures in accordance with the intentions of the Davidian academy, where ideological illustration is the intent, though this had long been prepared by the Academy in the 1670s.

The unconsidered aspect of figures is that as the painter paints they are living beings, that the painter disposes of at his pleasure or suffers with in their pains. It would need a special and deliberate distancing for a painter to be able to make a figure without imagining it as having a life, indifferent to whether the subject of drawing was a crocodile or a beautiful woman.

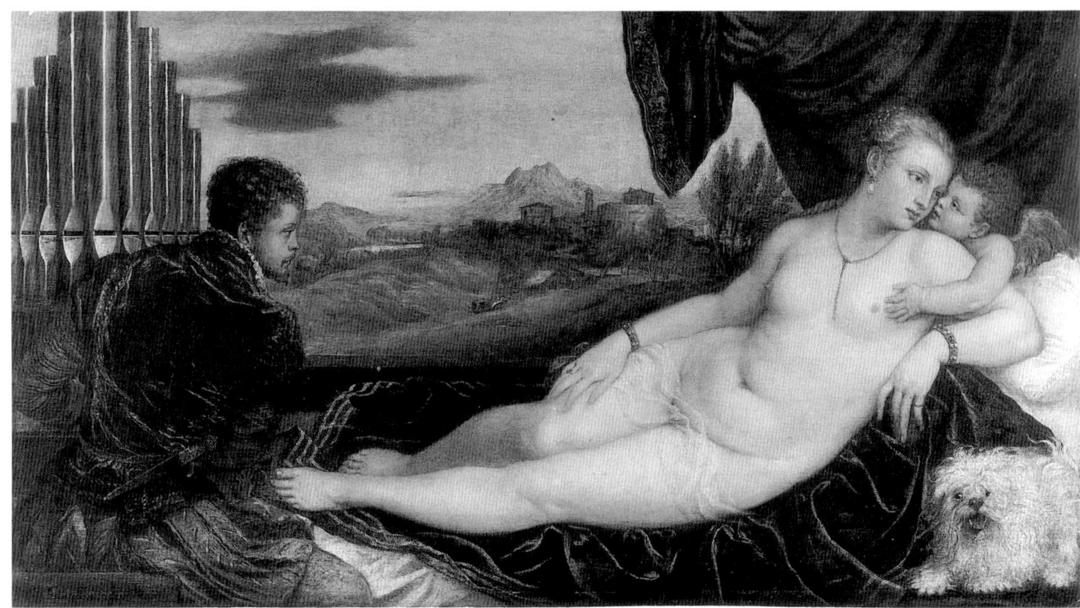

Titian. *Venus and Cupid with an organist*, 1548–50. Gemäldegalerie, Staatliche Museen Preußischer Kulturbesitz, Berlin (West).
This is one of the many versions Titian painted of the reclining figure of Venus; others include the *Venus of Urbino* in which her serving-women are removing her robe from a chest, and versions with a fountain, a park and a hunt.

Is it not likely that the meaning of paintings of Venus by Titian is something more than the symbols at his disposal? Can you imagine him singing along with the gondolier outside the window, as he put the paint on for the body of Venus very lovingly, and stroked the soft hairs of Venus' dog, with the most delicate touches. The robe that the women take out for her is of course fit for the Queen of Love, as is the exquisite palace the painter dreams up, or the hunt, the fountains, the lutenists and the organ-players, and, beyond all compare, her marvellous gardens, which Watteau and Proust knew as the Champs Elysées, the dizzy fields of Elysium.

Titian's painterliness encourages one to see the traces of the brush as they construct the figures for us to see as flesh, from the mere materials of brown ground, and red and white and yellow and black. There is a meaningfulness to the experience of being shown both the imagined scene and the means by which it is constructed. The conjuror performs a magic trick, and if we look we can see that it is a trick and how it is done. What we cannot see is the immense preparatory labour that goes into perfecting the trick, the mastery is only visible in the finished work.

Figure paintings are powerful objects, as much for the painter making them, seeing the figures of the imagination coming into a specific life, as for the beholder. Olivia, one of my three-year-old daughters, smashed her little plastic chair with a hammer. On the seat of the chair there was a picture of a boy and a girl. She hit the boy's eye with the hammer, because, as she explained, the boy had hit her in the eye with a dog.

Actually, the day before she had got into a lot of trouble, because she had hit her older brother in the eye with a necklace. Her comment is instructive, when you consider that she also said, when asked if the boy was her brother, no, it was just that boy (in the picture).

That is an index of the fascination of figures in pictures, especially if they have eyes. They seem to induce a kind of fear in the fearful and delight in those who live in hope.

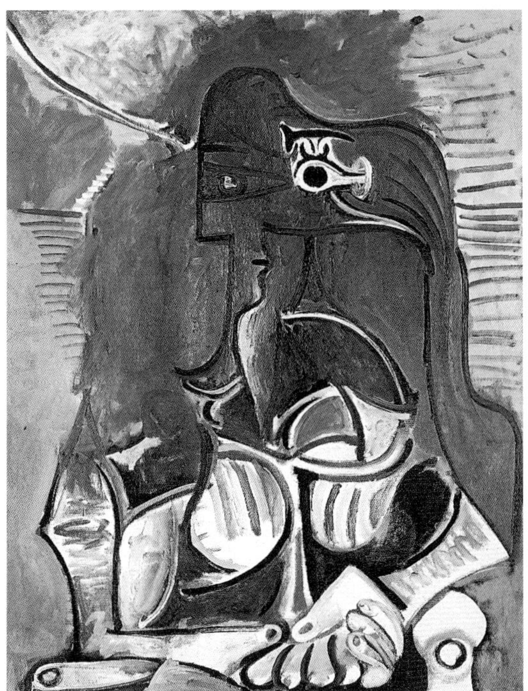

Picasso. *Woman with crossed hands*, 1961 (no.55).

What else to do with the portrait but to gaze into the eyes, and if it is the beloved, to long for the return, imagining how the beloved's eyes will turn to you, at last, as in the final cadence of a Mozart sonata.

It becomes clear in the 1930s that Picasso recognised that his figures were the figures of a continuing process of the mind at work, of the unconscious. In this way he forms ready connections with the Surrealists, as producers of the imagery, not of the rational simplification of consciousness, but of the revolutionary underside.

The Surrealists' ultimate conscious aim was to bring about a revolution in what constitutes our whole way of action, by letting the repressed return, freeing the mind from its shackles. That way you might get either blissful release from the rational tensions that restricted the poor old body, into its wildest sweetest erotic dreams, or the terrifying raging insanity of the holocaust and World War II. This too fulfills the equally erotic, forbidden, black dreams of the authoritarian mind.

The magic in the air, say, of Salvador Dalí's paranoid imagery, is the counter to the ideal dreams of Mondrian, and somewhere between comes Picasso, with his onslaught on the *Dream and Lie of Franco. Guernica*, is also a dream image: of the terror of German bombing technique let loose on a civilian Spanish population, in a Civil War between the idealistic dreamers of the Left and the power and punishment dreamers of the Right.

Picasso's later work is taken up more with the working out of the meaning of the figures that represent the subconsious. In this respect he returns to a kind of older history painting, with narrative content. But looking even at the Cubist phase paintings, he was always a painter of a gallery of figures.

There is a long meditation on mediation, through the figures of the artist and his model, in the *Vollard Suite* of prints, which has in recent times been mistaken for a tract on male domination of women. The question of a political ideology behind a figure art is always asked first, but without usually recognising the other messages. This is particularly true for people used to expecting the picture to tell its story at once.

Likewise, the long series of the late paintings recently on show in Paris and London has been taken journalistically as the sexist fantasies and meanderings of an aging man, regretting declining potency and other signs of approaching bodily death. These, however, parade, from a lifetime's experience and thought on the matter, not all of it happy or painless, the repertory of figures that suggests a discourse on love. Among the gallery of single figures, there is one recurrent figure: the embracing couple.

Will it suffice to say that Picasso here seems to join one of the oldest and richest traditions of erotic imagery, in which the central figure, among all the other images of actors in the drama, is the union of male and female? In alchemy, widely known and revived in the twentieth century among artists thanks to Carl Jung, the figure above all others is the Alchemic Wedding. And this figure can with some appearance of ease be made transparent and laid over figures from the mystical traditions of Jewish, Muslim and Christian origin, in which the exoteric language is that of love and lovers, while the esoteric is understood by initiates as a spiritual relation, in which the desire for union of Worshipper and Worshipped is figured forth.

* * * *

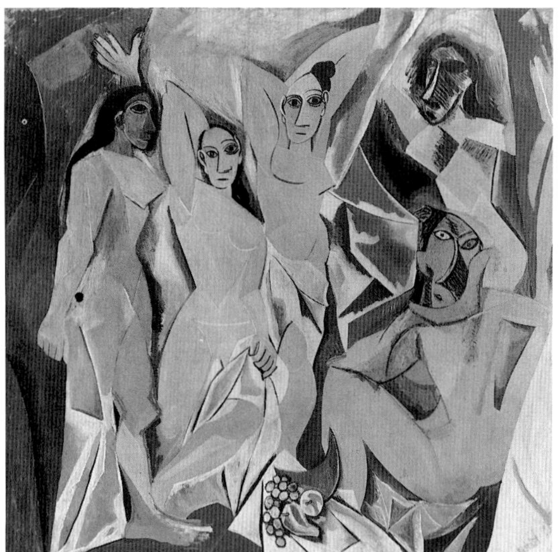

Picasso. *Les Demoiselles d'Avignon*, Paris, 1907. Oil on canvas, 243.9 × 233.7 cm. The Museum of Modern Art, New York. Acquired through the Lillie P. Bliss Bequest.

It is baffling to critics expecting a consistent personality to see the painter apparently shift style so frequently. It baffled everyone when he first changed style in the middle of painting a picture, and left it like that, supposedly finished: the *Demoiselles d'Avignon*. Even Braque, when he first saw it, thought it would ruin the moderns, by letting the side down.

One thought about it is that it changes the terms of representation of the figures, painting them as if they were somehow African or Polynesian carved figures with masks. At first this pseudo-primitive style was valued as an escape from a rule-bound classical drawing system, to the free-form creativity of the 'savage' world. All the alternatives to classical drawing were canvassed in the first part of this century, the art of children, of schizophrenics, of 'savages', of pre-classical Europe, of exotic civilisations, the Far East, Central America, and so on.

What was supposedly valuable in Picasso's famous picture has been thrown into doubt, in the past ten years especially, by the question of appropriation. Does his style-borrowing steal from some Pacific and African artists, thus keeping them in their places when he refused to give them anything in return? And their 'third world' places were such that they couldn't get a whisper out of a blade of grass that would tell anyone they were even alive, let alone artists of an equal vigour, which was certainly the case.

The arguments about the politics of appropriation take off from the painting's mask-like representations, and nothing more. They never return for a second look. Distracted by the political discourse, they do not notice that time disjuncture in Picasso's art is a deliberately conceived counter to an older European tradition. It therefore has little to do with the African and Polynesian arts, in which such a *raison d'être* is inconceivable, and in which the representational is not subjected to such a technique. This should be clear in New Zealand, amid the art of the Maori, where each figure or group of figures is remarkably consistent in style throughout.

But the interest of the *Demoiselles d'Avignon* goes beyond attempts to be child, madman, or savage, which was earlier a posture of many Romantics. Its inconsistency of style asks other art-historical questions, which can only be discussed in relation to a close look at the works and how they work on us. How can the painting be unified or finished, when it looks as if it is painted by more than one painter? How can it be understood at all if it is not answerable to one name, to one consistent person? What can it be saying, if it changes what it is saying in mid-air?

Picasso, unlike naïve painters, has many styles to hand, and uses them at will. In the end, he has no style that is uniquely his, adopted as such and adhered to as a form pre-conceived before beginning each work. Picasso has no style, but a lot of class.

As a result, the unique market-place feature is the signature, and only the signature. The artist's polymorphous 'I' is not a centre for the actual work of any of the paintings any more. But there is instead of the now exploded 'I' a reputation, a legend. Unfortunately for the promoters, they did not acknowledge how radical the work was. This shows particularly in the way they write. Nothing in his art gave them any doubts about the status of the sign-system they themselves relied on, that is the syntax of their writing-practice. That needed to be transformed by Picasso's attitude to paintings in an infinitely open time.

Picasso in New Zealand

Daniel-Henry Kahnweiler

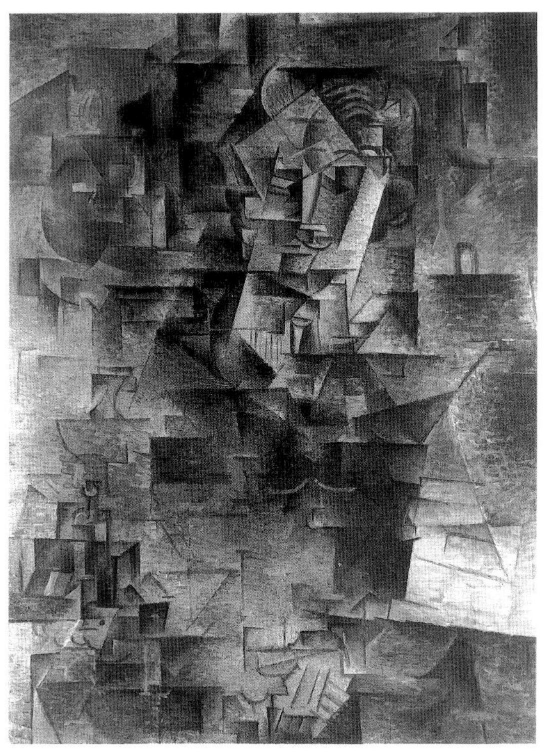

Picasso. *Daniel-Henry Kahnweiler*, Paris, 1910. Oil on canvas, 100.6 × 72.8 cm. The Art Institute of Chicago. Gift of Mrs Gilbert W. Chapman in memory of Charles B. Goodspeed, 1948.561.

I do not know if there is any knowledge in the Antipodes, of a certain aspect of modern painting – a strange epidemic which has spread throughout Europe and America since the end of the war. Its origins are in the past. It is precisely Pablo Picasso . . . who is, without any doubt, the point of departure of what is called *Abstract Art.* I hasten immediately to quote a reflection of this artist: 'Michelangelo is not responsible for the cupboards of the Renaissance.' One understands one ought not to make an artist responsible for what has been done by his followers who have misunderstood him. It is a great picture by Picasso, painted in the spring of 1907, *Les Demoiselles d'Avignon*, which stands at the beginning of a development in the plastic arts which has resulted today in the epidemic which I am about to discuss. I am able to explain here neither the reasons for the birth of Cubism – for this is the name history has given this style in the plastic arts – nor to show how it developed in the hands of four great painters – Picasso, Braque, Gris, Léger – but I will speak at least of what appears to me to be its particular innovation. Even if one has not been clearly aware of it – painting and sculpture have at all times been 'writings', that is to say the creation of signs in order to describe the outside world, but these signs have always been more or less imitative. Painters and sculptors truly see the outside world, and it is thanks to their works only that we others understand it in a plastic fashion and not simply as a combination of friendly or hostile forces as an animal does. It follows that each generation sees this world in a different manner. If the *writing* of artists changes considerably from one generation to another, as it happened during the last hundred years, it may be that their contemporaries cannot *read* the new writing immediately, that is to say they do not see what the artist has wished to describe. This was the case, strange to say, even with the Impressionists who had tried to invent signs as 'illusionistic' as possible. It occurred with their immediate successors, the Nabis, the Fauves, and naturally with the Cubists. These, in fact, no longer pretended to invent signs directly imitating the aspects of the outside world as the works of their elders had conceived it. They set out to describe objects, preserving an almost total liberty for their figurations. Thus it appears to me today, fifty years later, that Picasso's crucial gesture was the beginning of a liberation of plastic symbols. Let us understand quite clearly that by *writing* I understand a significant statement and not a calligraphy devoid of meaning. Never have the Cubist painters, nor those whom I consider as their legitimate heirs, renounced the divine aim of the plastic arts, the forming of the world of mankind.

But other artists and sculptors have been tempted by that aspect of Cubism which was very hard to read, to consider only the arrangement of coloured forms, and they have thus slid towards a kind of applied art, of hedonistic decoration. Such an 'art' necessarily can only aspire to please in one manner or another, having no message to transmit – the message of the plastic arts being the communication of an emotion of the artist confronted by the visible world, an emotion which he would like to share with everyone.

Derived directly from Cubism, a rigid, geometric abstract art was formed of which the first champion was Mondrian. What has often been called 'lyrical abstract' painting owed its origin more to certain of the Fauve painters (Matisse, Derain, Vlaminck, etc.) whose dazzling fireworks had been seen in Munich in 1909 at the very time when Kandinsky had painted his first abstract works. It was out of lyrical abstraction that Tachism was born a few years ago. Tachism has now invaded exhibitions of painting throughout the world.

Abstract art has assimilated certain ideas of Surrealism asking for the freedom of the instinct respecting the accidental. 'Automatic writing', which Surrealism had practised, is applied here in painting. No one will deny that this may provide a pleasant game for the author and even for the spectator, but never will I believe that this can be considered as painting, *cosa mentale*, as Leonardo da Vinci said.

This long preamble is intended simply to prevent a misunderstanding. I would not wish the works of Picasso which are being shown in New Zealand . . . to be regarded as abstractions. They are not exercises in style either. If Picasso is the greatest painter of our time – that is what I think and I am not alone in thinking it – it is because he has invented the most striking new symbols in order to make us share his enotion at the spectacle of life. To paint is to invent symbols.

Our epoch, after centuries during which painters were only painters, knows once more numerous artists who are painters, sculptors and engravers all at once, like the artists of the Renaissance.

Picasso is such a complete artist. He not only makes paintings, sculptures, prints, ceramics, mosaics, but there have been occasions during his life when he has had the need of words in order to externalise himself. He has written admirable poems in Spanish and French. In all this there is no frolic; according to circumstances he has felt the need of expressing himself by one or other of these means. Thus his lithographs . . . owe their existence to a banal fact of daily life. The winter of 1945–6 was very cold in Paris and stocks of coal had still not been replenished. Private homes were not heated and Picasso's studio was glacial. The Mourlot lithographic printing works, as an industrial building, had a coal allocation. Picasso went there to work one day and found himself at ease in this heated environment and he returned there to work every day for several months. It is thus that his first lithographs, printed by Mourlot, came to be born, and they constitute his real début in this technique. He had indeed made some before, but they were, rather, only drawings executed on stone. On the contrary, during this winter, as always when he touches something, he became excited over the technical possibilities, he refashioned the medium of lithography. To be precise, it was not a question of virtuosity in the new medium but of new possibilities (did he not say, one day, 'I do not search, I *find*'), new means to externalise himself in order to 'Donner à voir' (to give to seeing), if I may be allowed to use the beautiful title of a book by Paul Eluard, who was a close friend of Picasso. Let me explain. What is extraordinary is Picasso's memory of plastic forms, of innumerable visual expoeriences which store themselves in his mind.

One of our friends, André Beaudin, a younger painter of great talent, told me that he saw Picasso working one day in the studio of Lacourière, the printers. Picasso was in the process of engraving one of his illustrations – *The Frogs* – for Buffon's *Natural History*. 'One would have said,' Beaudin told me, 'that he had the animal in front of him. Each muscle was there!' In this way he makes us share in his treasure of images, and by them, the world around us is prodigiously enriched.

Engraving is not a subsidiary activity in Picasso's life. It plays as important a role as his painting and sculpture and it began as early as they did. It was in 1899 that he made his first etching – a picador. He called it *El Zurdo* (The left-handed man), for not knowing the medium too well he took no account of the fact that the engraved design on the plate was reversed in the paper: the picador holds his spear in his left hand. Engraving, at times, has even taken the place of drawing so that he has expressed himself only on to plate or stone. The life and art of Picasso are one. Everything which troubles his existence reflects itself in his art – his joys, his anxieties, his loves, his hates. Today one is entranced at Cannes in a huge dilapidated house, encumbered with a thousand objects, yet sparsely furnished. It looks over a fine sloping park. He hardly ever leaves house or work. He does not go anywhere except to the bullfights at Arles or Nîmes. He lives only for his work, and anything which might disturb it is thrust aside.

Hokusai, towards the end of his life, signed his work 'The old man mad with drawing.' I would give the same surname to Pablo Picasso – but he is so young, unbelievably young.

Written in 1958 as the introduction to the exhibition of Picasso lithographs and aquatints 1945–57 shown in Auckland, Dunedin, Wellington and Melbourne.

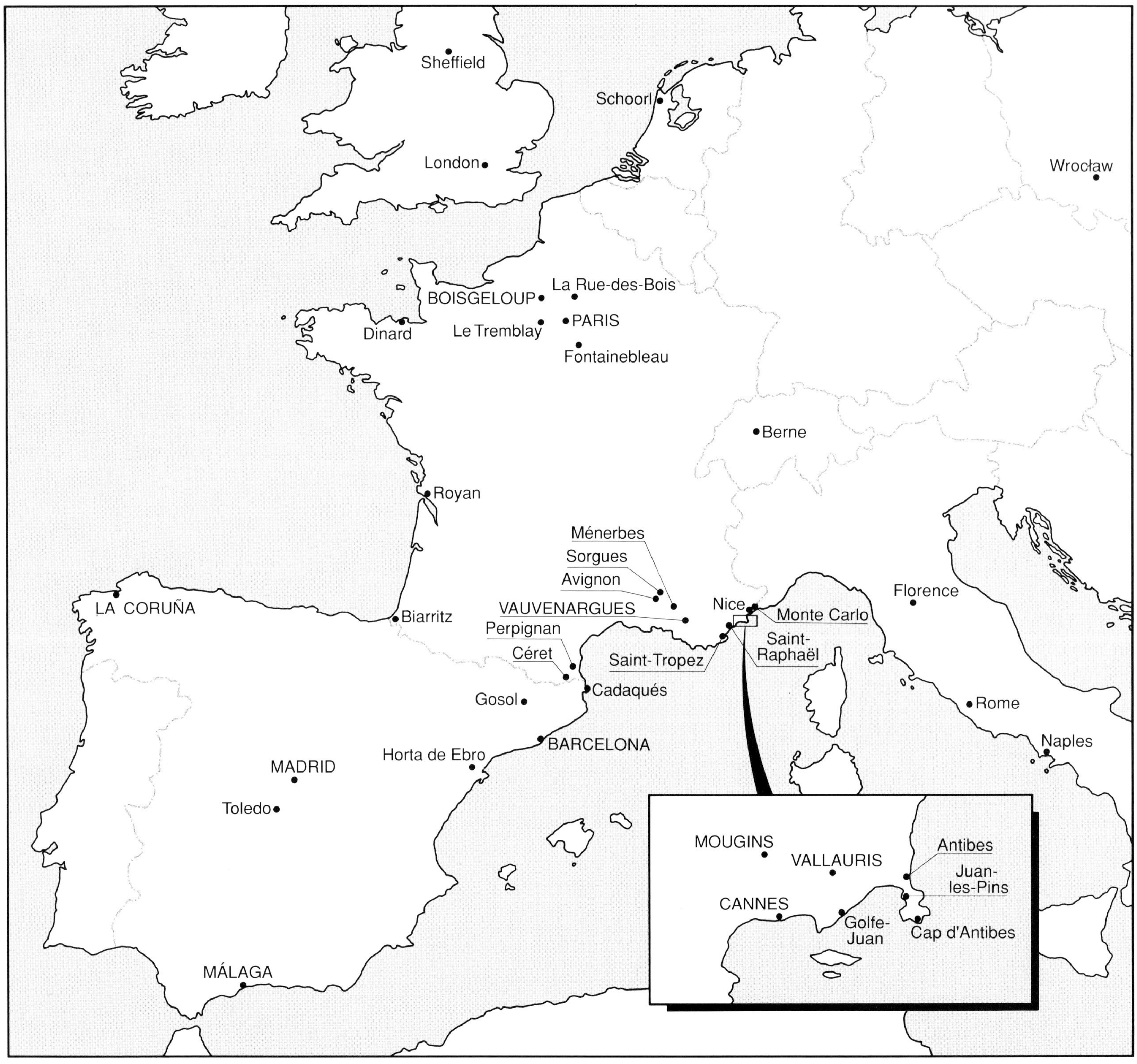
Sheffield
Schoorl
London
Wrocław
La Rue-des-Bois
BOISGELOUP
PARIS
Dinard
Le Tremblay
Fontainebleau
Berne
Royan
Ménerbes
Sorgues
Avignon
Florence
Nice
LA CORUÑA
VAUVENARGUES
Monte Carlo
Biarritz
Perpignan
Saint-Raphaël
Céret
Saint-Tropez
Cadaqués
Gosol
Rome
BARCELONA
Naples
Horta de Ebro
MADRID
Toledo
MOUGINS
VALLAURIS
Antibes
Juan-les-Pins
CANNES
Golfe-Juan
Cap d'Antibes
MÁLAGA

Chronology

Marilyn McCully

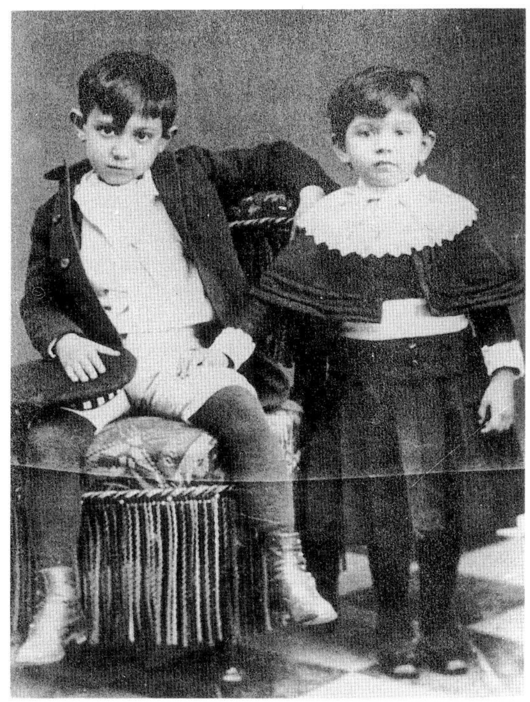

Pablo and Lola Picasso at the ages of seven and four. Picasso Archives, Paris.

Opposite: Map showing the principal places where Picasso lived or which he visited. Those places where he had permanent residences are shown in capital letters.

1881

On 25 October Pablo Diego José Francisco de Paula Juan Nepumuceno María de los Remedios Crispín Crispiniano Santísima Trinidad was born to José Ruiz Blasco, an art school teacher, and María Picasso López in Málaga, Spain, at 36, Plaza de Riego.

He is called Pablo Ruiz Picasso; but by 1901 he drops his father's surname in favour of his mother's.

Two sisters are born later: Lola (Dolores) in 1884, Conchita (Concepción) in 1887; the family moves to a larger apartment at No. 32 in 1883.

1881–1891

As a child, Pablo attends elementary school; and under his father's guidance, he begins drawing and making paper cut-outs.

His earliest known drawings depict pigeons (his father's own speciality as a painter), bullfights, and a full-length figure of Hercules.

1891–1894

In 1891 Picasso's father accepts a new position as professor in the School of Fine and Applied Arts (Instituto da Guarda) in La Coruña, and the family moves to an apartment at 24, Payo Gómez, just by the ocean.

Pablo attends secondary school and in 1892 is admitted to the Instituto, where he first studies drawing and later attends advanced classes with the sculptor and painter Isidoro Brocos as well as with his father.

His first dated oils – mainly portraits of family and friends – are painted in 1894.

1895

In January Picasso's sister Conchita dies of diphtheria, and the family begins to make plans to leave Galicia.

This spring Picasso comes of artistic age: his first patron, the eminent Doctor Ramón Pérez Costales buys small works; his father arranges models for him; and he exhibits twice in storefront windows – in February, two studies of heads, and in March, the *Beggar with a cap.*

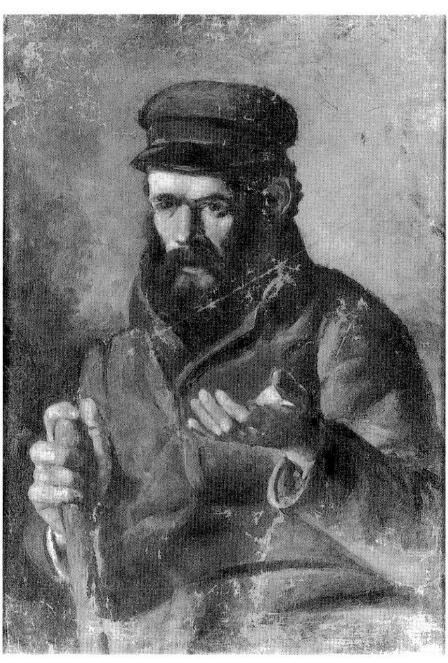

Picasso. *Beggar with a cap*, La Coruña, 1895.
Oil on canvas, 72.5 × 50 cm.
Musée Picasso, Paris.

The reviewer for *La Voz de Galicia* (21 February) predicts that 'if he continues in this [courageous and mature] manner, there is no doubt that he has days of glory and a brilliant future ahead of him.' Picasso was to keep this work and two others done in La Coruña, his portrait of Pérez Costales (Picasso Heirs Collection) and the *Girl with bare feet* (Musée Picasso, Paris) in his personal collection until his death.

In late spring Picasso's father obtains a position at the Art School in Barcelona, and the family leaves La Coruña. They travel through Madrid (where Pablo visits the Prado for the first time) to spend the summer in Málaga, staying with don José's brother Doctor Salvador Ruiz Blasco at 97, Calle Cortina del Muelle.

Picasso paints the harbour; his uncle arranges for an old fisherman, Salmerón, to model for him.

In September the family travels by boat to Barcelona; they reside at 4, Carrer Llauder, near the port.

Picasso passes the entrance examination for the Art School (known as 'La Llotja' as it is situated in the old Stock Exchange) where his father is teaching. He meets Manuel Pallarès, who becomes a lifelong friend; and through another classmate, Joaquim Bas, Picasso meets his first mistress, a circus equestrienne called Rosita de Oro.

1896

Don José arranges for his son to work in the studio of a colleague, Manuel Garnelo; later in the year, Pablo and Pallarès share a studio at 4, Carrer de la Plata. In addition to portraits of his family, Picasso paints and draws numerous religious subjects. These include *First Communion* (Museu Picasso, Barcelona), which is put on exhibition in Barcelona in April.

During the summer the Ruiz Blasco family moves to 3, Carrer de la Mercè.

They spend their summer holidays with Doctor Salvador in Málaga; Picasso paints a portrait of his Aunt Pepa (Museu Picasso, Barcelona).

Back in Barcelona in the autumn Picasso frequents the Eden Concert cabaret, where he meets the de Soto brothers, Angel and Mateu.

Late in the year he begins the large allegorical painting *Science and charity*, for which his father serves as model for the doctor.

1897

Science and charity is exhibited and wins an honourable mention in Madrid in the spring; and afterwards a gold medal in Málaga, where the family again spends the summer.

The Málaga painter Martínez de la Vega ceremoniously baptises Pablo as an artist by pouring champagne over his head. His family pools financial resources to send him to study in Madrid.

In October Picasso enters the Royal Academy of San Fernando in Madrid; he resides at 5, Calle de San Pedro Mártir.

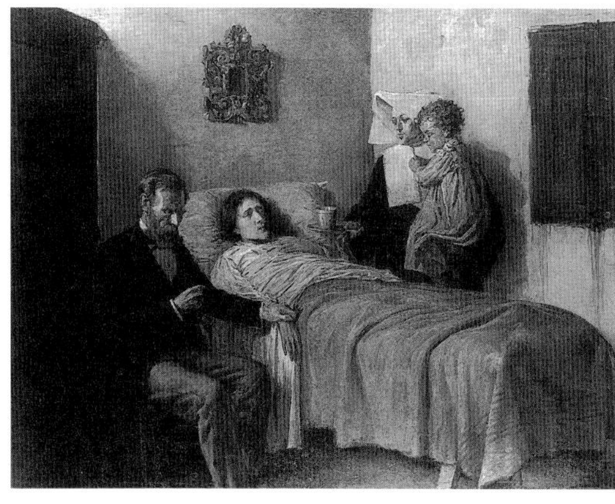

Picasso. *Science and charity*, Barcelona, 1897. Oil on canvas, 197 × 249.5 cm. Museu Picasso, Barcelona.

He spends little time in classes, preferring the company of the Argentinian painter Pancho Bernareggi, with whom he studies works by Velázquez, Goya and El Greco (in the Prado and in Toledo) and sketches in cafés and on the street.

1898

In March Picasso contracts scarlet fever and is attended in Madrid by his sister, Lola. In June he is well enough to return home.

He is then invited by Pallarès to convalesce at his family's farmhouse at Horta de Ebro. Over the next seven or eight months Picasso learns to speak Catalan, to live in the open (they camp and paint out of doors for weeks at a time) and to work in a house in the country. He later remarked: 'All that I know I learned in Pallarès's village.'

Some of his paintings are destroyed in a storm, but *Aragonese customs* (painted in Horta, now lost) is exhibited in Madrid and Málaga in 1899.

1899

Pablo returns to Barcelona early in the year; taking a studio with former classmates, the Cardona brothers, at 1 or 2, Escudillers Blancs. Later he works in the studios of the de Soto brothers and Ramon Pichot.

Apart from some support from his family and from friends, from now until the end of his life Picasso lives from his activities as an artist.

Picasso begins to go to the tavern Els Quatre Gats, the bohemian meeting place in Barcelona for Catalan artists and writers, whose artistic and political aspirations are in tune with Paris and northern Europe rather than tradition-bound Spain. His circle is broadened and includes the poet–painter Carles Casagemas and the poet–sculptor Jaime Sabartès (Picasso's future secretary and life-long friend), among many others.

Casagemas accompanies Picasso to Málaga in the summer for a small exhibition of his work, including a painting called *Last rites* (later renamed *Last moments*), a large canvas showing the visit of a priest to a dying woman.

Last moments will also be included in his first Barcelona solo exhibition and in the Spanish section of the Paris Exposition Universelle (both in 1900).

1900

In January Picasso and Casagemas take a studio at 17, Riera Sant Joan; both artists prepare first solo exhibitions at Els Quatre Gats. Picasso shows three paintings and between 50 and 150 portrait drawings (charcoal and other media on paper) of his Barcelona friends in February (Casagemas exhibits in March).

Picasso contributes drawings for publication in Catalan journals, including *Joventut* and *Catalunya Artística*; designs printed ephemera for Els Quatre Gats and other commercial establishments; and makes his first etching (*El Zurdo*).

He shows four bullfight pastels at Els Quatre Gats in July.

In October Picasso and Casagemas travel to Paris, where they take over the Montmartre studio of fellow Spaniard Isidre Nonell at 49, rue Gabrielle. Pallarès later joins them, as do three models (Odette/Louise Lenoir, who takes up with Picasso, Antoinette Fornerod and Germaine/Laure Florentin/Gargallo, who becomes involved with Casagemas and later marries Ramon Pichot).

In addition to visiting the painting section of the Universal Exhibition, the artists go to the Luxembourg and the Louvre. Picasso responds to French art, especially the work of Toulouse-Lautrec, in works such as the *Moulin de la Galette* (Guggenheim Museum, New York).

He signs a contract with the Catalan dealer Pere Mañach, who will represent him in Paris; Mañach immediately sells the dealer Berthe Weill three of Picasso's bullfight scenes. The state councillor Olivier Sainsère also begins to buy drawings; he continues to collect Picassos for over ten years.

Casagemas suffers depression over his failed love affair with Germaine; he and Picasso return to Barcelona and then travel to Málaga. After an unhappy visit, they go their separate ways.

1901

Picasso signs a one-year lease on a studio at 28, Calle Zurbano in Madrid; he works with Francisco de Assis Soler on the journal *Arte Joven* as art editor (5 issues appear, starting on 10 March).

In February Picasso learns that Casagemas has committed suicide in Paris. He decides to give up Madrid and abandons his painting *Woman in Blue* (Museo de arte contemporáneo, Madrid), which he has submitted to the General Exhibition of Fine Arts.

In early May he stops briefly in Barcelona, and – after he himself has left for Paris – a group of his pastels is exhibited at the Sala Parés there in June. To coincide with the show, a biographical article about Picasso by Miquel Utrillo appears in *Pèl & Ploma* with a portrait drawing by Ramon Casas.

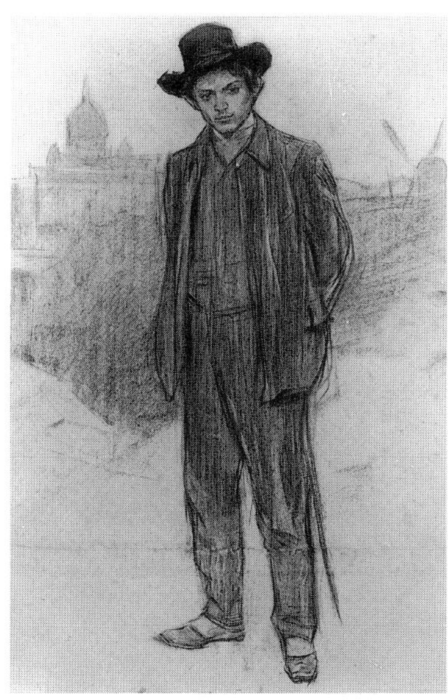

Ramon Casas. *Portrait of Picasso in Montmartre*, Barcelona, 1901. Charcoal and crayon on paper, 69 × 44.5 cm. Museu d'Art Modern, Barcelona.

In late May Picasso moves to 130*ter*, boulevard de Clichy, where the sculptor Manolo has resided since Casagemas's death; he and Picasso argue over Germaine, with whom both have affairs, and Manolo moves out. Little is known about Picasso's new mistress, a woman called Blanche.

In June, with the Basque painter Francisco Iturrino, Picasso exhibits some 64 paintings and drawings at Vollard's gallery on the rue Laffitte; these works show the influence of Van Gogh and French painting. Critics admire Picasso's energy, but fault him for lack of a personal style. Mañach, who has organised the show, introduces him to the poet and 'art critic' Max Jacob, who will play an important role in Picasso's life; Max teaches Picasso about French literature and esoteric thought, thus influencing the symbolism of the Blue and Rose periods.

In the autumn Picasso commemorates the death of Casagemas in several works, including *Evocation* (Musée d'Art Moderne de la Ville, Paris), and, according to him, 'the Blue period began.' Subjects of syphilitic whores and maternities are found in the Saint-Lazare women's prison.

1902

During January Picasso breaks his contract with Mañach and returns to Barcelona, where he works in the studio of Angel de Soto and Josep Rocarol at 10, Carrer Nou de la Rambla.

Major Blue period works, including the *Two sisters* (Hermitage, Leningrad), *La soupe* (Art Gallery of Ontario, Toronto) and his series of *Crouching women* (Art Gallery of Ontario, no.6; etc.) are done there.

In April in Paris Berthe Weill has a joint show of Picasso and Louis Bernard-Lemaire. Picasso's new work is not well received.

Before his twenty-first birthday Picasso's uncle, Doctor Salvador, buys him out of the draft for military service.

In the autumn an exhibition of ancient and mediaeval Catalan art (over 1,800 works) is held in the Barcelona Palace of Fine Arts.

In October Picasso returns to Paris for a few months. Life is difficult; he moves several times, staying at the Hôtel Maroc and finally sharing Max Jacob's small flat at 87, boulevard Voltaire.

Paintings by Picasso are shown again at Berthe Weill's gallery in November, and his work is discussed favourably in the *Mercure de France* by Charles Morice, who gives Picasso a copy of Gauguin's *Noa Noa* when they meet.

He studies Puvis de Chavannes and also Gauguin, whose works he sees both at Vollard's and in the studio of Paco Durrio, the Basque potter.

1903

In January Picasso moves back to Barcelona into the Riera Sant Joan studio (formerly shared with Casagemas), which he occupies with Angel de Soto.

He paints his most celebrated Blue period compositions during the next months (into 1904): *La Vie* – which he paints over his earlier canvas *Last moments* – *The old guitarist* (Art Institute of Chicago), *Tragedy* (National Gallery of Art, Washington, D.C.), *The blind man's meal* (Metropolitan Museum of Art, New York) and *La Celestina* (Private collection, Paris).

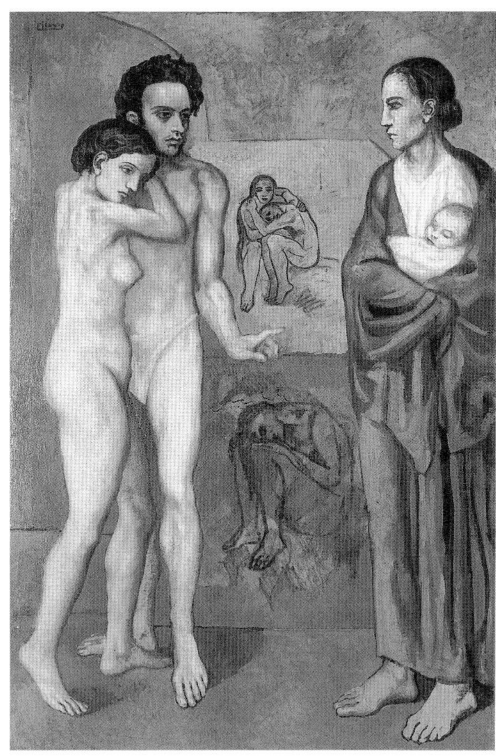

Picasso. *La Vie*, Paris, 1903. Oil on canvas, 196.5 × 129 cm. The Cleveland Museum of Art. Gift of Hanna Fund.

Els Quatre Gats closes in July.

Picasso is annoyed with de Soto's laziness and the continual presence of his friends in the studio; late in the year he takes over Pablo Gargallo's studio at 28, Carrer del Comerç (facing Isidre Nonell). His closest friends are Sabartès and the painter Sebastià Junyer-Vidal.

1904

In April he leaves Barcelona for Paris with Junyer-Vidal. They take over the studio of Paco Durrio in the so-called Bateau-Lavoir at 13, rue Ravignan (where Picasso will stay until 1909).

Picasso's work changes in response to new surroundings and people, including his mistress, a woman called Madeleine (who aborts Picasso's baby at the end of the summer), a neighbour, Fernande Olivier (whom he meets in August), and the writers Guillaume Apollinaire and André Salmon (whom he meets in October); they meet regularly at the café Le Lapin Agile.

In October he has his last exhibition at Berthe Weill's gallery.

Ricard Canals, another Barcelona painter who lives in Paris, encourages him to take up print-making again; he engraves *The frugal meal* (no.8), which is printed by Delâtre.

Transitional works between the Blue and Rose periods include *The woman ironing* (Guggenheim Museum, New York), *Les deux amies* (Private collection, Paris), *Woman with a crow* (Toledo Museum of Art) and *The marriage of Pierrette* (Private collection, Sweden).

At the end of the year Picasso starts work on the first of five stages of his huge painting *Family of saltimbanques*.

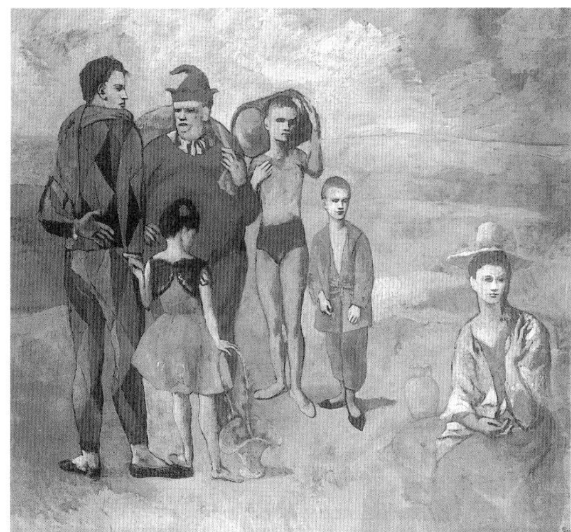

Picasso. *Family of saltimbanques*, Paris, 1905. Oil on canvas, 212.8 × 229.6 cm. National Gallery of Art, Washington, D.C. Chester Dale Collection.

1905

Working in close association with Apollinaire, Picasso develops the so-called Rose period; he exhibits a series of Saltimbanque engravings (see no.11) along with other works in a group show at the Galeries Serrurier (February–March). Morice writes the preface to the catalogue, and Apollinaire reviews the exhibition in *La Revue immoraliste* (April) and *La Plume* (May).

Picasso frequents the circle of *La Plume*, led by Paul Fort and Jean Moréas, with Apollinaire and André Salmon.

Picasso spends June and July in Holland at the invitation of the Dutch journalist and bohemian Tom Schilperoort; he stays first in Schoorl and then in the adjoining hamlet of Schoorldam on the Great Northern Canal.

A local girl poses for *La Belle Hollandaise* (Queensland Art Gallery). His sketchbooks indicate visits to nearby Alkmaar and Hoorn, but not Amsterdam.

Picasso returns to the Bateau-Lavoir in August, and Fernande Olivier moves into the studio within weeks.

The Salon d'Automne, which opens in October, features an Ingres retrospective as well as the 'Cage aux Fauves' (Picasso has already met Derain and Vlaminck, but not Matisse).

Picasso – who much later claimed he had already done his own 'fauve' paintings in 1901 – responds by abandoning the *Family of saltimbanques* and by beginning the search for a new style.

Around this time he meets Leo and Gertrude Stein, who buy the *Girl with a basket of flowers* (Private collection, New York). Gertrude becomes his friend and patron, and he begins her celebrated portrait (Metropolitan Museum of Art, New York; see ill. p.24).

He paints the *Woman with a Fan* (National Gallery, Washington, D.C.), the *Boy with a Pipe* (Whitney Collection) and, at the end of the year, *The Death of Harlequin* (Mellon Collection).

1906

New subjects, such as *The watering place* (never realised in oil), reflect Picasso's study of Ingres and Puvis de Chavannes and the challenge of the arcadian compositions – notably *Bonheur de vivre* (Barnes Foundation) – of Matisse, whom he meets through the Steins.

Later in the spring Picasso studies Iberian art exhibited at the Louvre.

In April Vollard buys virtually all Picasso's recent – Rose period – work, although the unfinished *Family of saltimbanques* remains in the studio. After 1907 Vollard loses interest in Picasso's work until he returns to a more classicising style in the war years.

The 2,000 gold francs he has received from Vollard enables Picasso to travel to Spain, and on 21 May he sets off with Fernande for Gósol, in the Pyrenees, stopping for a fortnight in Barcelona on the way.

At Gósol, where they stay in an inn, the Cal Tampanada, Picasso makes a decisive break with his previous work, abandoning symbolist overtones and concentrating on the physical representation of the human figure in such works as *The two brothers* (Kunstmuseum, Basle), using predominantly earth tones. He is inspired by the presence of Fernande and learns from his own sculpture and from his reductive studies of the old innkeeper Josep Fontdevila.

While he is there, he writes to the sculptor Enric Casanovas, who was intending to join them, requesting him to bring or send woodcarving tools as well as drawing paper; Fernande asks him to bring her perfume.

Fear of typhoid forces them to leave for Paris in mid-August.

Upon Picasso's return to the Bateau-Lavoir, he completes the portrait of Gertrude Stein; and embarks on a series of double-figure compositions, featuring hefty nudes inspired partly by Stein's physical presence. He also does drawings for sculpture, continues woodcarving and works in Durrio's studio, where he learns something of ceramic sculpture (*Head of Josep Fontdevila*).

He does several versions of a *Nude combing her hair*, in painting and sculpture (no.12), developing out of the Gósol composition *Harem* (Cleveland Museum of Art).

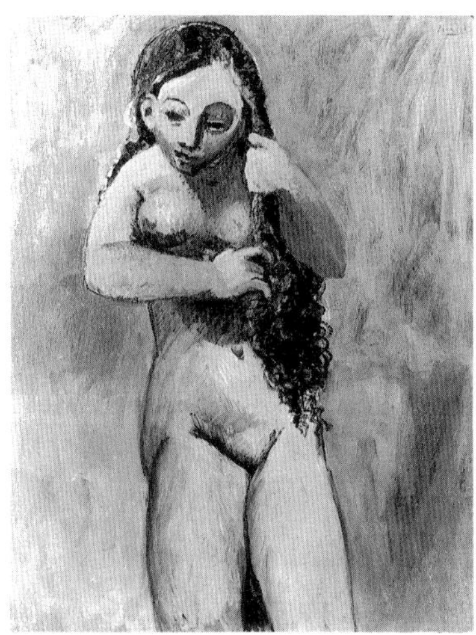

Picasso. *Nude combing her hair*, Paris, 1906. Oil on canvas, 104 × 80 cm. Norton Simon Inc. Foundation, Los Angeles.

Juan Gris, who initially comes to Paris to work as a cartoonist and illustrator, takes over Kees Van Dongen's studio in the Bateau-Lavoir; he and Picasso become friends.

1907

In March Matisse shows his *Blue nude* and Derain exhibits his large *Bathers* composition at the Salon des Indépendants. Picasso is also working on a brothel/bathers composition, which results in the work later called *Les Demoiselles d'Avignon*.

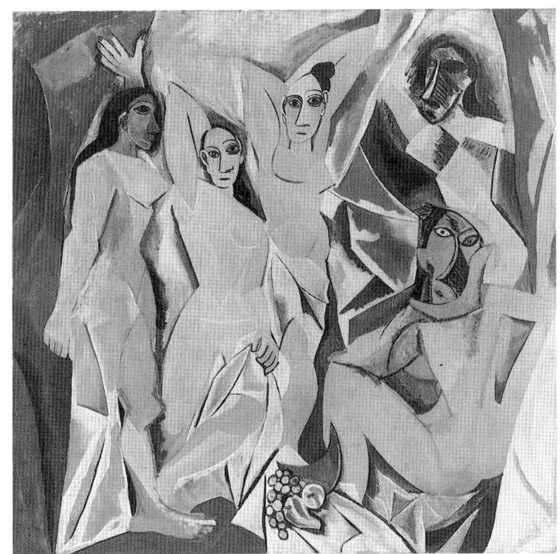

Picasso. *Les Demoiselles d'Avignon*, Paris, 1907. Oil on canvas, 243.9 × 233.7 cm. The Museum of Modern Art, New York. Acquired through the Lillie P. Bliss Bequest.

In late spring Picasso visits the Trocadéro ethnographic museum, where he studies African art.

He finishes the *Demoiselles* in July (although it is not exhibited until 1916). His future dealer D.-H. Kahnweiler comes to the Bateau-Lavoir to see the painting in the summer, as does his Russian patron Sergei I. Shchukin.

A retrospective exhibition of Cézanne (who had died the previous October) is held at the Salon d'Automne; Cézanne's work inspires Picasso and Georges Braque, who meet about this time, to develop his ideas (such as registering perspective through planar brushstrokes and colour) in their own work.

African influences are strong in works of this year, including *Woman in yellow* (Pulitzer Collection, St Louis), *The dancer* (Private collection) and sculptural masks.

1908

Beginning in the spring Picasso starts working on a large composition of *Three women*. He completes the final version (Hermitage, Leningrad) towards the end of the year.

The German artist Wiegels commits suicide in the Bateau-Lavoir in the summer; Picasso finds the body. As with the suicide of Casagemas, the death is reflected in Picasso's works, and skulls appear in some still-life compositions.

Picasso and Fernande spend several weeks in late summer in La Rue-des-Bois (some 30 miles north of Paris), where he paints landscapes influenced by Cézanne.

In November Kahnweiler mounts a large exhibition of Braque, who has had six recent paintings refused by the Salon d'Automne; Apollinaire writes the catalogue preface. The term 'Cubist' is applied to Braque's works (in September Matisse had said he was 'making little cubes', and now the critic Louis Vauxcelles describes his work as 'cubist').

In November Fernande and Picasso give a banquet at the Bateau-Lavoir for Douanier Rousseau.

In December–January three works by Picasso are included in an exhibition at the Galerie Notre-Dame-des-Champs.

During the year Kahnweiler has bought some forty paintings from Picasso. He makes an agreement with his artists that from now on he will not put on one-man shows, simply exhibit selections from gallery stock, and that they will not submit works to the official salons.

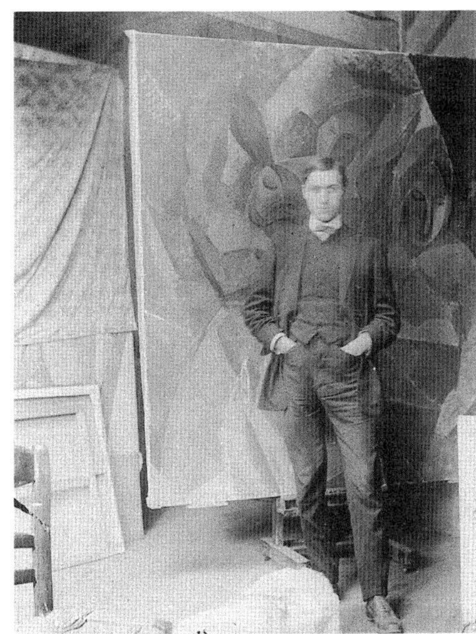

André Salmon standing in front of *Three women* at the Bateau-Lavoir, summer 1908. Picasso Archives, Paris.

1909

Picasso works on the large composition *Bread and fruit dish on a table* (Kunstmuseum, Basle) as well as painting various heads of Fernande.

They regularly attend Gertrude Stein's weekly salons; she encourages other collectors (such as the Cone sisters from Baltimore) to buy his work.

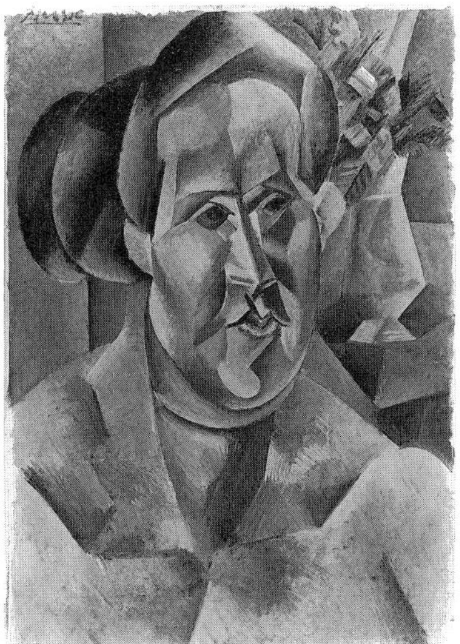

Picasso. *Portrait of Fernande*, Horta de Ebro, 1909. Oil on canvas, 61.8 × 42.8 cm. Kunstsammlung Nordrhein-Westfalen, Düsseldorf.

In the spring Picasso and Fernande travel to Barcelona, and then to Pallarès's village, Horta de Ebro, where they spend the summer. There Picasso paints (and photographs) the village and factory, and continues his paintings of Fernande: *Woman with a fan* (Pushkin Museum, Moscow).

Upon his return to Paris he moves to a new studio at 11, boulevard de Clichy; he also works on cubist sculpture (*Head of Fernande*) in Durrio's studio.

The close bohemian circle from the Bateau-Lavoir, which Fernande called 'la bande à Picasso' begins to break up; Picasso spends more time with Braque – 'Analytic Cubism' is fully underway in their work.

1910

Picasso does hermetic portraits of Vollard (Pushkin Museum, Moscow) and the German art enthusiast Uhde (Pulitzer Collection), followed in the autumn by one of Kahnweiler (Art Institute of Chicago; see ill. p.35); he also paints from the model – *Woman with a mandoline* (Museum of Modern Art, New York) – and increasingly depicts musical instruments in his compositions.

In May he exhibits recent (cubist) canvases at the Galerie Notre-Dame-des-Champs, and at the same time (April–May) four works are included in a group exhibition at the Müvészház Gallery, Budapest.

Fernande and Picasso spend July and August in a rented house in Cadaquès visiting the Pichots; the Derains are also there.

Picasso does a group of etchings to illustrate Kahnweiler's publication of Max Jacob's *Saint Matorel* (one of five books by Jacob he will illustrate over the next years).

They take the Derains on a brief visit to Barcelona, meeting Gargallo and Casanovas.

Back in Paris in the autumn Picasso and Braque begin to work in tandem in one another's studios.

As the recognised leaders of Cubism, their influence is far reaching; although Kahnweiler's exhibition policy means that Picasso seldom exhibits in Paris, the dealer ensures that works by his artists are included in many exhibitions abroad: this year Picasso and Braque are included in the Sonderbund exhibition in Düsseldorf in July–October, at the Galerie Thannhauser, Munich, in September, and at the end of the year in Roger Fry's exhibition 'Manet and the Post-Impressionists' at the Grafton Galleries, London.

Picasso does have a one-man show of recent work in Paris (at an unknown gallery), which opens in December and is reviewed by André Salmon.

He begins to enjoy some measure of financial success, thanks to Kahnweiler and to the Steins.

1911

Over the winter Picasso and Braque experiment with oval compositions.

In April Picasso has his first show in the U.S.A., at Stieglitz's Photo-Secession Galleries in New York; during the year works are also shown at the Galerie Paul Cassirer, Berlin, in the Berlin Secession exhibition and in 'Moderne Kunst Kring' at the Stedelijk Museum, Amsterdam.

In July Picasso travels alone to Céret to see Manolo, who is living in an eighteenth-century monastery (bought by his American art patron, Frank Havilland). Picasso takes over the first floor, where he lives with Fernande, who arrives in August with Max Jacob and Braque.

He and Braque begin to introduce lettering into their work: *L'Indépendant* (Private collection). The *Poet* (Peggy Guggenheim Collection) and the *Accordionist* (Guggenheim Museum, New York) are also painted at Céret.

Picasso returns to Paris in late August.

He gives back to the Louvre, through a newspaper, two stolen Iberian heads he had bought four years before (probably quite innocently); Apollinaire, who is implicated, is suspected of the theft of the *Mona Lisa* and spends five days in jail.

Soon after his return Picasso meets Eva Gouel (Marcelle Humbert) at the Steins, and she becomes his new mistress.

In Barcelona, despite his absence, Picasso is considered one of the principal forces in the new classicist movement in Catalan art; Eugeni d'Ors includes a Rose period engraving in his *Almanach dels Noucentistes* (Almanac of twentieth-century artists) in February; and in the following year the critic-poet Josep Junoy argues in his *Arte y artistas* that Picasso's Cubism is in fact a form of scientific analysis akin to classicism.

1912

Over the winter Picasso paints Eva: *Ma Jolie* (Museum of Modern Art, New York).

In 'Synthetic Cubism' he and Braque focus on still-life compositions, introducing collage elements in the spring; Picasso's *Still life with chair caning* includes a piece of oilcloth.

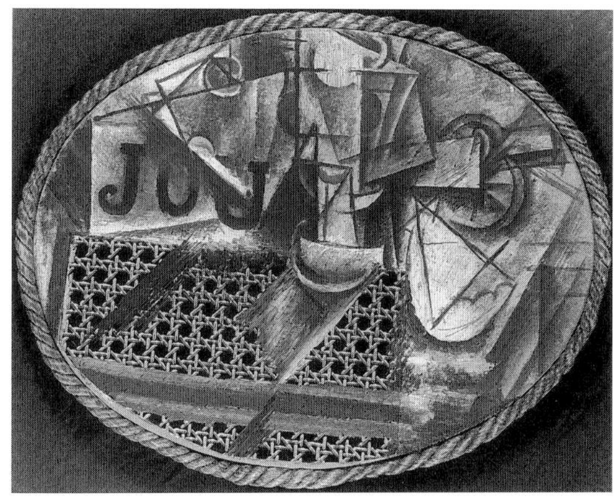

Picasso. *Still life with chair caning*, Paris, 1912.
Oil and oilcloth on canvas edged with rope, 29 × 37 cm.
Musée Picasso, Paris.

In May Picasso and Eva go to Céret, but when Fernande threatens to show up they go on to Avignon and settle six miles north in Sorgues-sur-l'Ouvèze. Picasso rents the Villa les Clochettes there for the summer; Braque, who has just married, and his wife join them, renting a villa nearby in July.

Kahnweiler is left to deal with Fernande and to make all Picasso's arrangements; he finds him a new studio at 242, boulevard Raspail in Montparnasse.

In September Picasso goes to Paris to install himself, returning to Sorgues to collect Eva. During his absence Braque makes the first of his *papiers collés*.

Picasso and Eva move into the studio together in October; Picasso too experiments with collage and construction.

Picasso's works are included for the first of several times in the annual exhibition of the Mánes Association of Visual Arts in Prague, where the art historian Vicenc Kramář becomes an avid collector of his work; in January four works are shown in Russia for the first time, at the 'Jack of Diamonds' exhibition; in February early works are shown at Dalmau's gallery, Barcelona; in April–May drawings are featured at the Stafford Gallery, London; and in May–September a special room is devoted to Picasso at the Cologne Sonderbund exhibition. His works are also included in other group exhibitions in Berlin, Munich, Leipzig, Amsterdam and London.

In December Picasso signs a three-year contract with Kahnweiler (who already has one-year contracts with Braque and Derain), giving him exclusive rights on all but five canvases a year.

1913

In February Picasso's first large retrospective is held at the Galerie Thannhauser, Munich; eight of his works are included in the 'Armory Show' (February–March) in New York (which travels to other American cities); and in the course of the year his work is shown at exhibitions in Vienna, Moscow, Budapest, Prague, Berlin, Dresden, Munich, Cologne and London.

In March Apollinaire publishes *Les Peintres cubistes*; Salmon also publishes his 'Anecdotal History of Cubism' in *La Jeune peinture française*. Vollard buys the plates of 15 etchings and engravings of 1904 and 1905 and reissues them as 'Les Saltimbanques'.

In mid-March Picasso and Eva return to Céret; Max Jacob later joins them.

On 3 May Picasso's father dies, and Picasso goes to Barcelona to attend the funeral. Max and Eva meet him in Catalonia and they return to Céret together.

In June Picasso and Eva fall ill and return to Paris for a few weeks, where they find a new studio at 5*bis*, rue Schoelcher. They go back to Céret at the end of July, but return to Paris in mid-August.

In the new studio Picasso paints *Woman in an armchair* (Private collection) and continues working on collages and constructions, some of which are published by Apollinaire in *Soirées de Paris*.

The Russian artist Tatlin visits Picasso at the end of the year, and begins to make his own constructions.

1914

Picasso develops his relief-constructions, introducing materials such as sand; he makes the painted bronze *Glass of absinthe* series.

In June he and Eva go to Avignon, where they live at 14, rue Saint-Bernard. Colour becomes livelier in his paintings.

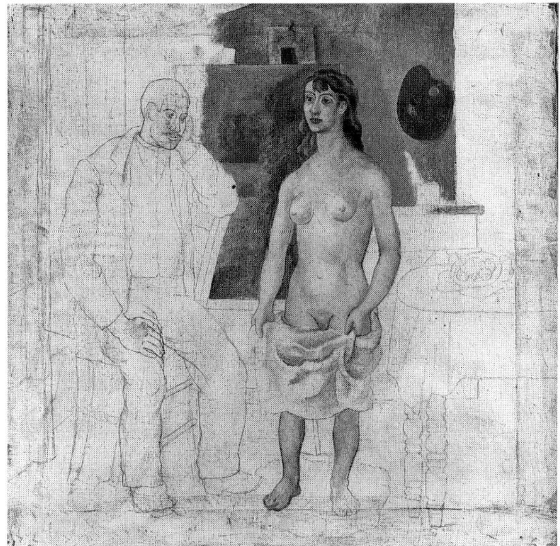

Picasso. *The painter and his model.* Avignon, 1914. Oil and crayon on canvas, 58 × 55.9 cm. Musée Picasso, Paris.

Although war is declared on 2 August, they stay in Avignon until late October or early November. Braque and Derain go to the front; Apollinaire follows at the end of the year. Most of his Spanish friends in Paris return home.

Picasso's work has been exhibited extensively in Germany during the spring and summer – in Berlin, Dresden (a one-man show at the Kunstsalon Emil Richter), Munich and Bremen – as well as in Vienna (a one-man show at the Galerie Miethke), Prague, Moscow, London and New York.

Kahnweiler is in Italy at the outbreak of war, and his Paris gallery on the rue Vignon is sequestered with all works, including Picassos and Braques; Kahnweiler, a German citizen, spends the war years in Switzerland. Gertrude Stein is in England.

The critic Gustave Coquiot classifies Picasso's work into categories, including 'blue period', 'red period' and 'black period', in *Cubistes, futuristes, passéistes.*

1915

In February, Picasso acts as Max Jacob's godfather at his baptism.

In the summer Eva becomes ill with tuberculosis; she is taken to a hospital in Auteuil in November and dies on December 14.

Picasso paints a sombre *Harlequin* (Museum of Modern Art, New York) during her illness.

In Kahnweiler's absence, Léonce Rosenberg begins to sell some of Picasso's pictures, including the *Harlequin.* Jean Cocteau visits Picasso's studio for the first time, where he sees the painting.

In May Braque is wounded; the following year he is invalided out of the army.

1916

Early in 1916 Picasso is in Barcelona with his family.

After his return to Paris, he proposes marriage (in February) to Gaby L'Espinasse (whom he had secretly courted, possibly in Avignon), but she turns him down.

In March Apollinaire returns from the war wounded.

In the spring Cocteau visits Picasso, dressed in Harlequin's costume, to suggest a collaboration with the Ballets Russes; his friend the Chilean art patron Eugenia Errazuriz brings Diaghilev to meet Picasso in May, and it is proposed that Erik Satie should compose the music for a ballet that Picasso will design.

In June or July Picasso moves to 22, rue Victor-Hugo, Montrouge.

In July André Salmon organises the first showing of *Les Demoiselles d'Avignon* at the Salon d'Antin in Paul Poiret's premises.

During the summer Picasso becomes friendly with Satie; Picasso and Matisse arrange a concert of music by Satie and Granados (who had died in March), and in August Picasso agrees to collaborate on *Parade.*

In November–December Cocteau organises a group show of Picasso, Matisse, Modigliani and Ortiz de Zarate at the Salle Huyghens.

1917

In early January Picasso returns to Barcelona, where he works 'without distraction'.

Some of his Parisian acquaintances, who are fleeing the war, are there, including Marie Laurencin, Albert Gleizes, Juliette Roche and Francis Picabia (the first number of whose journal *391* appears on 25 January).

Around 1 February Picasso returns to Paris.

On the 17th he travels with Cocteau to Rome to start work on *Parade.* He lives at the Hôtel de Russie and makes sketches for the décor and costumes in a studio at 53B Via Margutta.

His circle includes Diaghilev, Massine, Cocteau, Stravinsky and Bakst; he meets his future wife, Olga Kokhlova, among the dancers. While in Italy he also meets Italian artists, including Enrico Prampolini.

He visits St Peter's and the Borghese Gallery and also goes to Naples and Pompeii and to Florence, where he sees the Medici tombs.

In April the Diaghilev company returns to Paris, and *Parade* is first performed at the Théâtre du Châtelet on 18 May.

Afterwards Picasso accompanies the Ballets Russes to Madrid – where he meets King Alfonso XIII and visits the composer Manuel de Falla – and then to Barcelona.

His Catalan friends welcome him as a returning 'artistic' hero, and on 12 July a banquet is held in his honour.

Olga and Picasso stay behind while the company travels to South America. He lives at home; Olga stays at the Pension Ranzini, where Picasso paints and draws her as well as views of the port: *Passeig de Colom* (Museu Picasso, Barcelona).

He also paints a portrait of Leonide Massine as *Harlequin*; and he works in the studio of the painter Rafael Padilla, where he paints *La Salchichona* (Museu Picasso, Barcelona).

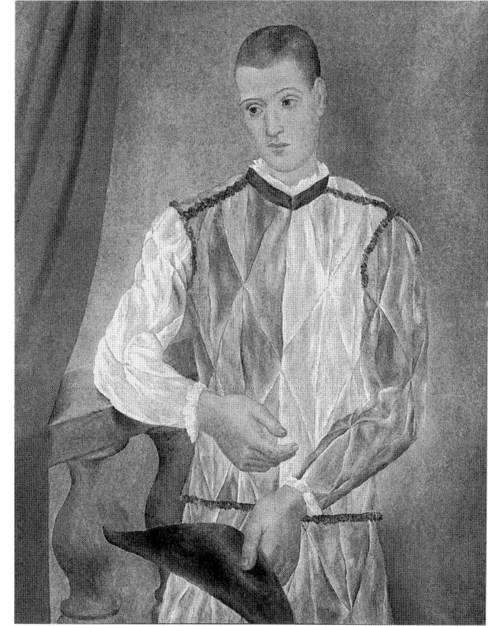

Picasso. *Harlequin.* Barcelona, 1917. Oil on canvas, 116 × 90 cm. Museu Picasso, Barcelona.

The great wartime exhibition of French art (over 1,460 works) is held in Barcelona in April–July; Vollard lectures on Renoir and Picasso at the Ateneu Barcelonès in May.

The Ballets Russes return in November to Barcelona; *Parade* is performed on the 10th; Joan Miró attends.

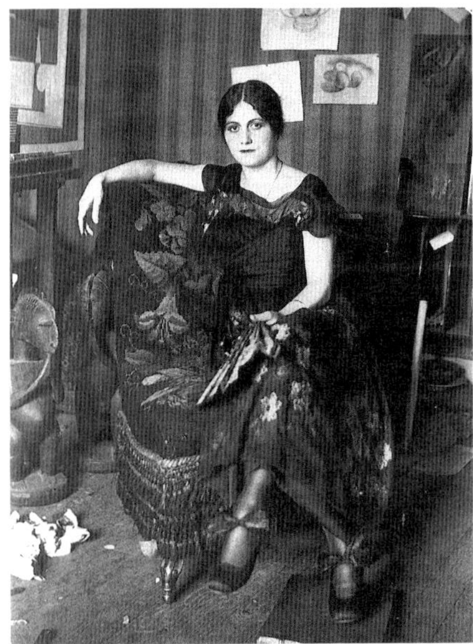

Olga Kokhlova photographed by Picasso, Montrouge, 1917. Picasso Archives, Paris.

Olga and Picasso leave for Paris in November, to live in his Montrouge studio.

Ivan Aksenov's *Picasso i okrestnosti* (written in 1915) is published in Moscow by Centrifuge.

1918

In January a Matisse–Picasso exhibition (catalogue preface by Apollinaire) is organised by Léonce Rosenberg at the Galerie Paul Guillaume; Cubist works, which are considered as 'art boche', are not included.

Later in the year he is included in a small group show of Barcelona artists in the Salon de Otoño at the Galeries Laietanes.

Picasso moves to the Hôtel Lutétia in the spring; he and Olga move in circles of high society; they marry on 12 July at the Russian church in Paris and honeymoon in Biarritz at the home of Mme Errazuriz, where Picasso meets Paul Rosenberg and Georges Wildenstein.

In the late summer Apollinaire writes to Picasso encouraging him to follow a new classicising direction in his work, citing his pointillist version of the *Peasant's Repast* by Le Nain (Musée Picasso, Paris).

The Picassos return to Paris in late September and move to 23, rue La Boëtie in mid-November. Picasso takes a floor for his studio, while Olga entertains on the floor below.

Paul Rosenberg becomes his dealer.

Apollinaire dies on 9 November.

1919

Most of the initiators of Dada begin to arrive in Paris. Although some of his writer friends participate in Dada events, Picasso remains attached to the society world of Diaghilev and his circle.

In May he travels to London to design the décor and costumes for the Ballets Russes production of *Le Tricorne* (music by de Falla). He and Olga, who rejoins the company, live at the Savoy Hotel.

He spends his time attending rehearsals and performances with Olga; being entertained by English society; meeting artists and writers (the Sitwells, Laura Knight and Clive Bell among many others); and in the company of his friend Derain, who is also there designing a ballet décor (*La Boutique fantasque).*

Picasso himself paints the drop curtain for *Tricorne* with Vladimir and Elizabeth Polunin in a studio on Floral Street.

Tricorne is first performed on 22 July at the Alhambra Theatre. (Later in the year he is invited to collaborate on *Pulcinella,* with choreography by Massine and music by Stravinsky.)

In June works done by Picasso in Barcelona (and left there) two years earlier, including his 1917 *Harlequin*, are exhibited with the Noucentista group 'Les Arts i els artistes'.

In August works by Picasso are included in a London exhibition of Modern French Art organised by Osbert and Sacheverell Sitwell at the Mansard Gallery, Heal's.

Late in the summer Picasso and Olga vacation at Saint-Raphaël on the Riviera. His work ranges from Ingres-influenced drawings and volumetric forms in his paintings to purified synthetic still lifes – especially a series of open window balcony views of Saint-Raphaël.

They return to Paris in the autumn, and in October he has an exhibition of drawings and watercolours at the Galerie Paul Rosenberg, next door to his apartment on the rue Boëtie; he does his first lithographs for the invitation and the catalogue. (His work is exhibited at the gallery almost every year over the coming years.)

1920

Tricorne is performed at the Opéra in Paris in February, *Pulcinella* in May. Picasso makes portrait drawings of his three composer-collaborators: Satie, Stravinsky, and de Falla.

Kahnweiler returns to Paris in February; his book, *The Rise of Cubism*, written during the war, is published in Munich, and in September he opens the Galerie Simon at 29*bis*, rue d'Astorg.

In March Joan Miró visits Picasso for the first time and they become friends.

Picasso and Olga spend the summer at Saint-Raphaël and then at Juan-les-Pins. Harlequin and Pierrot, as well as bathers and references to classical mythology, are principal subjects. The Picassos return to Paris in September.

During the year Picasso's work is exhibited at the Valori Plastici Gallery in Rome.

1921

In January an exhibition of works from 1902 to 1919 is held at the Leicester Galleries, London; Clive Bell writes the catalogue preface.

Paulo Picasso is born on 4 February.

In April Maurice Raynal's monograph *Pablo Picasso* is published in Munich (in Paris in 1922).

Picasso wins out over Juan Gris to design *Cuadro Flamenco* (with music arranged by de Falla) for Diaghilev; its only Paris performance is on 22 May at the Théâtre de la Gaîté-Lyrique.

On 30 May Uhde's collection (which had been confiscated by the French government during the

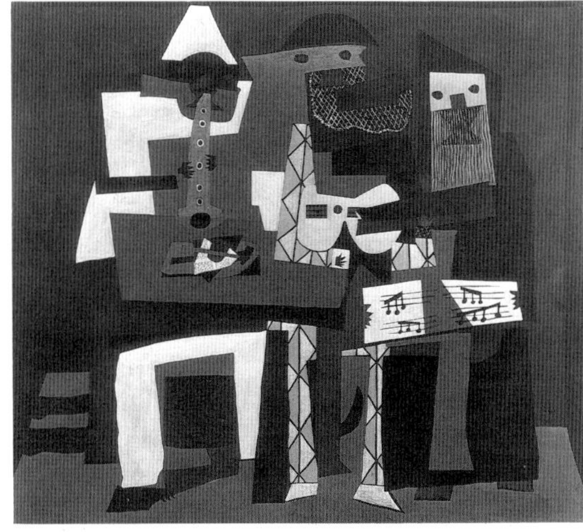

Picasso. *Three musicians.* Fontainebleau, 1921. Oil on canvas, 200.7 × 222.9 cm. The Museum of Modern Art, New York. Mrs Simon Guggenheim Fund.

war) is sold at auction; this is followed by the first (June) of four auctions (the others were in November 1921, July 1922 and May 1923) of works from Kahnweiler's gallery, including 36 by Picasso in the first sale and another 96 in all in the subsequent sales.

Picasso, his wife and baby spend the summer at a villa in Fontainebleau. Although he is ambivalent about his bourgeois surroundings, he works with enthusiasm: he completes two versions of the *Three musicians* (Museum of Modern Art, New York, and Philadelphia Museum of Art), *Three women at the spring* (Museum of Modern Art, New York) and numerous drawings of Olga and Paulo at the villa.

The Picassos return to Paris in September. His developing 'neo-classicism' manifests itself in giant nudes (begun in Fontainebleau), still lifes and a number of large compositions, such as *The village dance* (Musée Picasso, Paris), that are done in pastel on canvas.

1922

Early in the year André Breton (whom Picasso has not yet met) and Louis Aragon persuade Jacques Doucet to buy the *Demoiselles d'Avignon.* (The purchase is completed in 1924.)

Picasso, Olga and Paulo spend the summer at Dinard in Brittany, first in a hotel then in a rented villa; he works principally on still lifes. Olga becomes ill and they return to Paris.

In the autumn Picasso's work is shown at the Thannhauser gallery, Munich (his first exhibition in Germany since the war), and in Prague at the 60th Mánes exhibition; Kramár's preface to the Prague catalogue discusses Picasso's work from 1906 to 1921.

In December Picasso contributes the set design for Cocteau's *Antlgone*, performed at the Théâtre de l'Atelier in Paris. From this year until 1927 the Picassos are among the regular artistic and 'society' patrons of Le Bœuf sur le Toit, alongside Cocteau, Georges Auric, Francis Poulenc, Jean Hugo, René Crevel and many others.

1923

Picasso meets Breton; although he remains aloof from his activities or any other doctrinaire Dada/Surrealist programme, Picasso's work is championed by the Surrealists, and he contributes to many of their exhibitions and publications. In this year the Dadaist journal *Littérature* (new series, no.10) reproduces *Married couple*, a cubist painting Picasso signed in large script: 'Manet'.

In the summer the Picassos go to Cap d'Antibes, where their social circle is widened to include the American painter Gerald Murphy and the impresario Count Etienne de Beaumont (who produces *Mercure* the following year).

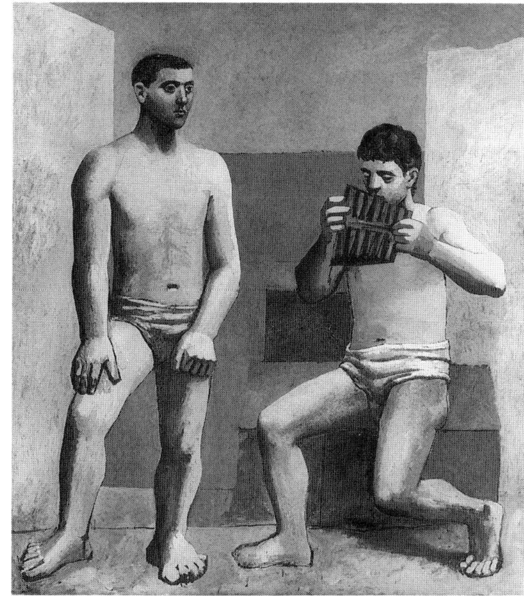

Picasso. *The pipes of Pan*. Antibes, 1923.
Oil on canvas, 205 × 174 cm. Musée Picasso, Paris.

Picasso paints *The pipes of Pan* and other neoclassical works, including portraits of Olga and Paulo and of the Barcelona painter Jacint Salvadó dressed in a Harlequin's costume given to Picasso by Cocteau (Kunstmuseum, Basle).

In the autumn the Thannhauser Gallery, Munich, exhibits works of 1906-13; and in December an exhibition of drawings is organised by Paul Rosenberg at the Arts Club of Chicago.

1924

The monumentality of Picasso's nudes extends to still lifes.

A selection of new works and 100 drawings is shown at Paul Rosenberg's in mid-April.

On 18 June the ballet *Mercure*, with choreography by Massine, music by Satie and décor and costumes by Picasso is first performed at the Théâtre de la Cigale, as part of the series 'Les Soirées de Paris'. Although some of the surrealists object to the fact that it is a benefit for Russian refugees (i.e., the aristocracy), Breton hails Picasso's designs, and an 'Hommage à Picasso', signed by other surrealists, is published in *Paris-Journal* (20 June).

On 20 June *Le train bleu* (scenario by Cocteau, music by Milhaud) is put on by Diaghilev at the Théâtre des Champs-Elysées; Picasso's *Women running on the beach* (enlarged from a small work of 1922) is used as the drop curtain.

In the summer the Picassos vacation at Villa La Vigie, Juan-les-Pins, where he works on his constellation drawings; two pages are reproduced in the 15 January 1925 issue of *La Révolution surréaliste*.

Picasso paints his son: *Paulo as Harlequin* (Musée Picasso, Paris); he will paint him as Pierrot in 1925.

André Breton's *Manifeste du surréalisme* is published in October; the review *La Révolution surréaliste* begins to appear in December (reproducing a sheet-metal and wire construction by Picasso as well as a photo of him by Man Ray).

1925

In the spring Picasso and Olga visit Monte Carlo for the Ballets Russes season; it is the last time they see Diaghilev.

In June he completes the *Three dancers*, incorporating the profile of his old friend Ramon Pichot, who has died suddenly.

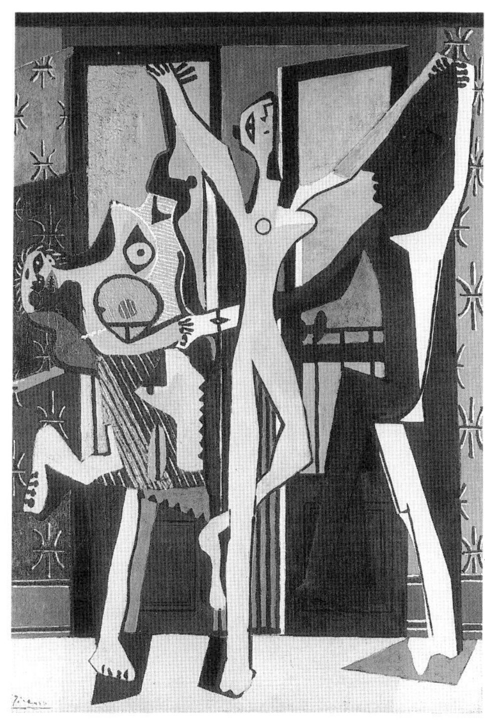

Picasso. *Three dancers*. Monte Carlo, 1925.
Oil on canvas, 215 × 142 cm. Tate Gallery, London.

La Révolution surréaliste (no. 4, 15 July) publishes the work, along with *Les Demoiselles d'Avignon*; in the same issue Picasso's recent work is considered as authentic 'dream painting' and is used to counter opponents of Breton, who believe surrealist painting does not exist. Picasso never officially joins the surrealist movement, but he is given a prominent place in their first group exhibition, *La Peinture Surréaliste* (Galerie Pierre, November), although he does not offer any recent works, and he contributes to most of the subsequent surrealist exhibitions well into the 1930s.

The Picassos again spend the summer in Juan-les-Pins, where he paints the *Studio with plaster head* (Museum of Modern Art, New York) and the *Embrace* (Musée Picasso, Paris).

1926

In early 1926 Christian Zervos founds *Cahiers d'art*, which will often feature Picasso's art; in June the Galerie Rosenberg shows works from last twenty years.

Picasso works on the *Milliner's workshop* (Musée National d'Art Moderne, Paris) and a series of collages employing cloth and nails; *La Révolution surréaliste* (15 June) reproduces one in which a knitting needle is thrust into an irregularly torn piece of cloth tacked onto board (Musée Picasso, Paris).

The Picassos are in Juan-les-Pins and Antibes in the summer and visit Barcelona in October; there Picasso sees the work of Dalí at the autumn salon at the Sala Parés.

Picasso advises Diaghilev to commission Miró and Ernst to do the décor for Constant Lambert's *Romeo and Juliet*, provoking their attempted 'expulsion' from the surrealist group by Breton and Aragon.

Jean Cocteau's essay 'Picasso' is published in *Rappel à l'ordre.*

1927

In January Picasso meets seventeen-year-old Marie-Thérèse Walter; their affair is kept secret for several years, although references to her begin to appear in his work.

Picasso spends an unhappy summer in Cannes with Olga and Paulo; he is reunited with Marie-Thérèse in Paris in the autumn.

Eroticism in his work – such as the *Metamorphoses* series of drawings made in Cannes of biomorphic bathers – reflects the sensuality of his new mistress and also the influence of literary surrealism.

A set of illustrations is commissioned by Vollard for an edition of Balzac's *Le Chef-d'œuvre inconnu*; Picasso does a series of engravings and some woodcuts based on the constellation drawings of 1924 (the book is published in 1931).

Exhibitions are held in Paris (Galerie Rosenberg, July, and Galerie Pierre, December–February), in New York (Wildenstein) and Berlin (Galerie Flechtheim).

1928

Picasso turns once again to sculpture, modelling his *Bather* (based on the Cannes drawings of the previous summer) early in the year. He renews his acquaintance with the sculptor Juli González, who teaches him welding techniques in his studio on the rue de Médéah.

In July Picasso returns with Olga and Paulo to Dinard; Marie-Thérèse is installed in a local *colonie de vacances* (for children). Sketchbooks look ahead to sculptural projects and subjects of bathers and bathing-huts.

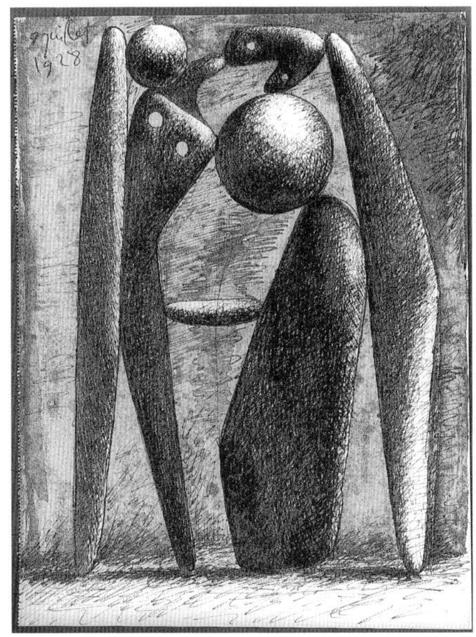

Picasso. *Bathers (design for a monument).* Dinard, 1928. Pen, ink and wash on paper, 30.2 × 22 cm. Musée Picasso, Paris.

Back in Paris in the autumn, Picasso continues working in González's studio and finishes his *Wire construction* (Musée Picasso, Paris), the first of four metal-rod constructions; early the next year he works on *Woman in a garden* (Musée Picasso, Paris).

Dalí, on an assignment from a Barcelona newspaper, visits Picasso on his first trip to Paris. Although they never become close friends, Picasso admires his early work.

Uhde's *Picasso et la tradition française*, in which Picasso is considered as a 'gothic' artist, is published; also André Level's study *Picasso.*

Over the winter of 1928/9 aggressive, threatening women, sometimes superimposed with the artist's profile, reflect problems in Picasso's marriage and Olga's erratic behaviour.

1929

Studies for a *Crucifixion* appear in a sketchbook done at the rue La Boétie studio in February.

Picasso returns to Dinard for the summer; his August sketchbook includes drawings of double-profile women who appear first as Marie-Thérèse and are then transformed into skull-like, screaming Olgas.

With the death of Diaghilev, Picasso's association with the Ballets Russes and the social circle around it, comes to an end; an exception is Jean Cocteau, who remains a friend until the end of his life.

1930

In February Picasso completes his painting of the *Crucifixion* (Musée Picasso, Paris); according to Breton, this work shows the influence of Miró.

In June Picasso buys the château of Boisgeloup (near Gisors, some 40 miles north-west of Paris).

He once again spends his summer vacation with Olga and Paulo in Juan-les-Pins, but upon his return to Paris he and Marie-Thérèse live together at 44, rue La Boëtie, which he has rented for her.

He begins a series of etchings to accompany Ovid's *Metamorphoses* (it is published by Albert Skira in 1931).

In anticipation of his fiftieth birthday, a special number of *Documents* (April) is dedicated to the artist, including articles by twenty contributors.

Exhibitions are held in New York (with Derain at the Reinhardt Galleries, January–March; Museum of Modern Art group show, January–March; John Becker Gallery, October–November; and again at the Reinhardt Galleries in November); and at the Chicago Arts Club (March–April).

1931

In April a thirty-year retrospective is held at Alex Reid & Lefevre Gallery, London; works are also shown in New York and Paris.

In May he sets up a sculpture studio in the stables at Boisgeloup; for some years he does large sculptures, based upon the head of Marie-Thérèse, who is not only his companion-mistress but the inspiration for the highly-charged erotic work of this period. He also works in González's studio, where he starts incorporating real objects in his sculpture.

While vacationing at Juan-les-Pins in the summer, Picasso works on engravings (later to form a large part of the 'Vollard Suite').

In October Picasso is fifty.

1932

In the first few months of the year Picasso produces some of his classic portraits of Marie-Thérèse, including *Girl before a mirror* and several versions of her sleeping or reading.

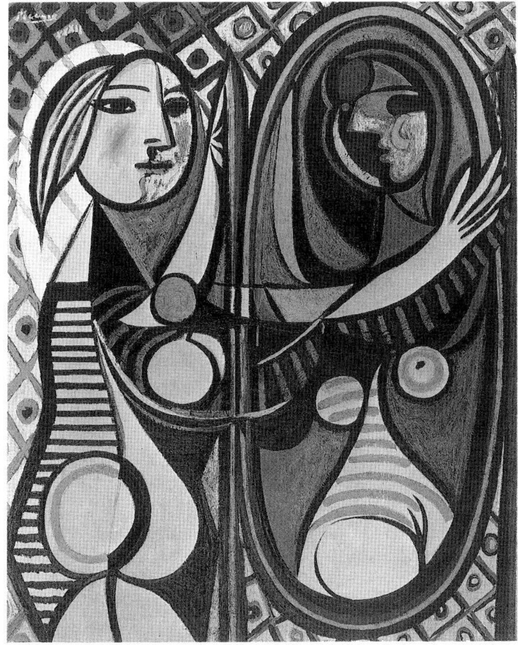

Picasso. *Girl before a mirror.* Boisgeloup, 14.3.1932 Oil on canvas, 162.3 × 130.2 cm. The Museum of Modern Art, New York. Gift of Mrs Simon Guggenheim.

They spend the summer together at Boisgeloup; among their visitors there are Kahnweiler, Braque, González and their wives.

During these years Picasso's regular café is the Dôme, where he meets the photographer Brassaï; they become good friends for the rest of their lives, and Brassaï takes many photographs both of Picasso and of his work, including sculpture made at Boisgeloup.

A major retrospective is held in June–July at Galeries Georges Petit; Picasso chooses the 236 works himself (the show travels in augmented form to the Kunsthaus, Zurich).

A special issue of *Cahiers d'art* appears (Vol. 7, no. 3-5) to coincide with the show, and in October the journal issues the first volume of the Picasso *Catalogue raisonné* edited by Christian Zervos.

In October works by Picasso and Ramon Casas are shown at the Galeria La Pinacoteca, Barcelona, and in November–December etchings by the artist are shown alongside objects by Joseph Cornell at the Julien Levy Gallery, New York.

1933

Etchings for the *Sculptor's studio* are completed in the spring (1933); these and others acquired or commissioned by Vollard – 100 in all when completed in 1937 – comprise the 'Vollard Suite'. He also produces many monotypes (92 in January alone).

On 1 June the first issue of *Minotaure* is published (by Skira and Tériade) with a collage by Picasso as the cover; his so-called 'hybrid-object' (forged iron, festooned with children's toys, a real butterfly, etc.) is also illustrated.

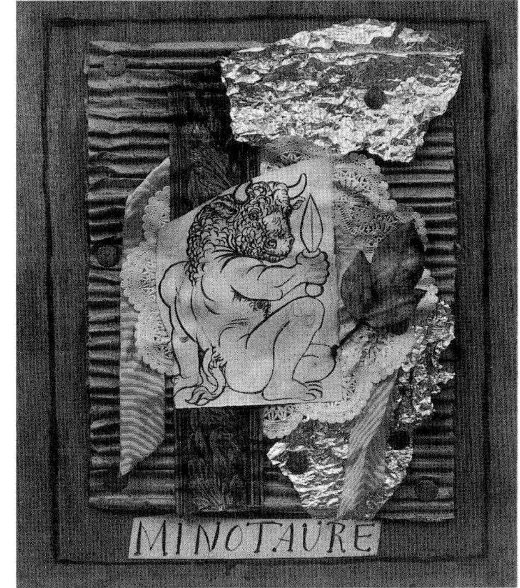

Picasso. *Minotaure.* Paris, 1933. Collage of pencil on paper, corrugated cardboard, silver foil, ribbon, wallpaper painted with gold paint and gouache, paper doily, burnt linen leaves, tacks and charcoal on wood, 48.5 × 41 cm. The Museum of Modern Art, New York. Gift of Mr and Mrs Alexandre P. Rosenberg.

In the summer Picasso vacations with Olga and Paulo in Cannes, and they then visit Picasso's family and friends in Barcelona, returning to Paris in early September.

During the autumn he works in Paris and at Boisgeloup.

Fernande Olivier publishes *Picasso et ses amis*, the first of two memoirs (her *Souvenirs intimes* was published posthumously in 1988); also the first volume of Bernhard Geiser's *catalogue raisonné* of printed work, *Picasso, peintre-graveur*, appears.

1934

Coinciding with visits to Spain in 1933 and 1934, Picasso returns to the subject of the bullfight; the Minotaur and bullfight subjects merge in his graphic work.

On the last trip he was to make there – in the late summer, accompanied by Olga and Paulo – he stops in San Sebastián, Burgos, Madrid, Toledo, Zaragoza and Barcelona.

In Barcelona he visits the new installation of the Museum of Catalan art in the Palau Nacional; he sees the Romanesque frescoes transferred from Catalan churches and also the recently acquired Plandiura collection, which includes works from his own early period.

In mid-September Picasso is once again in Paris; he finishes a series of *Blind Minotaur* prints.

1935

In February–March the Galerie Pierre, Paris, exhibits his *papiers collés* (catalogue preface by Tristan Tzara).

From May until February 1936 he does no painting, but begins writing experimental poetry; collections of his poems are published in 1936 in a special number of *Cahiers d'art* and in *Gaceta de arte* (Tenerife).

In June Picasso and Olga separate; they never divorce.

Marie-Thérèse gives birth to a daughter, Maya, on 5 September.

In November Jaime Sabartès returns from Guatemala to act as Picasso's personal secretary (a position he holds until his death in 1968).

1936

ADLAN (Friends of New Art) organises a Picasso exhibition (January–February) in Barcelona (where his work had been suppressed during the Spanish Dictatorship in the twenties); the poet Paul Eluard attends the opening and gives a lecture on communism and surrealism. The close friendship

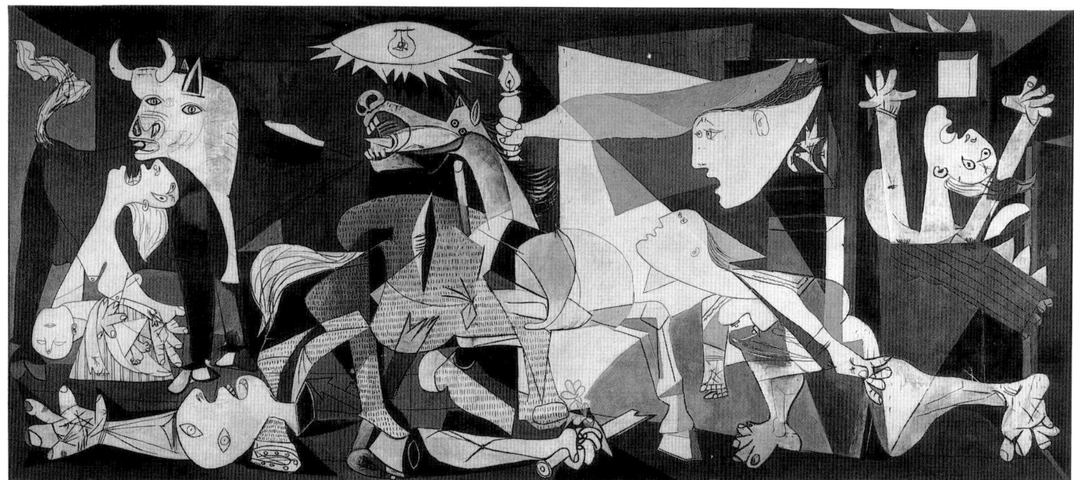

Picasso. *Guernica*. Paris, 1937. Oil on canvas, 349.3 × 776.6 cm. Museo del Prado, Madrid

of Picasso and Eluard begins at this time. The exhibition travels to Bilbao, Málaga and Madrid.

In March works by Picasso are included in the Museum of Modern Art exhibition *Cubism and Abstract Art*; during the year he also has several one-man shows, in Paris, London and New York.

Picasso, Marie-Thérèse and Maya spend late March through April at the Villa Sainte-Geneviève in Juan-les-Pins, where Picasso continues the theme of the Minotaur.

They return to Paris in mid-May; he works in Lacourière's print studio on illustrations to Buffon's *Histoire naturelle* (eventually published in 1942). Picasso designs the drop curtain for Romain Rolland's *14 Juillet* at the Alhambra music-hall.

On 17 July Spanish anti-Republican forces under General Franco in Morocco begin a revolt, and the Spanish Civil War ensues; Picasso opposes the Nationalists, and the Republicans name him director of the Prado.

In early August, Picasso goes for the first time to Mougins (in the hills above Cannes), where a number of friends visit him, including Paul and Nusch Eluard, Christian and Yvonne Zervos, Roland Penrose, Lee Miller, Man Ray and the photographer Dora Maar.

Later in the year he experiments with photographic shadow prints with Dora Maar's assistance.

Picasso discovers the village of Vallauris, a potters' settlement since ancient times.

In the autumn he is forced to give up Boisgeloup as part of the division of property with Olga; he works for a time in a studio at Vollard's house at Le Tremblay-sur-Mauldre, where he installs Marie-Thérèse and Maya (who will live there until 1940).

1937

In January Picasso etches the *Dream and lie of Franco* – two plates, divided into nine scenes, and a poem – to be sold to benefit the Republican cause.

He is commissioned to paint a mural for the Republican pavilion at the Paris World's Fair; apparently in exchange, he acquires a new studio, which Dora Maar finds for him, at 7, rue des Grands Augustins.

In February–March he is with Marie-Thérèse and Maya in Le Tremblay.

After the bombing of the historic Basque town of Guernica by German aircraft on 26 April, Picasso takes this outrage as the theme of his mural. Dora Maar, now his mistress, photographs and helps him paint *Guernica* in May.

The Spanish pavilion opens on 12 July; works by Miró, Calder and González and two sculptures by Picasso are also displayed as well as *Guernica*.

Picasso and Dora Maar vacation in Mougins, returning to Paris in late September.

In mid-October Picasso travels to Switzerland on family business; he meets Paul Klee in Berne.

Upon his return to Paris, he paints a series of *Weeping women* (Tate Gallery, Musée Picasso, National Gallery of Victoria).

In November he has two retrospective shows in New York: works from 1901-37 at the Valentine Gallery and from 1903-23, including *Les Demoiselles d'Avignon*, at Jacques Seligmann's gallery; there are also exhibitions in London and Paris.

In December he paints the gouache *Woman crying* (Musée Picasso, Paris).

1938

Picasso begins *Seated woman* series of paintings, inspired both by Marie-Thérèse and Dora Maar.

In the summer he and Dora Maar again stay at Mougins, where they are joined by Paul and Nusch Eluard. In late September they return to Paris; some weeks later he visits the Zervoses at Vézelay.

Penrose arranges for *Guernica* and studies to be shown at the New Burlington Galleries in London in October in support of the Republican cause; afterwards, they are shown at Whitechapel Gallery, London, in Leeds and Liverpool. In October–November Picasso and Matisse are featured at the Museum of Fine Arts, Boston; and in November Picasso again shows at the Valentine Gallery, New York.

1939

In January, 33 still lifes from 1936-38 are shown at the Galerie Rosenberg, Paris.

Picasso's mother dies on 13 January. He does not return for the funeral because of the war; Barcelona falls to Franco on the 26th. After the Civil War is over, he helps his nephews who seek refuge in France, and he assumes self-imposed exile from Spain for the rest of his life.

In the spring he works for long periods with the printer Lacourière; his prints include six coloured aquatint portraits of Dora.

In early July Picasso and Dora visit Man Ray in Antibes; Sabartès is also there.

His former dealer and friend Vollard dies on July 22; Picasso makes a brief visit to Paris for the funeral.

In August he paints *Night fishing at Antibes* (Museum of Modern Art, New York).

Picasso and Dora Maar return to Paris in late August.

On 1 September Picasso and his entourage go to Royan (in western France on the Garonne estuary), where Marie-Thérèse and Maya are also installed; his studio is in the Villa Gerbier des Joncs.

Two days later Britain and France declare war on Germany. The war is reflected in violent still lifes and tortured skull-like heads of Dora Maar; he paints Sabartès as a Spanish grandee.

Picasso makes several trips to Paris: for a day in September to get a residence permit for Royan, for two weeks in October and for a further two weeks in December.

Guernica and studies are exhibited in the United States: at the Valentine Gallery, New York; in Los

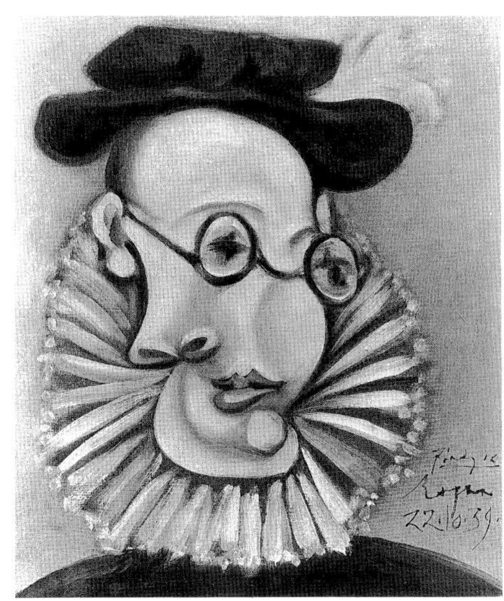

Picasso. *Portrait of Jaime Sabartès.*
Royan, 1939. Oil on canvas, 46 × 38 cm.
Museu Picasso, Barcelona.

Angeles, Chicago and San Francisco; and finally at the Museum of Modern Art, New York, as part of the retrospective *Picasso: Forty Years of His Art* organised by Alfred Barr Jr. This show then travels to eight cities in the U.S.A. in 1940–41.

Guernica remains at the Museum of Modern Art until it is installed in the Prado in 1981; a generation of young painters, including Jackson Pollock and Dutchman Willem de Kooning are influenced by the work.

1940

In January Picasso hires a new studio at Royan in the Villa Les Voiliers, but he spends most of the month of February and some eight weeks in March–May in Paris; in April-May he has an exhibition there at Yvonne Zervos's gallery.

He begins a series of *Woman dressing her hair* (final version: Mrs Bertram Smith Collection); disturbing distortions of the female nude reflect a new depth of expression in his work.

Paris falls to the Germans on 14 June; Royan is occupied nine days later.

In late August, after completing the painting *Café at Royan* (Musée Picasso, Paris; no.40), Picasso and Dora return to the capital, leaving Royan for good; he moves first to his rue la Boëtie studio and then in the autumn to the rue des Grands Augustins; Dora Maar keeps her own studio on rue de Savoie, while Marie-Thérèse and Maya remain in Royan.

Many of Picasso's friends are in the Resistance and consider Picasso's anti-fascist politics sympathetic with their own (Cocteau is the exception). His dealer Paul Rosenberg, whose collection is confiscated by the Nazis, goes to the United States.

Picasso is said to have handed out photographs of *Guernica* as souvenirs to Germans who visit his studio. One of Hitler's preferred artists, the sculptor Arno Breker, later claims that he prevented the Gestapo from bothering Picasso.

Picasso makes six etchings to illustrate a collection of sonnets, *Afat*, by the Russian poet Iliazd (Ilya Zdanevich); this is the first of nine collaborations 1940–1972.

He also spends time during the war in the Bibliothèque Nationale, copying by hand his friend Ramon Reventós's stories, 'El centaure picador' and 'El capvespre d'un faune', which are finally published in Catalan in 1947 with the artist's illustrations.

1941

Picasso continues to see Marie-Thérèse and Maya on a weekly basis in an apartment he finds for them on boulevard Henri-IV after they return from Royan in the spring.

Dora, however, dominates his work of this year, including sculptures made in his Paris studio; friends help have his work cast in bronze in spite of wartime restrictions – a fact that later leads to suggestions of collaboration.

In January he writes the play *Le Désir attrapé par la queue*.

One of the wartime meeting places for Picasso and his friends, including Eluard, Robert Desnos, Braque, Leiris, Sartre, Simone de Beauvoir and Georges Auric, is the restaurant Le Catalan on rue des Grands Augustins.

Exhibitions of Picasso's work continue to be put on in the U.S.A. during the war years.

1942

Picasso begins drawings for the *Man with a sheep* sculpture, and in April he paints *Still life with steer's skull* (Kunstsammlung Nordrhein-Westfalen, Düsseldorf), in May *L'Aubade* (Musée National d'Art Moderne).

In June Vlaminck's denunciation of Picasso in *Comœdia* for having led French painting into a dead end gains Picasso the sympathy of members of the Resistance. Eluard, who rejoins the Communist party in the summer, introduces him to the circle around the underground paper *Les Lettres françaises* (first issue, September).

The preferred café during the winter of 1943/4 is the Flore; regulars include Picasso and Dora Maar, Sartre, poets Jacques Audiberti and Jacques Prévert, the Leirises, playwright Arthur Adamov and, for a time, the sculptor Giacometti.

1943

In May the young painter Françoise Gilot visits Picasso for the first time; she begins to appear in his work towards the end of the year.

In the Grands Augustins studio Picasso produces the bronze *Tête de mort* (skull), *Head of a bull* (an assemblage of a bicycle saddle and handlebars; Musée Picasso, Paris) and *Man with a sheep*. Pigeons once again begin to appear in his work (he had done them as a child following the example of his father).

Picasso continues to see his friends, including Brassaï (whom he invites to photograph his recent sculpture) and the poet Pierre Reverdy (with whom he will collaborate on the publication of *Le Chant des morts* – poems by Reverdy of 1944–8 and lithographs by the artist – in 1948).

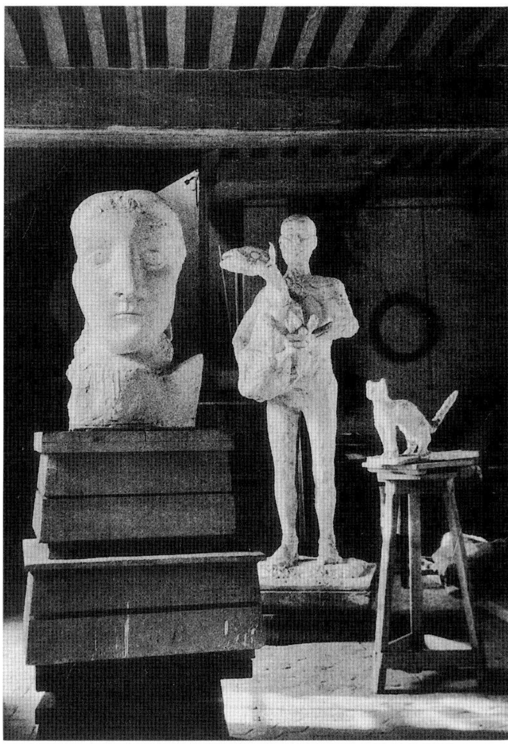

Picasso's studio on the rue des Grands-Augustins, Paris, with *Head of Dora Maar* (1941), *Man with a sheep* (1943) and *Crouching cat* (1943); photograph by Brassaï, 1943.

1944

Some of his friends, including Surrealist writer Robert Desnos and Picasso's godson Max Jacob, are arrested. Cocteau and others, but not Picasso, try in vain to save Jacob, who dies in Drancy concentration camp in March. Desnos dies in the camp at Terezin the following year.

In March *Le Désir attrapé par la queue* is given a reading in the Leiris's apartment, under the direction of Albert Camus.

Some of Picasso's poems appear in *Poemas y Declaraciones*, published in Mexico City, where in June a retrospective exhibition is held.

In August, during the Paris uprising, Picasso moves in with Marie-Thérèse and Maya; he works on a watercolour and gouache (which later disappears from the studio) based on Poussin's *Bacchanal*.

He returns to the rue des Grands-Augustins after the Liberation of Paris on 25 August; his studio becomes a gathering place for old friends and for British and American soldiers, including young painters like Cleve Gray.

Around this time he meets Geneviève Laporte, then a young student, later his mistress.

In October Picasso joins the Communist party; this leads to demonstrations against him at the *Salon de la Libération* in October, which incorporates a retrospective exhibition of his work.

In November he resumes oil painting with a series of still lifes.

1945

Picasso begins the *Charnel house* (Museum of Modern Art, New York); in February–March, works in private collections are shown at the Buchholz Gallery, New York.

André Malraux visits Picasso in May; Brassaï and the Eluards are also there.

In June Picasso designs the curtain for *Le Rendez-vous*, a production of the Ballets des Champs-Elysées (décor by Brassaï, choreography by Roland Petit) at the Théâtre Sarah Bernhardt, Paris.

In June recent works are exhibited at the Galerie Louis Carré, Paris.

Picasso and Dora go to Cap d'Antibes in July; he buys her a house in Ménerbes (paying for it with a painting).

He returns to Paris in August, but is back again in Antibes at the beginning of October. During November he is again in Paris and begins making lithographs in the studio of Fernand Mourlot.

Françoise rejoins him at the end of the month.

Works by Picasso and Matisse are exhibited in December at the Victoria and Albert Museum, London.

Paul Eluard's tribute *A Pablo Picasso* appears.

1946

In February–March Picasso exhibits two works of political inspiration – the *Charnel House* and *Hommage aux espagnols morts pour la France* (Picasso Heirs Collection) – in the *Art et Résistance* exhibition in Paris; in April a Matisse–Picasso exhibition is held in Amsterdam (it travels to Brussels in May); and in June–July, nineteen recent paintings are shown at the Galerie Louis Carré, Paris.

In mid-March Picasso and Françoise are together in Golfe-Juan (at the home of the printer Louis Fort); they visit Matisse in Nice.

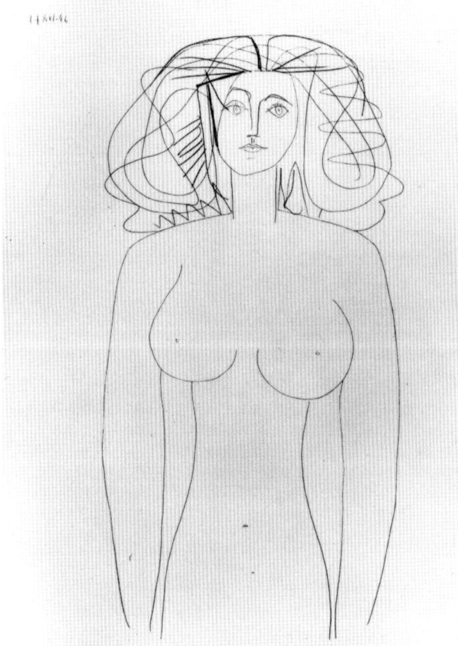

Picasso. *Françoise Gilot*. Paris, 27 April 1946.
From Paul Eluard, *Picasso Dessins* (Paris, 1952).

Françoise begins to live with Picasso in Paris beginning in late April; the next month he paints her as *Woman-Flower* (Françoise Gilot Collection).

In early July they travel to Ménerbes, where they stay in the house he has given Dora. At the end of the month they visit the collector Marie Cuttoli in Cap d'Antibes and then move into Louis Fort's home in Golfe-Juan early in August.

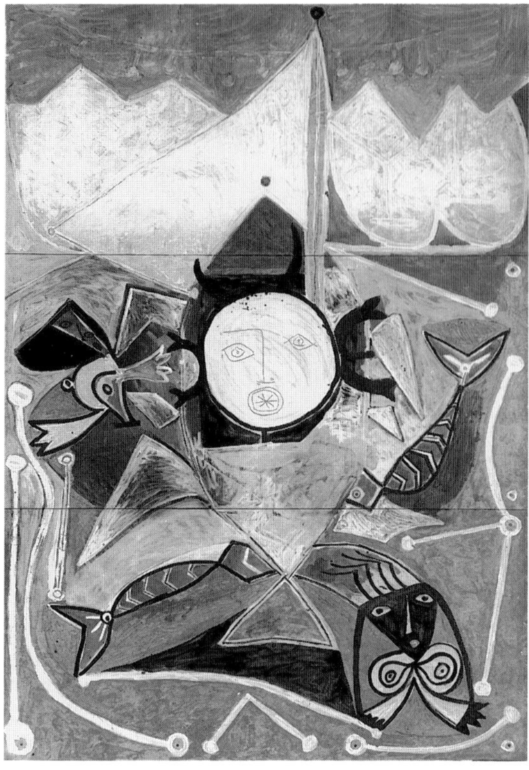

Picasso. *Ulysses and the Sirens*, Antibes, 1946-7.
Oil and glycerophthalic on three panels of fibro-cement, 360 × 250 cm. Musée Picasso, Antibes.

While there Picasso accepts an invitation from Romuald Dor de la Souchère to paint the museum at Antibes (the Château Grimaldi – renamed the Musée Picasso later that year); mythological and Mediterranean themes dominate his work of that autumn, all of which remains in the museum.

He sees the Eluards and also Breton, returned from exile in the United States, but because of Picasso's Communist party affiliation, Breton will have no more to do with him.

Françoise and Picasso return to Paris in November. Jaime Sabartès's book *Portraits et souvenirs* is published.

1947

Early in the year Picasso begins to use the owl motif in his work; he spends much time in Mourlot's printing studio, and at the end of March he makes a series of lithographs after Cranach.

Lithographs are featured in exhibitions in New York, Stockholm, Amsterdam, Hanover, London and in a travelling exhibition in Great Britain during 1947 and 1948.

In May Picasso gives ten major paintings to the Musée National d'Art Moderne – the first significant public holding of his work in France.

Claude, Françoise and Picasso's first child, is born on 15 May.

They go to Golfe-Juan at the end of June.

In August Picasso begins working at the Ramiés' Madoura pottery in Vallauris; he works with their technicians and a local chemist at the chemical works in Golfe-Juan, and employs personal experimentation in the ceramic process; he works with enormous enthusiasm, producing over 2,000 pieces in one year alone.

Apart from one brief trip to Paris, he spends the winter in the Midi with Françoise and the baby.

From November 1947 to August 1948 Picasso is at work on his Jarryesque play, *Les Quatre petites filles*; in December he does the décor for Sophocles' *Oedipus Rex*, directed by Pierre Blanchard at the Théâtre des Champs-Elysées, Paris.

1948

Early in the year Paul Haesaerts films Picasso at Vallauris and in the Antibes museum: *Visite à Picasso*.

In March Picasso returns for a short time to Paris, where he completes his illustrations for Reverdy's *Le Chant des morts* and the 41 etchings for the publication of Góngora's *Vingt poèmes*.

He returns to Vallauris, and in July he moves with Françoise and Claude to La Galloise, a villa above Vallauris.

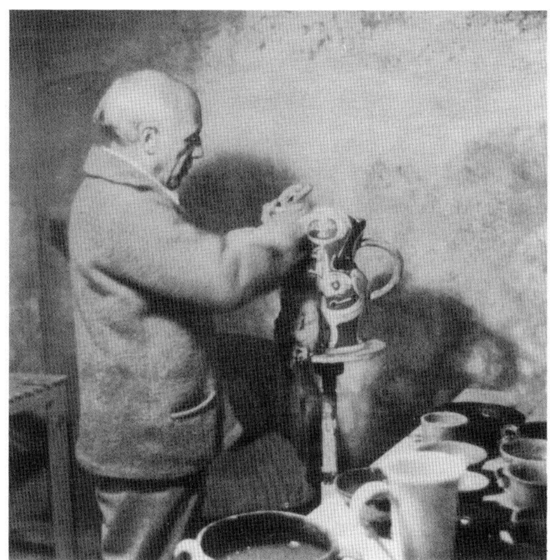

Picasso decorating a pot at Vallauris, 1947.

In August he attends the Congress of Intellectuals for Peace at Wrocław in Poland; he meets Ilya Ehrenburg and visits Cracow and Auschwitz.

He returns to Vallauris in September and the next month goes with Françoise and Claude to Paris.

In October Kahnweiler (whose gallery was bought during the war by his sister-in-law Louise Leiris and now bears her name) exhibits works done in Provence 1945-8; it is his first Picasso exhibition in France.

In November an exhibition of 149 ceramics is held at the Maison de la Pensée Française. A two-week Picasso exhibition is held over the turn of the year at the Galeries Laietanes in Barcelona.

1949

Picasso and Françoise remain in Paris until their second child, Paloma, is born on 19 April.

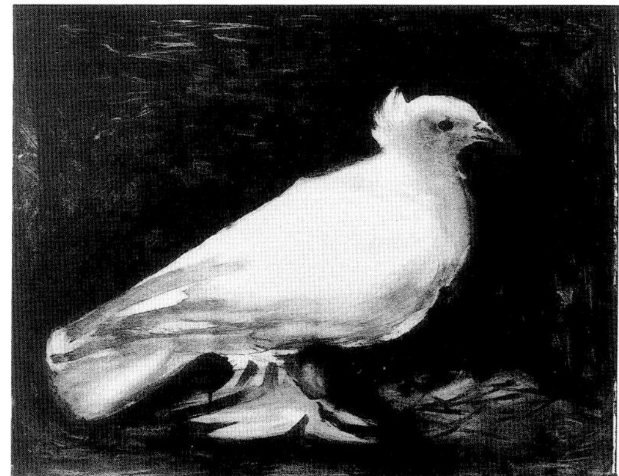

Picasso. *The dove*, Paris, 9 January 1949. Lithograph, 56 × 75 cm. Musée Picasso, Paris.

He spends much of the time working on lithographs with Mourlot. Aragon chooses a lithograph of a dove (done in January) for the poster to announce the Peace Conference in Paris, which opens on 20 April.

In January a book of his sculptures (text by Kahnweiler, photos by Brassaï) is published. In February–March 38 engravings are published in an edition of Mérimée's *Carmen*; and in March–April, recent works (including bronzes) are exhibited at the Buchholz Gallery, New York.

In the late spring the family returns to Vallauris, and Picasso rents a studio on rue du Fournas, where he paints and sculpts; a series of *Pregnant woman* sculptures (e.g. no.46) is developed.

In July, 64 recent works are exhibited at the Maison de la Pensée Française, Paris.

1950

In January the Museum of Modern Art, New York, holds an exhibition *Picasso: the Sculptor's Studio*.

Early in the year Picasso does a portrait 'après Greco' (Rosengart Collection, Lucerne) and a version of Courbet's *Women on the banks of the Seine* (Kunstmuseum, Basle); he also does paintings of Claude and Paloma at play. In sculpture, he revives the technique of assemblage, (*Woman with baby carriage* etc.) as well as continuing his ceramic work (owls).

In the summer Henri Langlois (founder of the Cinémathèque Française) persuades Picasso to direct a film; the artist creates specially designed objects, like a bullring in cut paper painted with watercolour, which is animated by light. The film is edited and screened the following year.

A cast of *Man with a sheep* is placed in the main square of Vallauris; Laurent Casanova, from the Communist party, presides at the inauguration.

In October Picasso attends the Second World Peace Conference in Sheffield, England; he visits the former Ballets Russes dancer Lydia Lopokova in London and Roland Penrose at his farm in Sussex.

In November he is awarded the Lenin Peace Prize.

In November–January an exhibition of sculpture and drawings is held at the Maison de la Pensée Française (catalogue preface by Aragon).

1951

In response to the Korean War, Picasso paints *Massacre in Korea* (Musée Picasso, Paris), which he bases on Goya's *Third of May, 1808*.

He returns to Paris at the end of February after an absence of nearly two years. *Massacre in Korea* is exhibited at the Salon de Mai.

In June Picasso and Françoise attend Eluard's marriage in Saint-Tropez to Dominique Lemor (his third: his first wife, Gala, had left him for Dalí in 1929, and Nusch had died in 1946).

Later they visit Vence to see Matisse, whose chapel there is inaugurated on 25 June.

Picasso also spends part of the summer in Saint-Tropez with the poet Geneviève Laporte, who has become his mistress. Her collection of poetry *Les Cavaliers de l'ombre* is illustrated with seven drawings by him (published 1955).

During the summer he is evicted from the rue La Boëtie in Paris and takes two apartments on the rue Gay-Lussac.

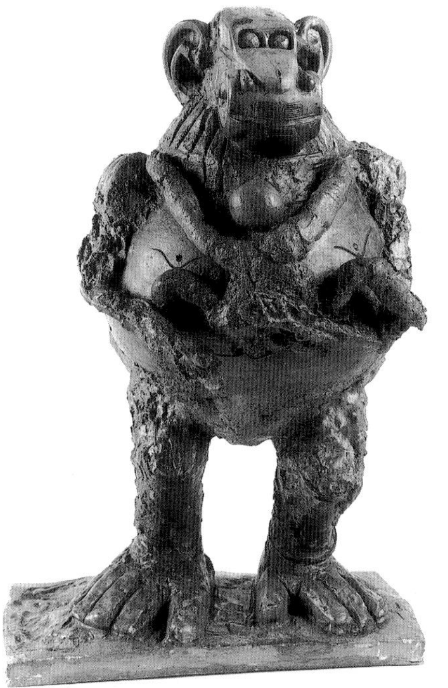

Picasso. *Baboon with young*, Vallauris, 1951. Pottery, two model cars, metal and plaster, ht: 71 cm. Musée Picasso, Paris.

In August a Picasso exhibition is held in Tokyo.

Picasso is in Vallauris in the autumn and in Paris in the winter with Françoise and the children. He makes the *Baboon with young* , one of his many sculptures to incorporate found objects.

1952

Picasso, Françoise and the children remain in Paris until July.

In the spring he starts working there on plans for the decoration of a gothic chapel in Vallauris as a temple of peace.

He continues working on sculpture, including the *Crane*, and paints a portrait of his friend Hélène Parmelin, wife of the painter Edouard Pignon.

In April Françoise has an exhibition at the Galerie Louise Leiris.

In May–June Picasso works on engravings with Lacourière.

In the summer Picasso meets Jacqueline Roque Hutin at the Madoura pottery in Vallauris (though she does not appear in his work until 1954).

Picasso travels to Paris alone (because of troubles with Françoise) in October; he attends Paul Eluard's funeral in November and returns in early December to Vallauris.

He completes the *War* and *Peace* panels (installed in the Vallauris chapel in 1954 and dedicated in 1959); he revises his play *Les Quatre petites filles*; he also makes a series of lithographs of the family and a painting of *Paloma asleep* (Mrs Bertram Smith Collection).

A special issue of the magazine *Le Point* appears in October to celebrate the artist's seventieth birthday; many of his friends contribute, including Raynal, Reverdy, Kahnweiler and Pignon.

1953

Around the middle of January Picasso is once again in Paris, where he works on lithographs with Mourlot.

Les Demoiselles d'Avignon and Cubist work is included in a major Cubism exhibition at the Musée National d'Art Moderne, Paris (January–April).

He returns to Vallauris in mid-February.

In March a disagreement with officials of the Communist party over his portrait of Stalin, reproduced in *Les Lettres françaises* at the time of the Russian leader's death, leads him to distance himself from the party.

At the end of March Françoise takes the children and leaves Picasso, though they return in the summer. Meanwhile, Picasso continues working in the rue du Fournas sculpture studio.

In the autumn Picasso works on a series of drawings 'after' Altdorfer (made at the suggestion of Kahnweiler).

In May–June recent works are shown at the Galerie Louise Leiris.

A major retrospective is held in Rome at the Galleria Nazionale d'Arte Moderna (May–July), which includes *War* and *Peace*. It is put on in Milan later in the year in enlarged form, to include *Guernica*, the *Charnel house* and *Massacre in Korea*. In June a retrospective is held in Lyons; and in December–February, a retrospective, again including *Guernica*, is shown at the Museu de Arte Moderna, São Paulo.

In August Picasso and his daughter Maya go to Perpignan at the invitation of the Lazerme family, friends of Totote Manolo; later they go to Paris to bring back his son Paulo and nephew Javier Vilató to join them.

In mid-September Picasso returns to La Galloise, and Françoise and her children finally leave at the end of the month; they return to Paris, where they live in the rue Gay-Lussac studio (when Picasso goes to Paris, he now stays at the rue des Grands Augustins). Picasso paints violent still lifes with a cat killing a cock (no.50).

In October he breaks with Geneviève Laporte, and he now lives as an 'eligible bachelor'. His son Paulo begins to spend more time with him, principally as his chauffeur.

At Christmas he is visited by the Lazermes.

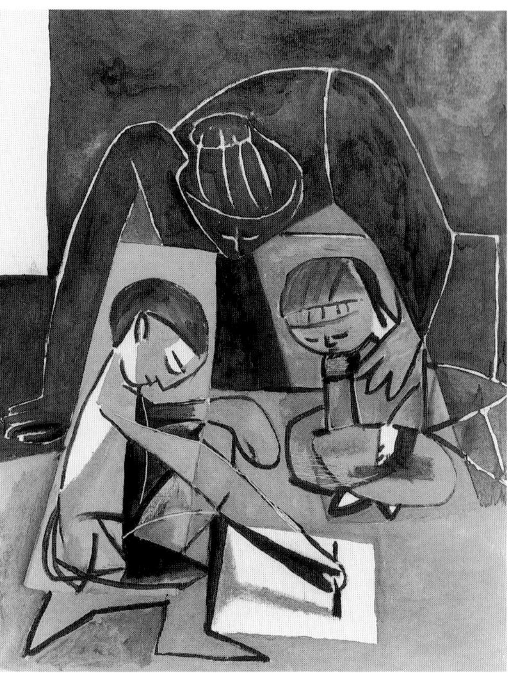

Picasso. *Claude drawing, Françoise and Paloma*, Vallauris, 1954. Oil on canvas, 116 × 89 cm. Musée Picasso, Paris.

1954

Picasso incorporates old themes of harlequin, the circus and Spain into the subject of the *Artist in his studio*; he begins what becomes a characteristic of the late period – sequences in one medium that develop personal subjects and are made intensively over a short period (e.g. 180 drawings of the artist and entourage in his studio, made between 28 November 1953 and early February 1954).

During the year Kahnweiler publishes Picasso's *Poèmes et lithographies*.

In April Picasso meets the 20-year-old Sylvette David (Lydia Corbett) and paints a series of portraits of her.

In May–June a comprehensive exhibition of his engravings is organised at the Kunsthaus, Zurich.

In early June Picasso paints three portraits of 'Madame Z' (the reference is to Jacqueline Roque's villa Ziquet at Golfe-Juan).

During the summer he also begins his variations on Manet's *Déjeuner sur l'herbe*; these continue into the 1960s.

In early July and again in August Picasso pays visits to the Lazermes in Perpignan with Maya and Paulo. Françoise and her children also come to stay there in the late summer, as do Jacqueline and her daughter Catherine and many of Picasso's friends.

In July an exhibition of two periods (1900–14 and 1950–54) is held at the Maison de la Pensée Française.

At the end of September Picasso returns to Vallauris with Jacqueline, and she moves with him to the rue des Grands Augustins in Paris.

Picasso makes numerous lithographic posters over the next years, including the announcements for Vallauris bullfights.

After Matisse dies on 3 November, Picasso jokes to Penrose that Matisse has 'left him his Odalisques', and in December he begins his series of variations on Delacroix's *Algerian women*, claiming that one of Delacroix's models reminds him of Jacqueline.

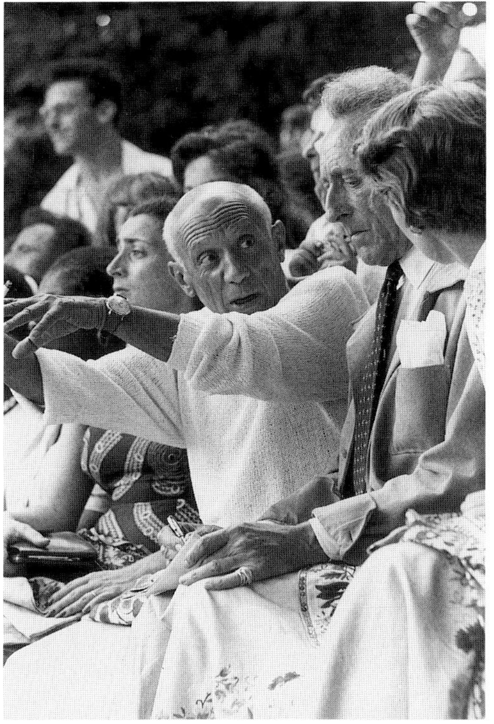

Picasso and Jacqueline with Jean Cocteau at a bullfight at Vallauris, 1955. Photo by Brian Brake.

1955

Olga dies in February; though some of his former mistresses reappear in the hopes of marriage, Picasso escapes Paris with Jacqueline (apart from a visit to hospital in 1965, he never returns to Paris again).

They stay with the Lazermes in May, and in June they move into a turn-of-the-century villa, 'La Californie', above Cannes. Their guests there include the bullfighter Luís-Miguel Dominguín, Kahnweiler, the Leirises and Jean Cocteau.

In the summer Henri-Georges Clouzot films *Le Mystère Picasso*, which shows the artist at work in a film-studio in Nice; many works, done in coloured inks on absorbent paper, are filmed from behind, so that the pictures are seen as they are painted.

Picasso, Jacqueline and the Pignons go to see Manet's *Lola de Valence* in Nice during the summer; afterwards he does drawings of Jacqueline as Lola.

Claude and Paloma, as well as Maya, visit him, and he takes them to a bullfight at Vallauris along with Jacqueline and Cocteau; they are photographed by Brian Brake.

In May–June an exhibition is held at Marlborough Fine Art Ltd., London; in June–October a retrospective is held at the Musée des Arts Décoratifs, Paris (and later in Munich, Cologne and Hamburg).

1956

Picasso begins working again in earnest on the theme of bathers; he also continues his 'indoor landscapes' (based on his studio at La Californie) and his series of *Woman by a window* (Museum of Modern Art, New York, no.52; etc.). References to old masters, including Rembrandt, Velázquez and Cranach, begin to appear more frequently, especially in his graphic work.

In the summer he constructs the *Bathers* from an assemblage of wood; it is later cast in bronze.

The Sala Gaspar in Barcelona holds its first Picasso exhibition in October; they will continue to exhibit his work regularly over the coming years.

Picasso's seventy-fifth birthday is also celebrated at the Madoura pottery, Vallauris; and in Moscow, where Ilya Ehrenburg organises an exhibition of works belonging to the State.

In November Picasso and the Pignons are among the signatories of a protest letter to the Central Committee of the French Communist party concerning the situation in Hungary (the letter is published in *Le Monde*).

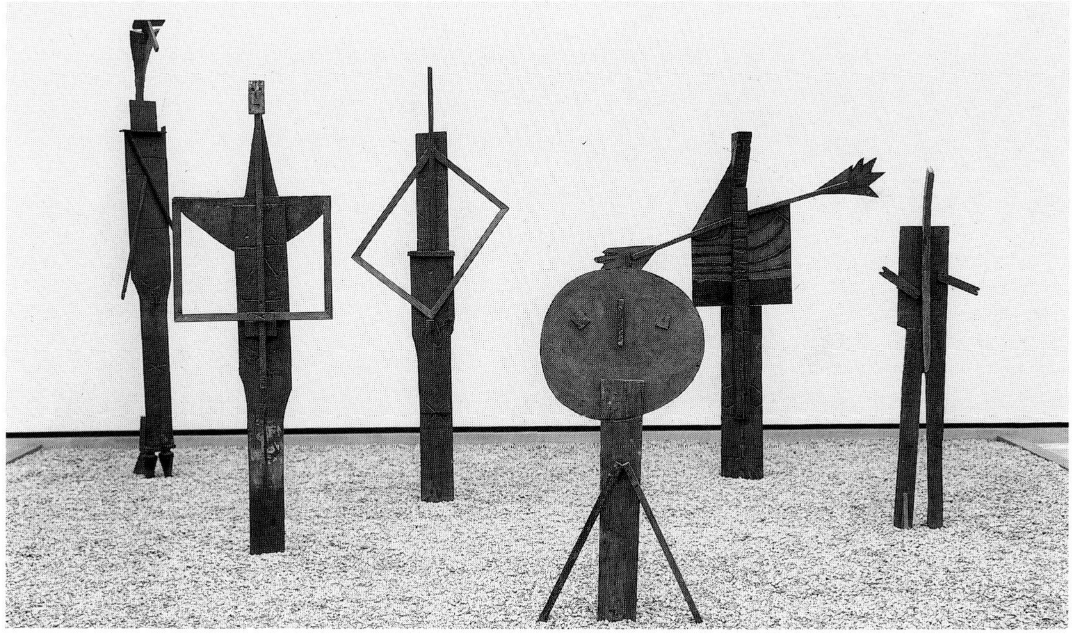

Picasso. *Bathers*, Cannes, 1956. Group of six wooden figures: woman diver (ht: 264 cm); man with clasped hands (ht: 214 cm); fountain man (ht: 227 cm); child (ht: 136 cm); woman with outstretched arms (ht: 198 cm); young man (ht: 176 cm). Staatsgalerie, Stuttgart.

1957

In March Kahnweiler and Louise Leiris move their gallery to 47, rue de Monceau, Paris; they open with an exhibition of Picasso's works of 1955–6; from now until the end of his life, the gallery will show Picasso's most recent works on a regular basis, holding twelve exhibitions in all between 1957 and 1973.

In May–September, the *Picasso 75th Anniversary* exhibition is held in New York at the Museum of Modern Art; it later travels to Chicago and Philadelphia; in July–September, a retrospective exhibition of works on paper (1898–1957) is shown at the Musée Réattu, Arles.

In the summer Vice-President Nixon declines the suggestion of the photographer David Douglas Duncan that Picasso should be invited to the U.S.A. as a guest of the government, in order to deliver 'a cultural body-blow to the Communists'.

In August Picasso begins his series of variations after Velázquez's *Las Meninas,* working from a postcard.

At the end of the year he works on studies for a wall decoration for the UNESCO building in Paris.

During the year Picasso begins to collaborate with the Norwegian Carl Nesjar, who uses a sand-blasting technique to realise Picasso's drawings or maquettes (in wood or cut-out sheet metal) in large sculpture; the first of these is for a government building in Oslo.

1958

At the end of January Picasso completes the UNESCO panel, later called *The fall of Icarus*; it is installed in September. He develops a further series of *Bathers* sculptures made from assemblages of wood.

In the spring an exhibition of 150 ceramics is held at the Maison de la Pensée Française. An exhibition of lithographs and aquatints (catalogue introduction by Kahnweiler) tours Auckland, Dunedin, Wellington and Melbourne.

With the help of his friends Douglas Cooper and John Richardson, Picasso sets about to collect Degas monotypes (specific references to these in Picasso's work surface some ten years later in a series of brothel scenes); these he adds to a fairly large collection, assembled throughout his life, of erotic art and works by other artists, including Corot, Victor Hugo, Seurat, Cézanne, Rousseau, Matisse, Miró and many of his friends.

At the end of the year, Picasso buys the château of Vauvenargues at the foot of Mont Sainte-Victoire.

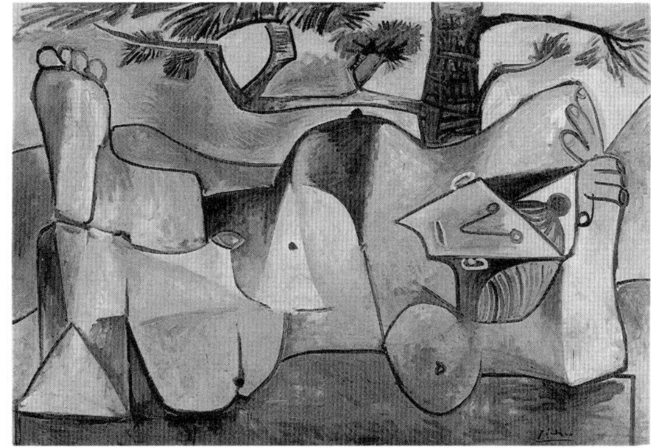

Picasso. *Nude under a pine tree*, Vauvenargues–Cannes, 1959. Oil on canvas, 182.9 × 244 cm.
The Art Institute of Chicago. Grant J. Pick Collection.

1959

Early in the year Picasso and Jacqueline begin to alternate residence between La Californie and Vauvenargues.

He paints *Nude under a pine tree* as a tribute to Cézanne (the contour of her body echoes the Mont Sainte-Victoire), and he works on further variations of Manet's *Déjeuner sur l'herbe* and a series of linocuts – a technique he has learned from the printer Arnéra in Vallauris – on Mediterranean themes.

In May–June the *Las Meninas* series is exhibited at the Galerie Louise Leiris (catalogue introduction by Michel Leiris).

In June the *Monument to Apollinaire* – a bronze head of Dora Maar (1941) on a stone base – is dedicated in the churchyard of Saint-Germain-des-Prés.

Picasso and Jacqueline and Luís Miguel Dominguín and his wife make a brief appearance in Cocteau's film *Le Testament d'Orphée*.

1960

A retrospective exhibition at the Tate Gallery is held in June–July.

Picasso continues making maquettes for sheet metal cut-outs; some of these are realised in a foundry in Vallauris with the assistance of the dealer and art enthusiast, Lionel Prejger.

1961

In March Picasso and Jacqueline marry, and in June they move into Notre-Dame-de-Vie, a farmhouse in Mougins; her image dominates the late work, a period which has been called 'l'époque Jacqueline'.

Celebrations for his 80th birthday are held in Vallauris on 25 October; he invites many Spaniards, who have come to pay homage, to a celebration lunch the next day.

Over 170 works are exhibited in *Happy Birthday Mr Picasso* at the UCLA Art Gallery, Los Angeles, in the same month.

Trozo de piel, a group of Picasso poems, is published in *Papeles de Son Armadans* (Mallorca); and David Douglas Duncan publishes *Picasso's Picassos*, containing photographs of works by the artist in his own collection.

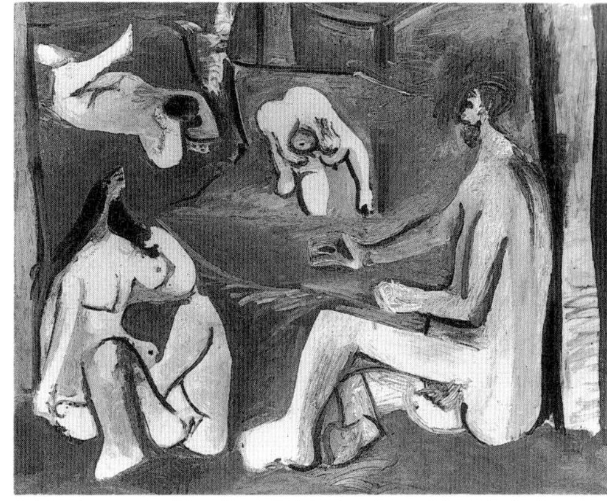

Picasso. *Le Déjeuner sur l'herbe after Manet*, Mougins, 1961. Oil on canvas, 60 × 73 cm.
Musée Picasso, Paris.

1962

In January–February an exhibition of paintings made at Vauvenargues (1959–61) is held at the Galerie Louise Leiris, Paris; in June the *American Tribute to Picasso* exhibition is held at nine galleries (each showing different periods of work) in New York, and a birthday exhibition is staged at the Museum of Modern Art.

In May Picasso is awarded the Lenin Peace Prize for the second time.

In August Picasso does a series of drawings of a rape scene for the drop curtain for Serge Lifar's *L'Après-midi d'un faune*; these are rejected by the director of the Paris Opéra, his old friend Georges Auric. Lifar also invites the artist to design a set for the ballet *Icare*, for which he makes a gouache.

Picasso works from slide projections (on a studio wall at Notre-Dame-de-Vie) of David's *Rape of the Sabines* and Poussin's *Massacre of the Innocents*; he begins to paint his versions of *Rape of the Sabines* employing elements borrowed from both works.

1963

Early in the year Picasso completes the final version of the *Rape of the Sabines* (Museum of Fine Arts, Boston); he also works on a series of portraits of Jacqueline and a sequence of the *Artist and his model*. In the spring he does drawings after Rembrandt's *Bathsheba*.

The Museu Picasso, with Sabartès's personal collection as its base, opens in Barcelona in March on carrer Montcada.

Towards the end of the year Picasso begins a fruitful collaboration with the brothers Piero and Aldo Crommelynck, master-printers whom he had met in Lacourière's workshop in the 1940s and who set up an engraving studio in an old bakery at Mougins.

In the last decade Picasso's life becomes more reclusive; many of his friends have died, others (such as Douglas Cooper) become alienated. Jacqueline increasingly prevents Picasso's children (with the exception of Paulo) having access to their father, but she allows a few visitors, including the Leirises, biographers Roland Penrose and John Richardson, Spanish friends Pallarès, Dominguín and Rafael Alberti, and the photographers David Douglas Duncan, Roberto Otero and Edward Quinn, as well as a few collectors and art historians.

1964

In January–February a retrospective exhibition, *Picasso and Man*, is held at the Art Gallery of Toronto; and another retrospective travels in Tokyo, Kyoto and Nagoya, Japan; 102 linocuts are shown at the Auckland City Art Gallery.

During this year, in addition to printmaking, Picasso does a series of paintings on the theme of *Nude with cat* and a new series of *Artist and his model*. He makes the maquette for the Chicago *Woman's head* (it is unveiled in l967).

Much to Picasso's displeasure, Françoise Gilot's *Life with Picasso*, written with Carlton Lake, is published in the spring (Picasso attempts unsuccessfully to stop the French edition in the following year). Brassaï's *Conversations avec Picasso*, illustrated with his photographs of the artist, also appears.

1965

For the Salon de Mai, Picasso presents a group composition that he and Pignon had arranged from 12 separate canvases of nudes and painters as *Twelve canvases in One. One canvas in Twelve.*

An exhibition, *Picasso et le Théâtre*, is held at the Musée des Augustins, Toulouse, in the summer, as well as a major show at the Sala Gaspar, Barcelona.

Newly invigorated themes appear in his work, including landscapes, and man and child/family; illness interrupts this period. In November Picasso undergoes an operation in the American hospital in Neuilly.

1966

In the spring the subject of the musketeer appears in full force in drawings and paintings; and in August he once again begins working in earnest on printmaking. On a visit made (some time later) by Edward Quinn, Picasso challenges the photographer to film him etching, to prove the steadiness of his hand at the age of almost ninety.

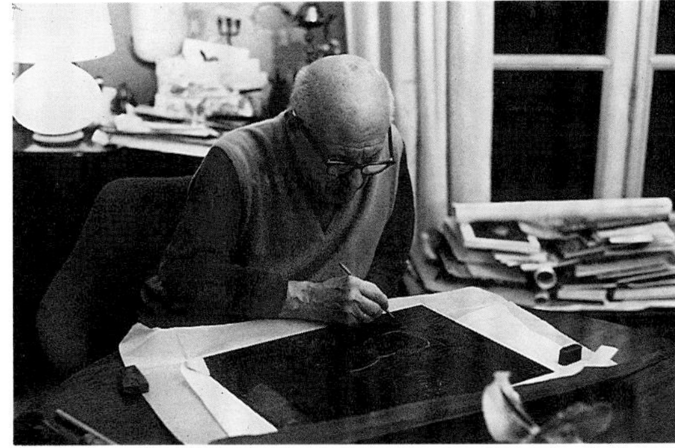

Picasso etching a plate at Notre-Dame-de-Vie in the late 1960s. Photo by Edward Quinn.

In November an *Hommage à Picasso* with over 700 works is held at the Grand Palais, the Petit Palais and the Bibliothèque Nationale in Paris.

During the year ten aquatints (from the *Artist and his model* series, 1963–4) accompany the posthumous publication of Pierre Reverdy's last poem *Sable mouvant*.

1967

Picasso is at work on a series of male figures and dramatically foreshortened female nudes.

In the spring he is evicted from the rue des Grands Augustins studio, since he no longer lives there; the contents are transported to his houses in the Midi.

He turns down the Légion d'Honneur.

The first retrospective of his sculptures and ceramics is held at the Tate Gallery, London, and the Museum of Modern Art, New York.

1968

Early in the year he does paintings on the theme of *Nude with bird*, and drawings of the *Turkish bath*.

Jaime Sabartès dies on 13 February; Picasso gives the *Las Meninas* series to the Museu Picasso, Barcelona, in his memory.

Between 16 March and 5 October, working with the Crommelynck brothers, he carries out the *Suite 347*, engravings of highly personal content: bullfights, musketeers, commedia dell'arte characters, the Celestina, as well as erotic variations on Raphael and the Fornarina; they are exhibited at the Galerie Louise Leiris at the end of the year.

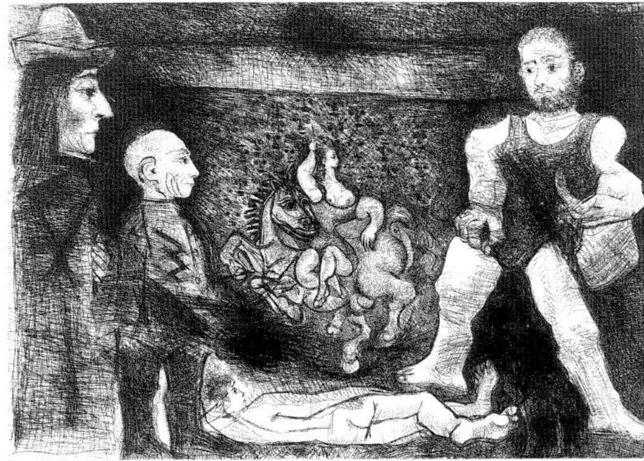

Picasso. Plate 1 of *Suite 347*, with self-portrait of the artist, Mougins, 16–22 March 1968. Etching, 39.5 × 56.5 cm. Musée Picasso, Paris.

Eroticism, always an element in Picasso's art, is allowed full and energetic expression in the late paintings: most of them of Jacqueline, sometimes of the artist himself – the palette pierced by a brush becomes a metaphor for his sex.

Picasso and the Crommelyncks realise an illustrated edition of *Le Cocu magnifique* by their father Fernand Crommelynck with engravings dating from 1966; in the following year Picasso's own play (written in 1957–8) *El entierro del Conde de Orgaz* is published with a set of engravings dating from 1966-7 and a preface by the Spanish poet Rafael Alberti (no.63).

Dibujos y escritos and the complete version of *Trozo de piel* are published (Faro de Cullera).

The first volume of Georges Bloch's *L'Œuvre gravé de Picasso* appears.

1969

Picasso works ever more intensely, especially in painting and graphic techniques: still lifes, nudes, musketeers (with echoes of Rembrandt and of the golden age of Spanish painting), the theme of

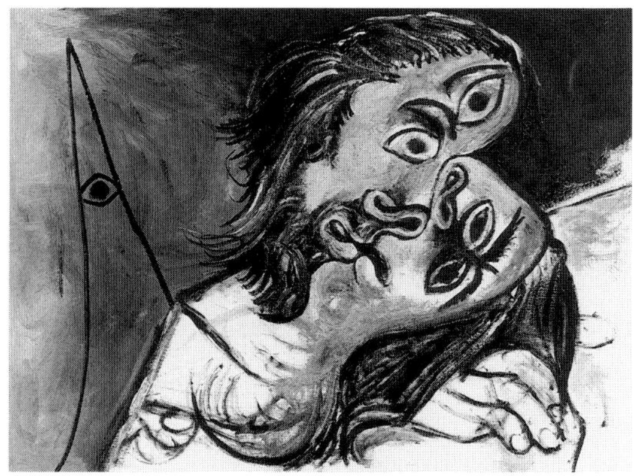

Picasso. *Kiss*, Mougins, 24 October 1969. Oil on canvas, 97 × 130 cm. Private collection, Switzerland.

the kiss and staring figures. Because he rarely goes out, he finds inspiration in old television movies (such as *The Lives of the Bengal Lancers*), and in 'Catch' (all-in wrestling).

1970

In January the Picasso family agrees to donate to the Museu Picasso, Barcelona, works left by the artist in Spain, some 2,000 drawings and paintings from the early period and from the summer of 1917, when Picasso lived for the last time in Barcelona.

In the early months of the year he is again intensely involved in printmaking.

The exhibition of late work in the Palais des Papes at Avignon (organised by Christian and Yvonne Zervos, both of whom die in the course of the year) opens in May.

The Bateau-Lavoir is destroyed by fire on 12 May, shortly after Malraux (Minister of Culture since 1959) had declared it a national monument.

In October, after attending a bullfight at Fréjus, Picasso paints versions of a *Black matador* from Mozambique, which represents his farewell to the bullring.

In December–March 1971, Picasso's work from the collections of Gertrude Stein and her family are included in the *Four Americans in Paris* exhibition at the Museum of Modern Art, New York.

1971

Between February and June he does another 97 new prints. In April–June 194 drawings of 1969–71 are shown at the Galerie Louise Leiris.

Some of Picasso's new paintings reflect his deep roots in Spanish tradition, especially saint- or Christ-like busts. A series of full-length figures – *Standing bather*, *Nude man and woman* (both in private collections) – reveal that he is still extending the limits of his medium.

In October the Louvre exhibits a selection of his works in honour of his ninetieth birthday.

1972

Picasso's last paintings and drawings are intensely personal: sometimes his own head appears as a skull, one painting seems to be a kind of Entombment, and there is a certain poignancy to works of sexual themes.

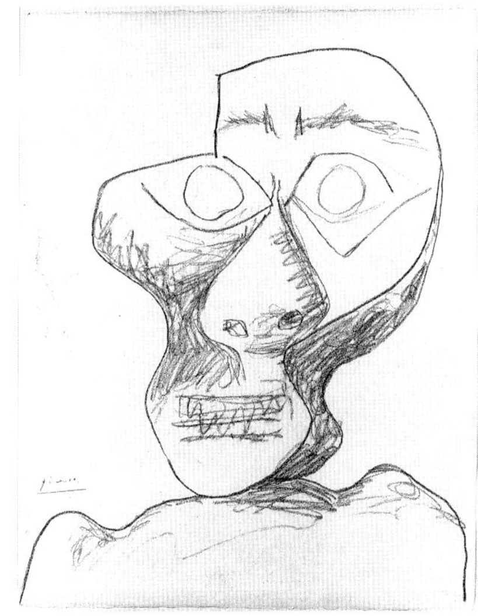

Picasso. *Self-portrait*, Mougins, 1968. 65.7 × 58.5 cm. Private collection, England.

His last dated works are done in this year, the last painting, *Embrace* (Private collection), on 1 June, the last drawing, of reclining figures, on 5 November.

1973

In January-February 156 engravings (1970–72) are shown at the Galerie Louise Leiris.

On 8 April Picasso dies at Notre-Dame-de-Vie; he is buried on 10 April in the wall of the château de Vauvenargues.

Picasso's own selection of late work (1970–72) is exhibited at the Palais des Papes in Avignon in May–September.

Bibliographic Note

A full bibliography of Picasso would comprise many thousand items, but for the guidance of visitors to the exhibition who are interested in finding more information about the artist, the following may be of special interest:

Reference Works:

Christian Zervos, *Pablo Picasso*, 33 vols., (1932–78); a basic work reproducing most paintings and some drawings in black and white.

Detailed catalogue raisonnés of paintings and drawings of the early period include: Pierre Daix & Georges Boudaille, *Picasso: The Blue and Rose Periods, 1900–1906* (1967); Pierre Daix & Joan Rosselet, *Picasso: The Cubist Years, 1907–1916* (1979); Josep Palau i Fabre, *Picasso, 1881–1907: Life and Work of the Early Years* (1981).

Catalogues and studies of works in other media include: Georges Bloch, *Pablo Picasso: Catalogue of the Graphic Work 1904–67*, (1968); Bernhard Geiser, *L'Œuvre Gravé de Picasso*, 2 vols., (1933 and 1968); Douglas Cooper, *Picasso: Theatre* (1968); Arnold Glimcher & Marc Glimcher, *Je Suis Le Cahier: The Sketchbooks of Picasso* (1986); Sebastian Goeppert, Herma Goeppert-Frank & Patrick Cramer, *Pablo Picasso: The Illustrated Books* (1983); Fernand Mourlot, *Picasso Lithographe*, 4 vols., (1949–64); Georges Ramié, *Céramique de Picasso* (1974); Werner Spies, *Picasso: Das Plastische Werk* (1983).

For catalogues of major holdings of works by Picasso: *The Musée Picasso, Paris*, vols. I-II (1988); *Picasso: Catàleg de pintura i dibuix* (Museu Picasso, Barcelona, 1984); *L'Œuvre de Picasso à Antibes* (Musée Picasso, Antibes, 1981); William Rubin, *Picasso in the Collection of the Museum of Modern Art* (1972).

Memoirs, including personal recollections and photographic memoirs:

Brassaï, *Picasso & Co.* (1966); David Douglas Duncan, *The Private World of Pablo Picasso* (1958); *Picasso's Picassos* (1971); *Goodbye Picasso* (1975); *The Silent Studio* (1976); *Picasso and Jacqueline* (1988); Françoise Gilot & Carlton Lake, *Life with Picasso* (1964); D.-H.Kahnweiler, *Mes galeries et mes peintres* (1961); *Confessions esthétiques* (1963); Geneviève Laporte, *Sunshine at Midnight* (1975); Fernande Olivier, *Picasso and his Friends* (1964); *Souvenirs Intimes* (1988); Roberto Otero, *Forever Picasso* (1964); Hélène Parmelin, *Picasso Plain: An Intimate Portrait* (1963); *Picasso Says . . .* (1968); *Voyage en Picasso* (1980); Jacques Prévert, *Portraits de Picasso* (1981); Edward Quinn, *Picasso at Work, an Intimate Photographic Study* (1965); Jaime Sabartès, *Picasso: an Intimate Portrait* (1949); *Picasso Documents iconographiques* (1954); Gertrude Stein, *The Autobiography of Alice B. Toklas* (1933).

Statements by the artist and his friends:

Dore Ashton, *Picasso on Art: A Selection of Views* (1972); Marilyn McCully, *A Picasso Anthology: Documents, Criticism, Reminiscences* (1981).

Biographies:

Pierre Daix, *La Vie de Peintre de Pablo Picasso* (1977); *Picasso Créateur* (1987); Roland Penrose, *Picasso: His Life and Work* (1958); Antonina Vallentin, *Pablo Picasso* (1957); Gertrude Stein, *Picasso* (1939); the first volume of John Richardson's *A Life of Picasso* is due to appear in 1990.

Critical works:

Many of the most useful contributions to the critical study of Picasso's work have appeared in exhibition catalogues, including: Jürgen Glaesemer, *Der Junge Picasso: Frühwerk und blaue Periode* (Kunstmuseum, Bern, 1984); *Les Demoiselles d'Avignon*, 2 vols. (Musée Picasso, Paris, 1988); *Late Picasso* (Tate Gallery, 1988); William Rubin, *Pablo Picasso: A Retrospective* (Museum of Modern Art, New York, 1980).

Other useful studies include:

Lydia Gassman, *Mystery, Magic and Love in Picasso 1925–1937* (Thesis, Ann Arbor, 1981); John Golding, *Picasso in Retrospect* (1973); and Gert Schiff, *Picasso in Perspective* (1976).

Note on the Catalogue

Dimensions are given in centimetres; height precedes width.
References at the end of each entry are to standard catalogues of Picasso's works (see adjacent Bibliographic Note) and/or to the catalogues of the Picasso Museums in Paris and Barcelona:

Z: Christian Zervos. *Pablo Picasso*. 33 vols. (1932–78).

Bloch: Georges Bloch. *Pablo Picasso: Catalogue of the Graphic Work* (1968).

Geiser: Bernhard Geiser. *L'Œuvre Gravé de Picasso*. 2 vols. (1933, 1968).

Spies: Werner Spies. *Picasso: Das plastische Werk* (1983).

MPB: Inventory number in the Museu Picasso, Barcelona.

M.P.: Inventory number in the Musée Picasso, Paris.

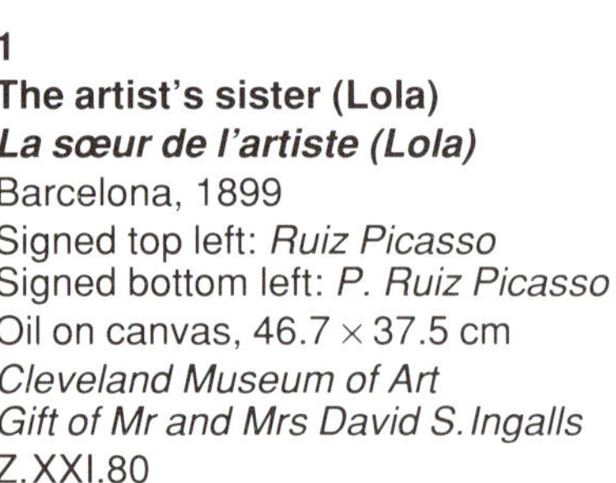

1
The artist's sister (Lola)
La sœur de l'artiste (Lola)
Barcelona, 1899
Signed top left: *Ruiz Picasso*
Signed bottom left: *P. Ruiz Picasso*
Oil on canvas, 46.7 × 37.5 cm
Cleveland Museum of Art
Gift of Mr and Mrs David S. Ingalls
Z.XXI.80

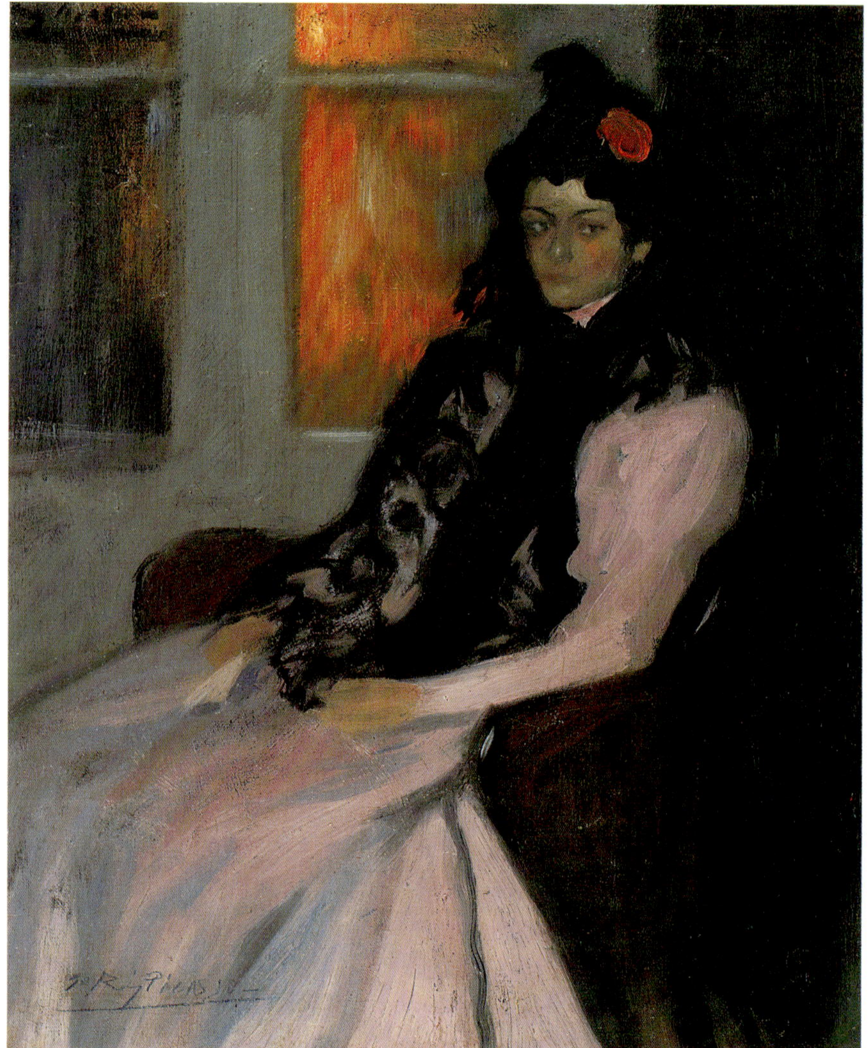

1

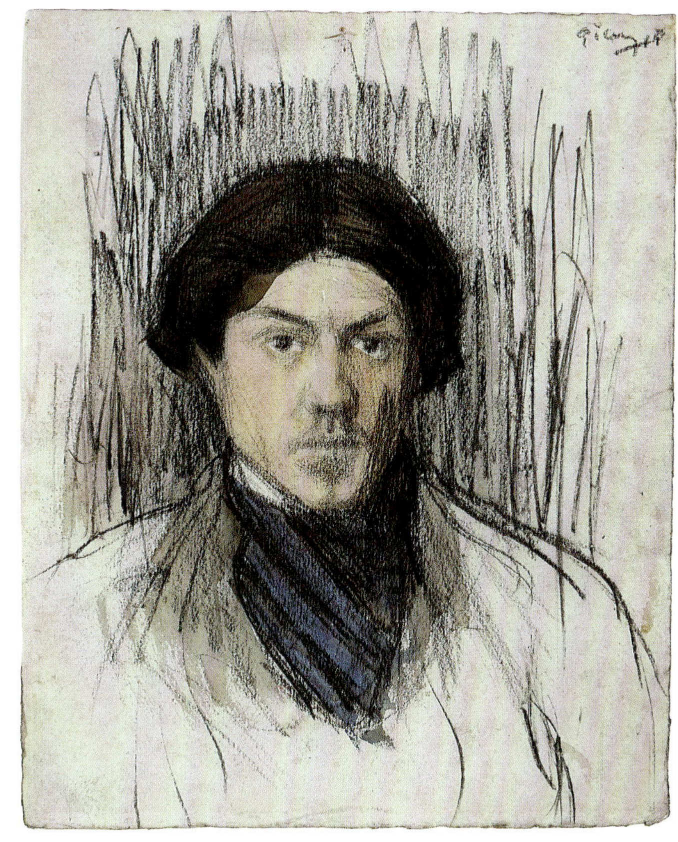

2

2
Self-portrait
Autoportrait
Paris, 1901–02
Black crayon with colour washes on paper, 30.2 × 23.8 cm
National Gallery of Art, Washington, D.C. Ailsa Mellon Bruce Collection (1970.17.164)
Z.XXI.336
The signature is false; on the verso is a charcoal drawing of a *Walking Woman*

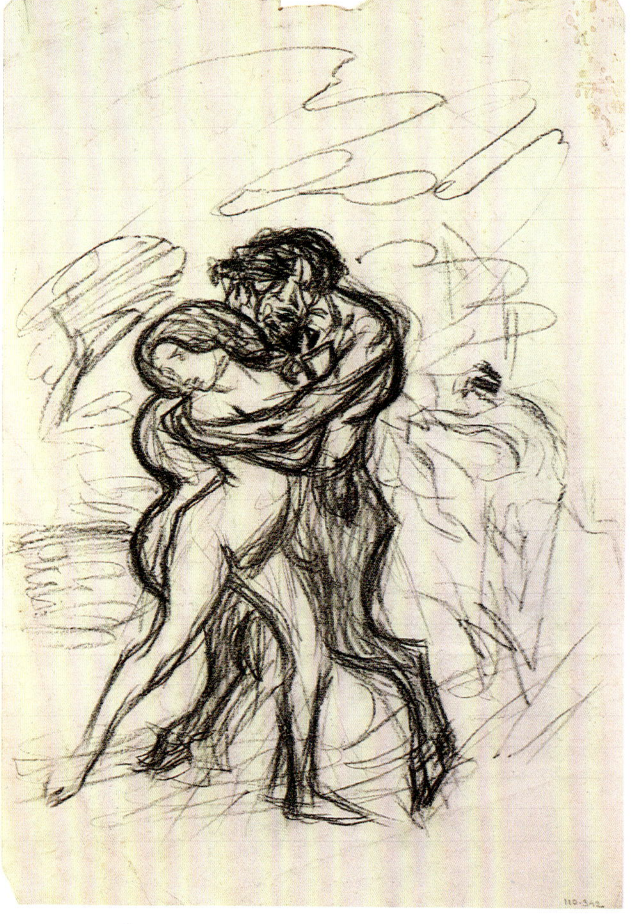

3

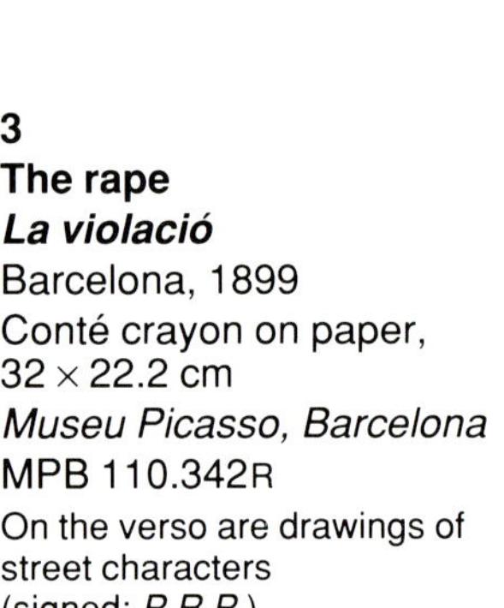

3
The rape
La violació
Barcelona, 1899
Conté crayon on paper, 32 × 22.2 cm
Museu Picasso, Barcelona
MPB 110.342R
On the verso are drawings of street characters (signed: *P.R.P.*)

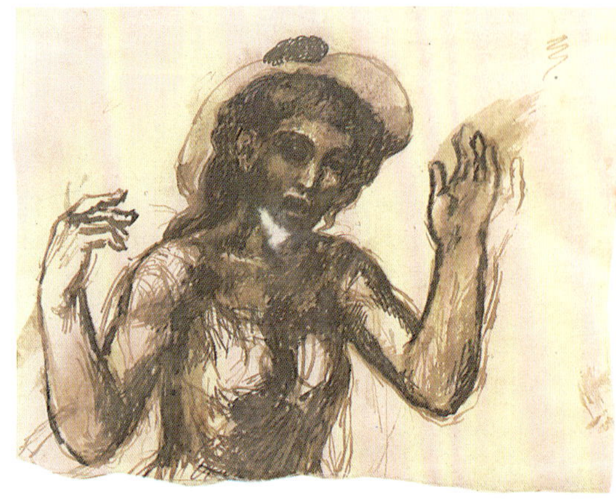

4

4
Bust of a woman
Buste de femme
Paris, December 1902
Dated (verso): *D 02*
Pen and wash on paper, 14.8 × 18.3 cm
Museu Picasso, Barcelona
MPB 110.469

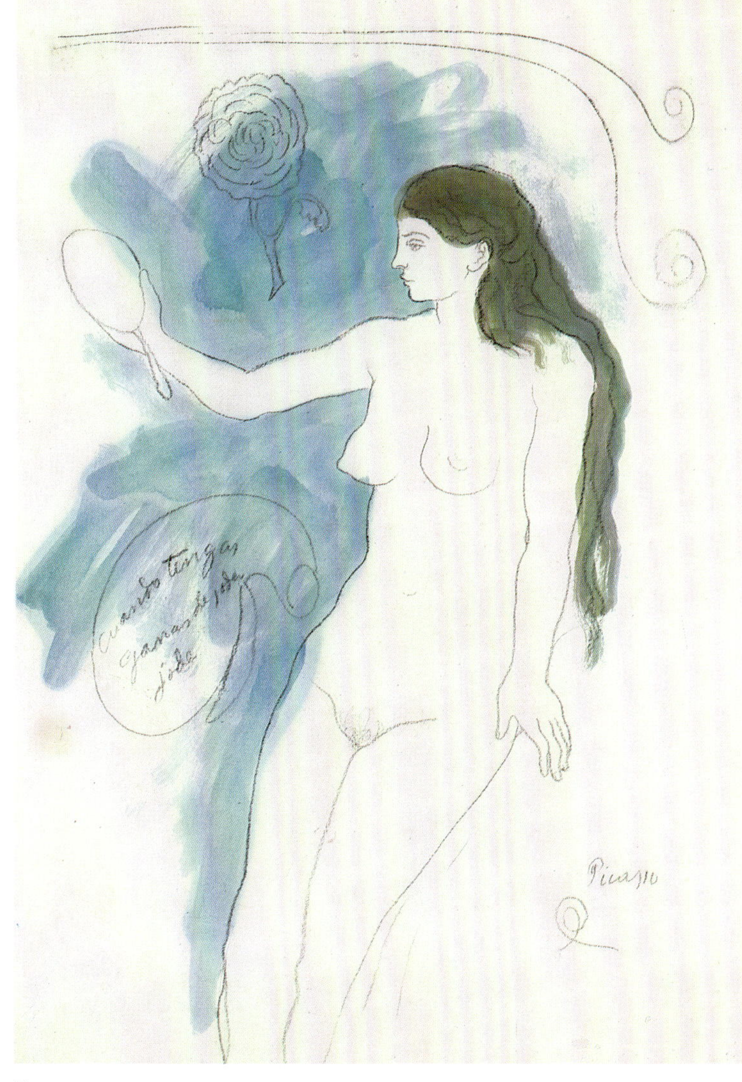

5

5
Woman with a mirror
Femme au miroir
Barcelona, 1902
Signed lower right: *Picasso*
Inscribed: *Cuando tengas ganas de joder, jode*
Crayon and gouache on paper, 38 × 26 cm
Courtesy of the Lefevre Gallery, London
Z.XXI.343

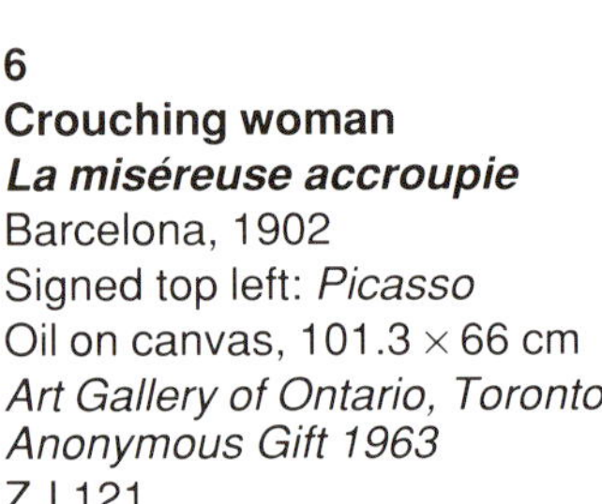

6

6
Crouching woman
La miséreuse accroupie
Barcelona, 1902
Signed top left: *Picasso*
Oil on canvas, 101.3 × 66 cm
Art Gallery of Ontario, Toronto
Anonymous Gift 1963
Z.I.121

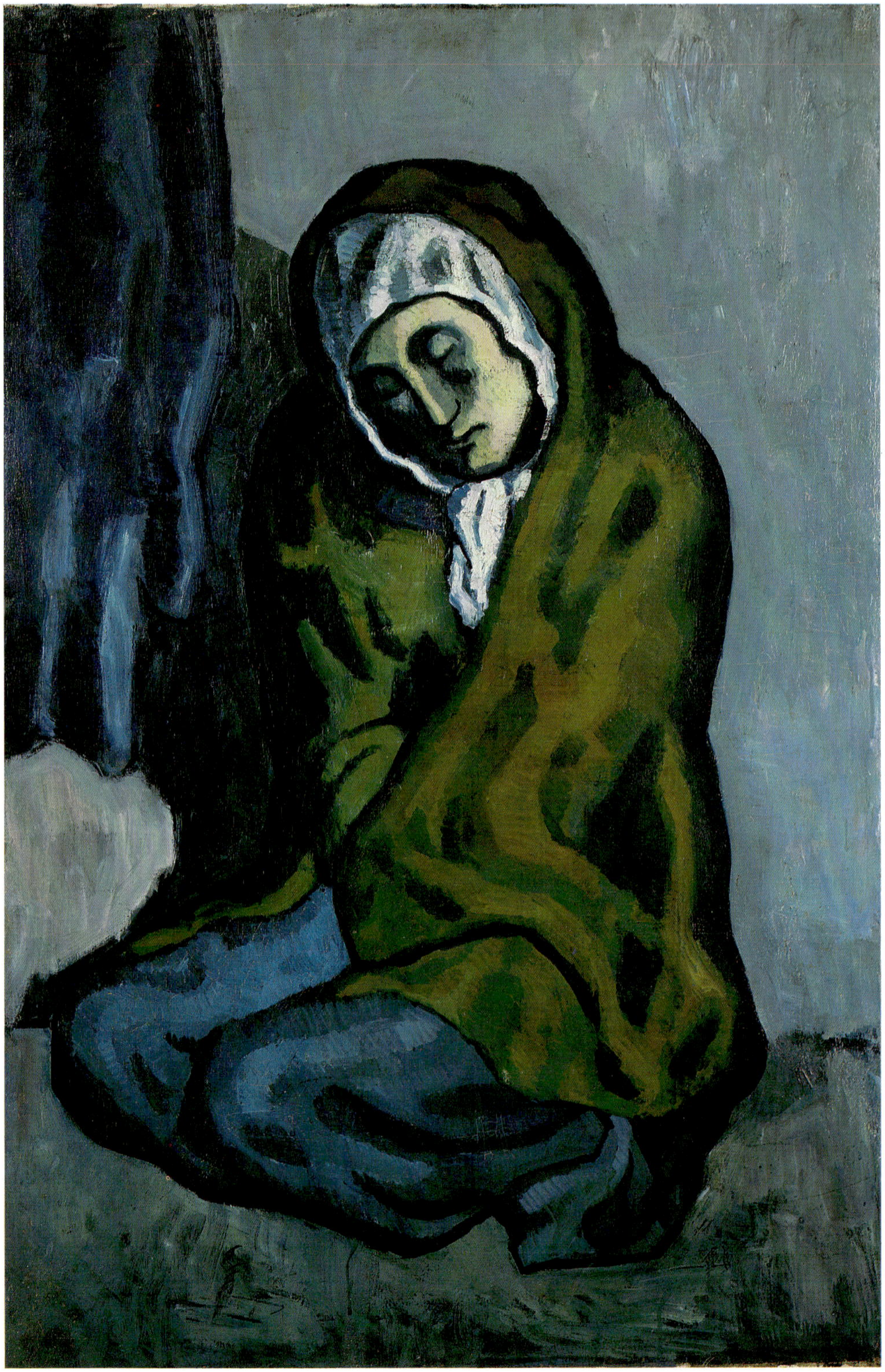

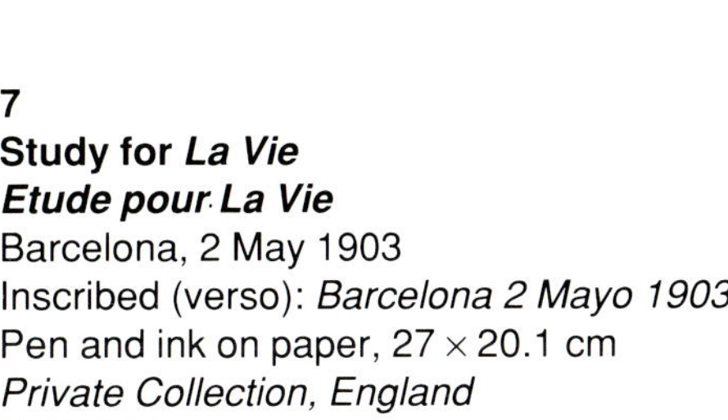

7
Study for *La Vie*
Etude pour La Vie
Barcelona, 2 May 1903
Inscribed (verso): *Barcelona 2 Mayo 1903*
Pen and ink on paper, 27 × 20.1 cm
Private Collection, England
Z.XXII.44

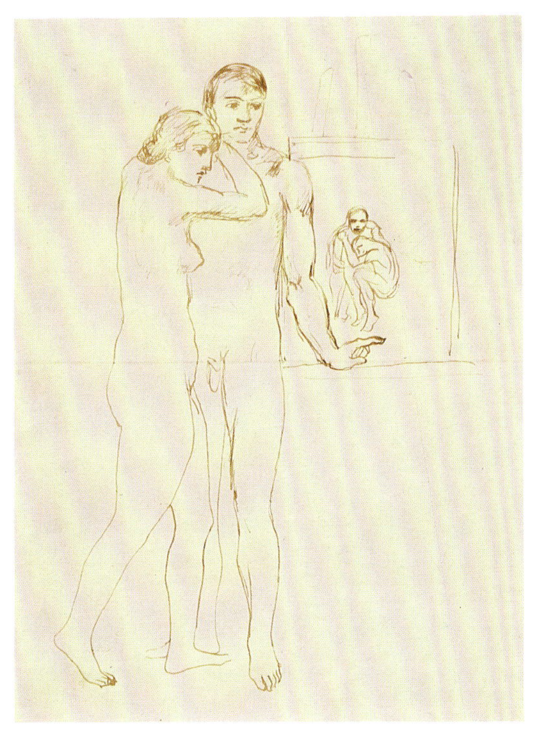

7

8
The frugal meal
Le repas frugal
Paris, 1904
Etching, 46.3 × 37.7 cm
National Gallery of Victoria, Melbourne
Geiser 2/II/b. Bloch 1

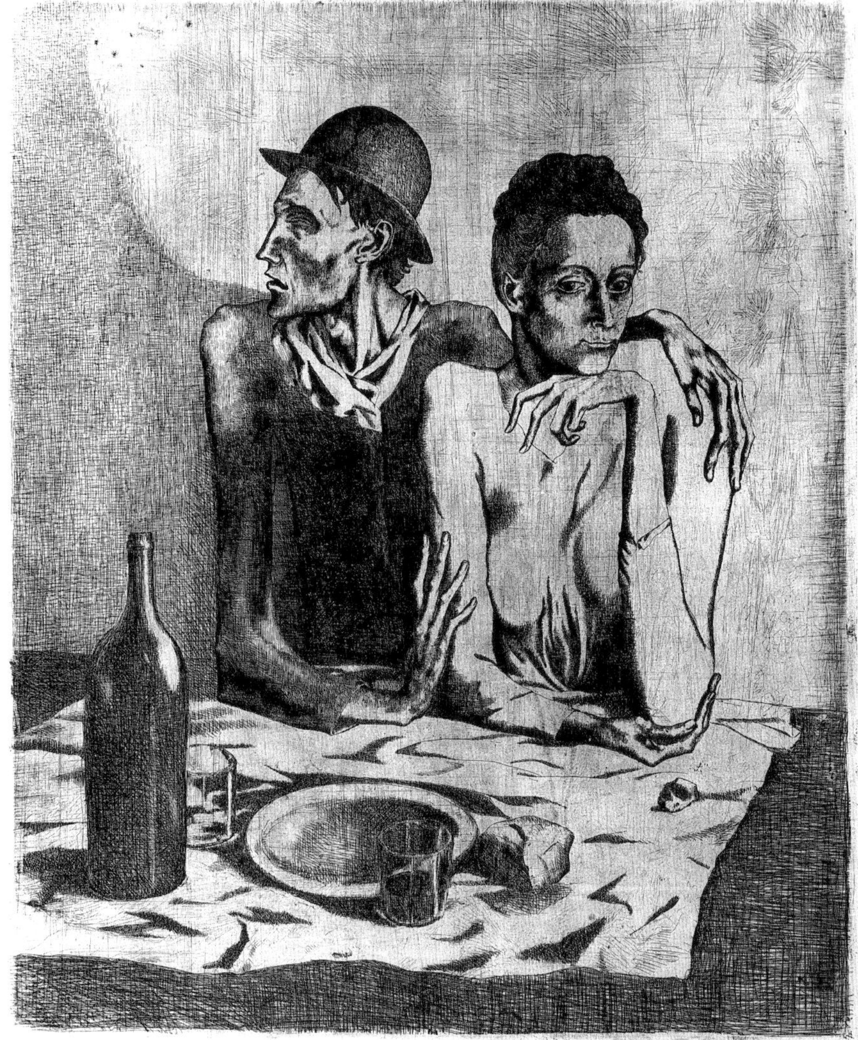

8

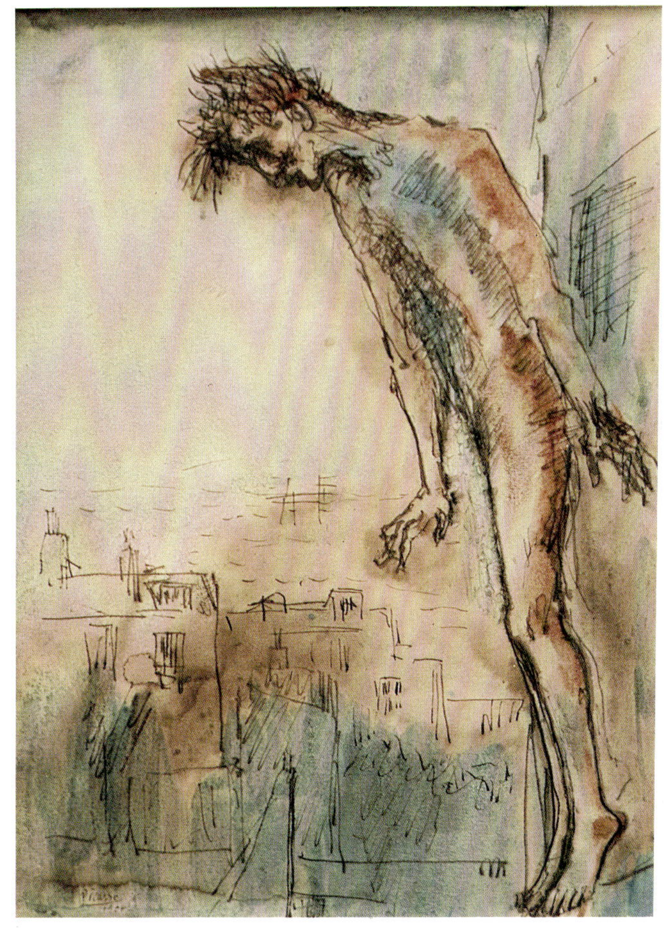

9

9
The Christ of Montmartre
Le Christ de Montmartre
Paris, 1904
Signed and dated bottom left: *Picasso/ 1904*
Indian ink and watercolour on paper, 36 × 26 cm
Foundation Prince M., Zurich
Z.VI.617

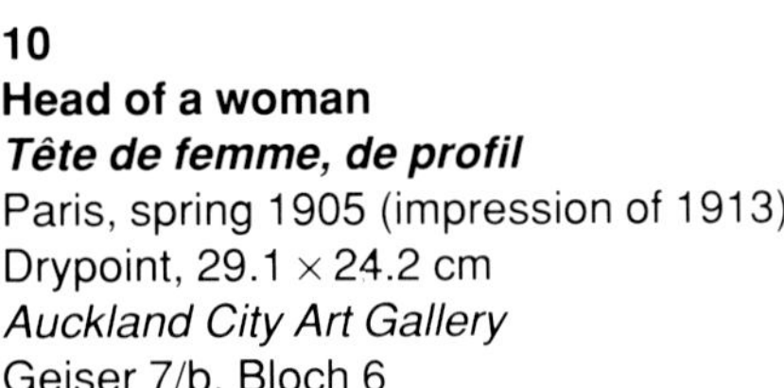

10
Head of a woman
Tête de femme, de profil
Paris, spring 1905 (impression of 1913)
Drypoint, 29.1 × 24.2 cm
Auckland City Art Gallery
Geiser 7/b. Bloch 6

11
Two saltimbanques
Les deux saltimbanques
Paris, March 1905 (impression of 1913)
Signed and dated on the plate upper left:
1905P/ Picasso
Drypoint, 12.2 × 9.1 cm
Private Collection, Sydney
Courtesy Rex Irwin Art Dealer, Sydney
Geiser 6/b. Bloch 5

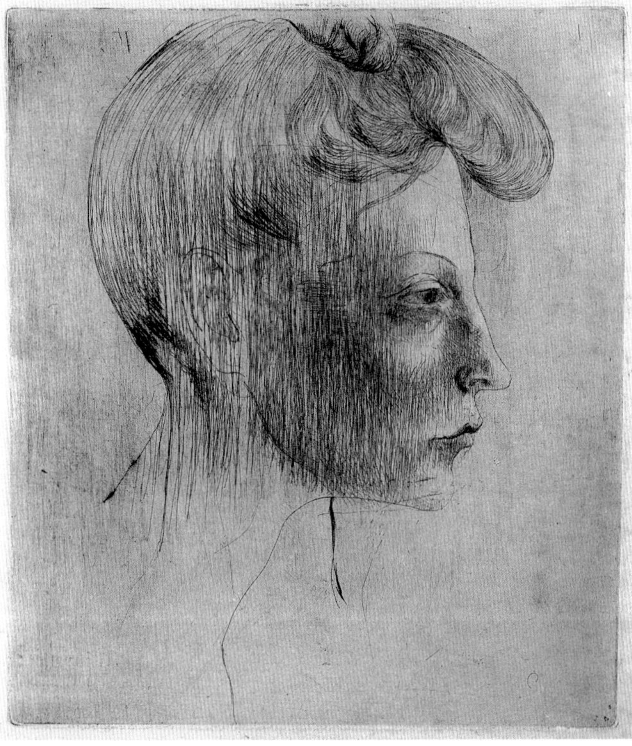

10

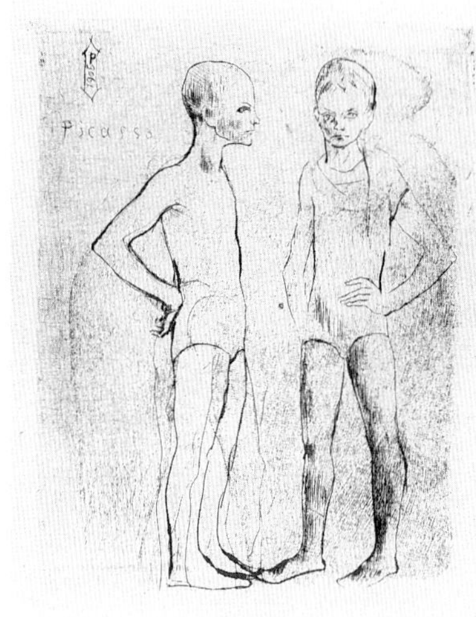

11

12
Kneeling woman combing her hair
Femme se coiffant
Paris, 1906
Bronze, 41.2 × 26 × 31 cm
Hirshhorn Museum and Sculpture Garden, Smithsonian Institution
Gift of Joseph H. Hirshhorn, 1972
Spies 7

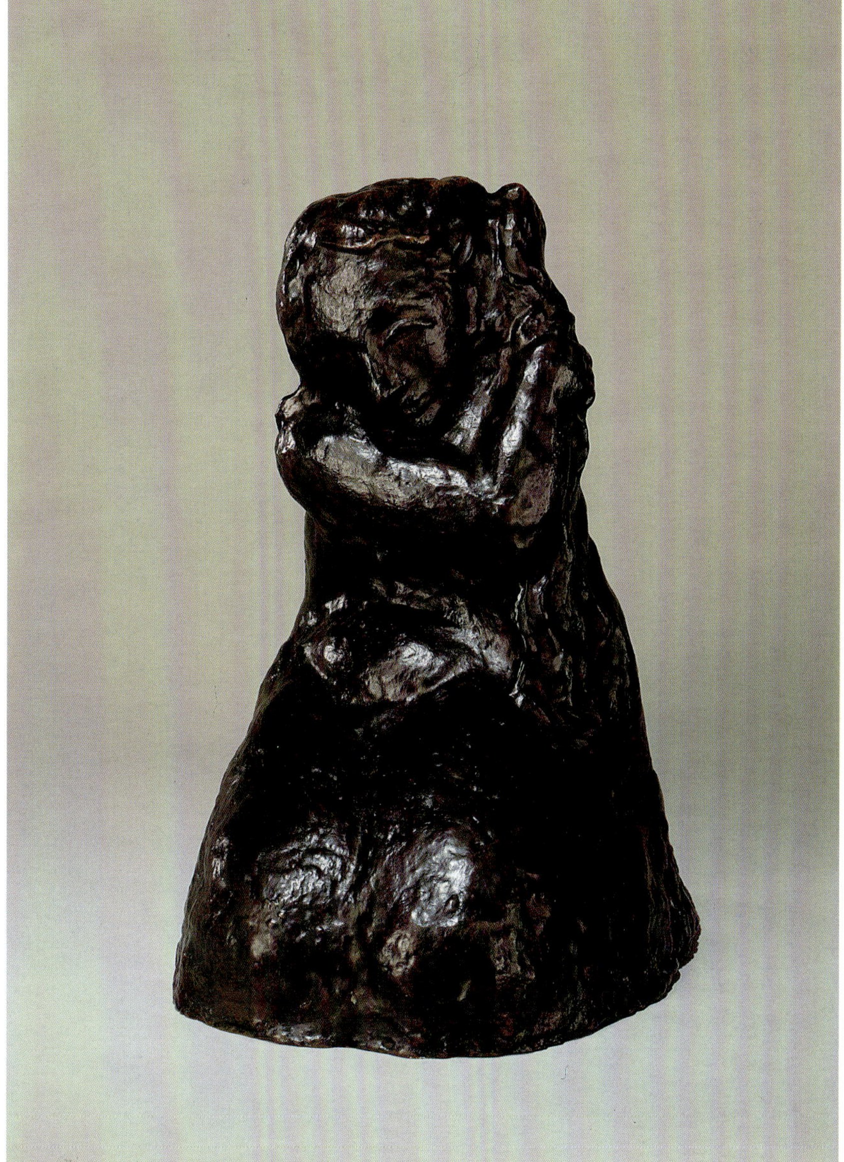

12

13
Woman with clasped hands
Femme aux mains jointes
(Study for *Les Demoiselles d'Avignon*)
Paris, spring 1907
Oil on canvas, 90.5 × 71.5 cm
Musée Picasso, Paris
Z.II**662. M.P.16

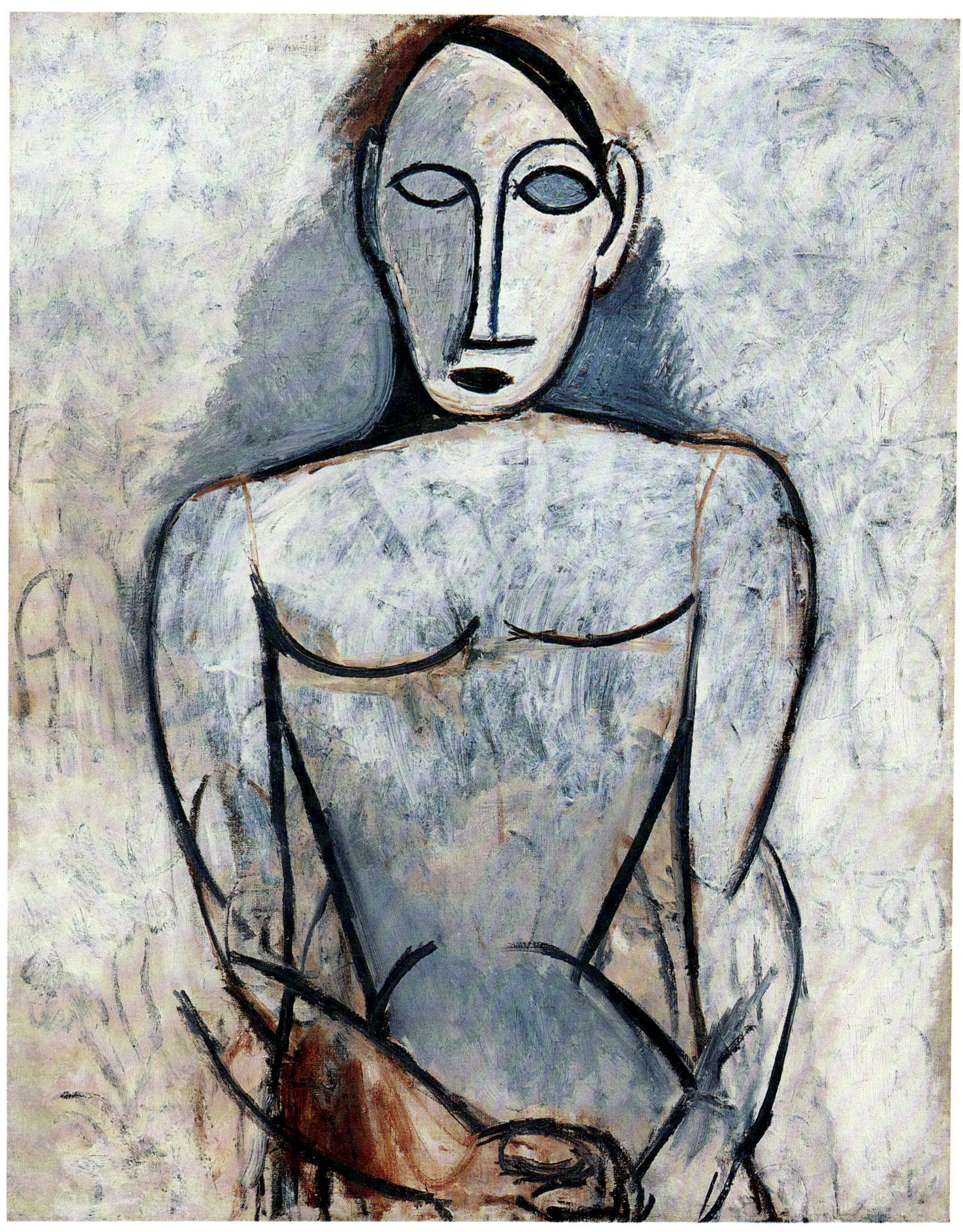

13

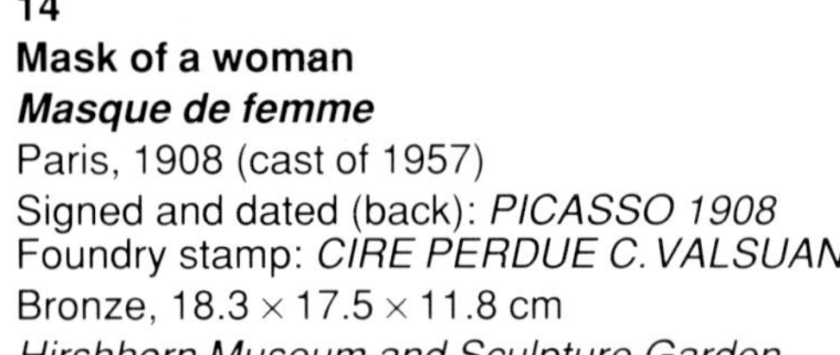

14
Mask of a woman
Masque de femme
Paris, 1908 (cast of 1957)
Signed and dated (back): *PICASSO 1908*
Foundry stamp: *CIRE PERDUE C. VALSUANI*
Bronze, 18.3 × 17.5 × 11.8 cm
Hirshhorn Museum and Sculpture Garden,
Smithsonian Institution
Gift of Joseph H. Hirshhorn, 1966
Spies 22

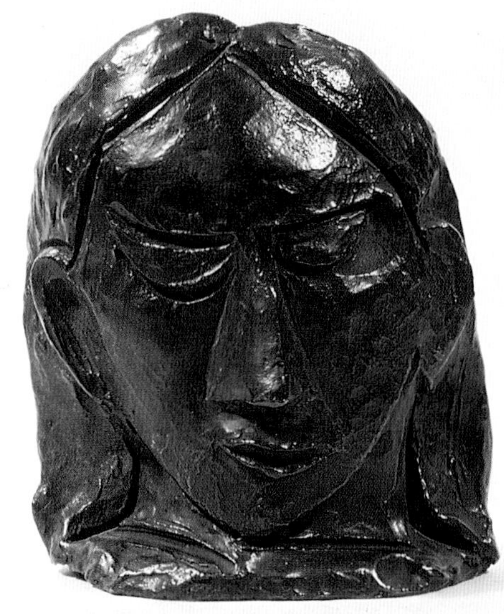

14

15
Head of a man
Tête d'homme
Paris, 1908
Signed bottom right: *Picasso*
Pencil and watercolour wash on paper, 31.4 × 24.4 cm
Queensland Art Gallery
Major Harold de Vahl Rubin Gift
Z.II**716

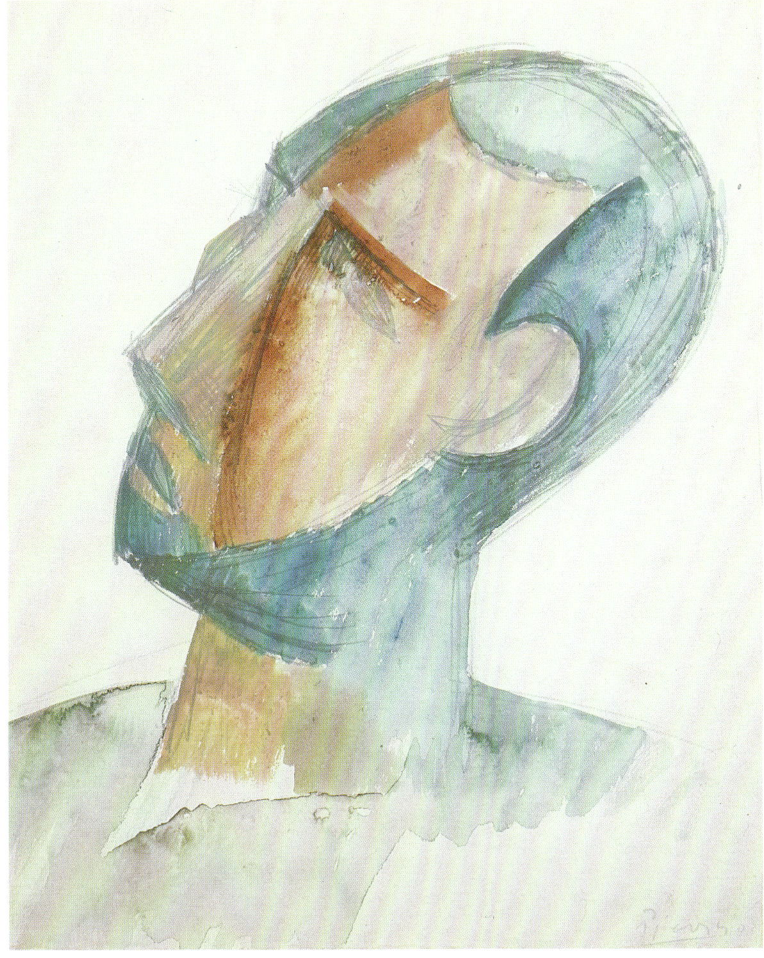

15

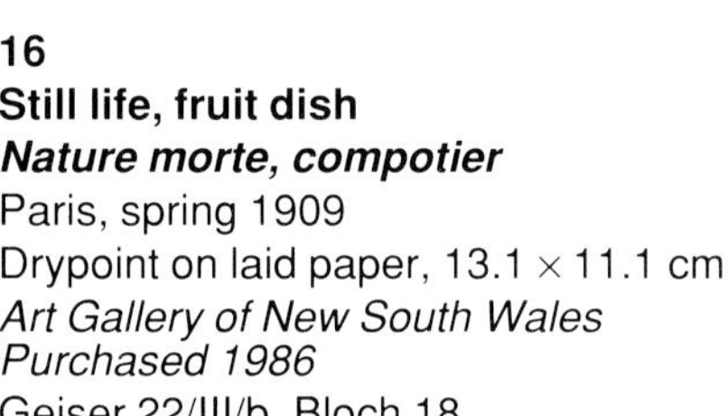

16
Still life, fruit dish
Nature morte, compotier
Paris, spring 1909
Drypoint on laid paper, 13.1 × 11.1 cm
Art Gallery of New South Wales
Purchased 1986
Geiser 22/III/b. Bloch 18

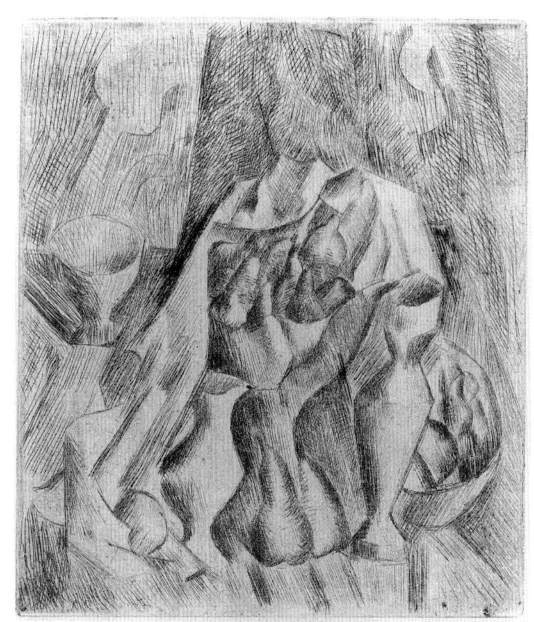

16

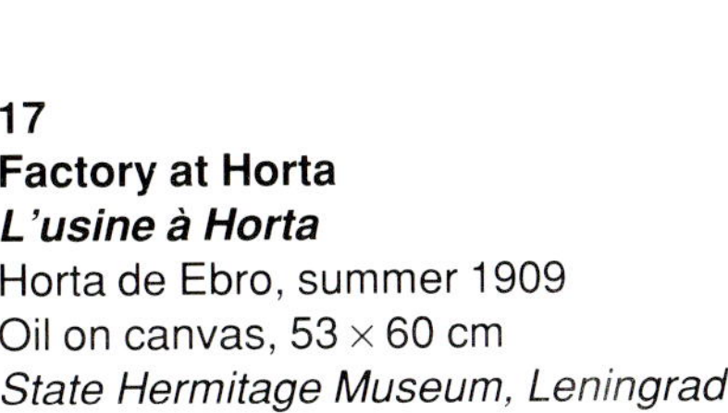

17
Factory at Horta
L'usine à Horta
Horta de Ebro, summer 1909
Oil on canvas, 53 × 60 cm
State Hermitage Museum, Leningrad
Z.II**158

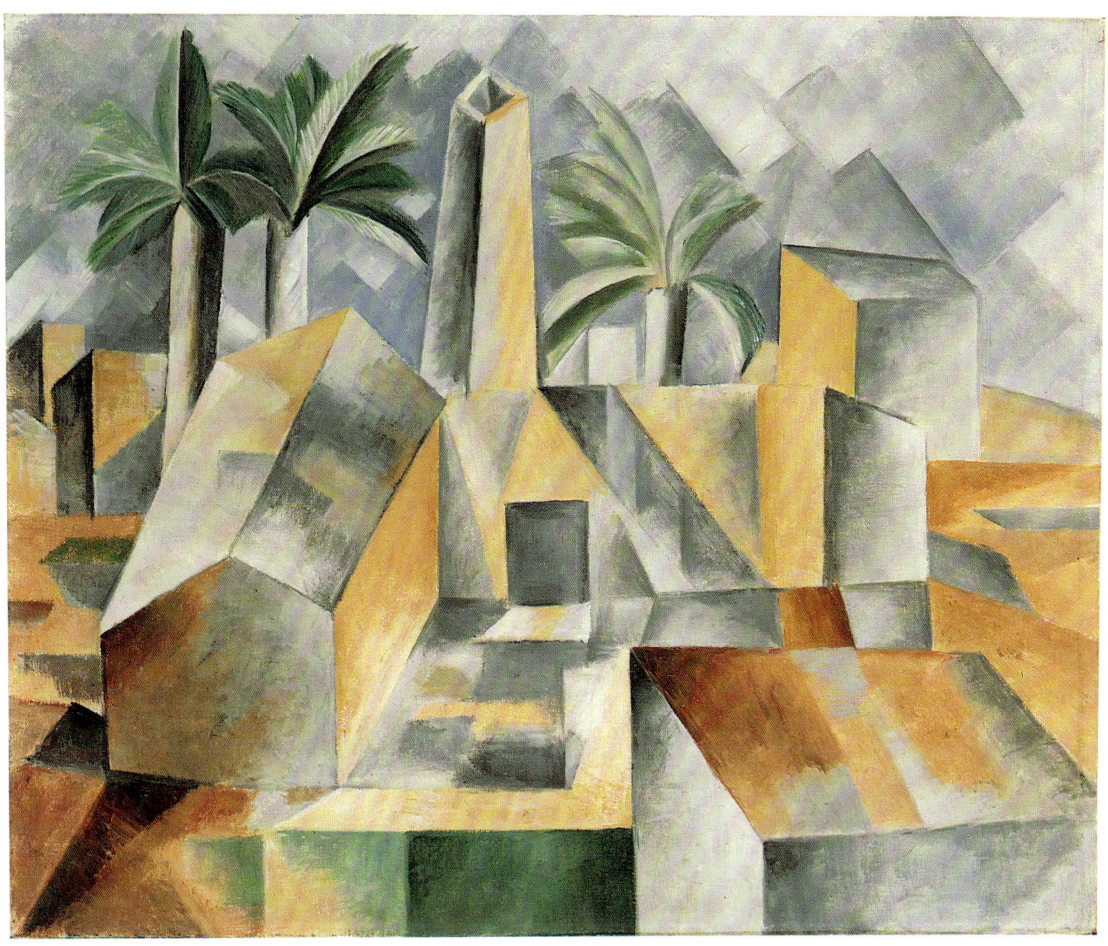

17

18
Half-length female nude
Femme nue debout
Paris, autumn 1910
Signed (verso): *Picasso*
Oil on canvas, 98.5 × 77 cm
Philadelphia Museum of Art
Louise and Walter C. Arensberg Collection
Z. II*225

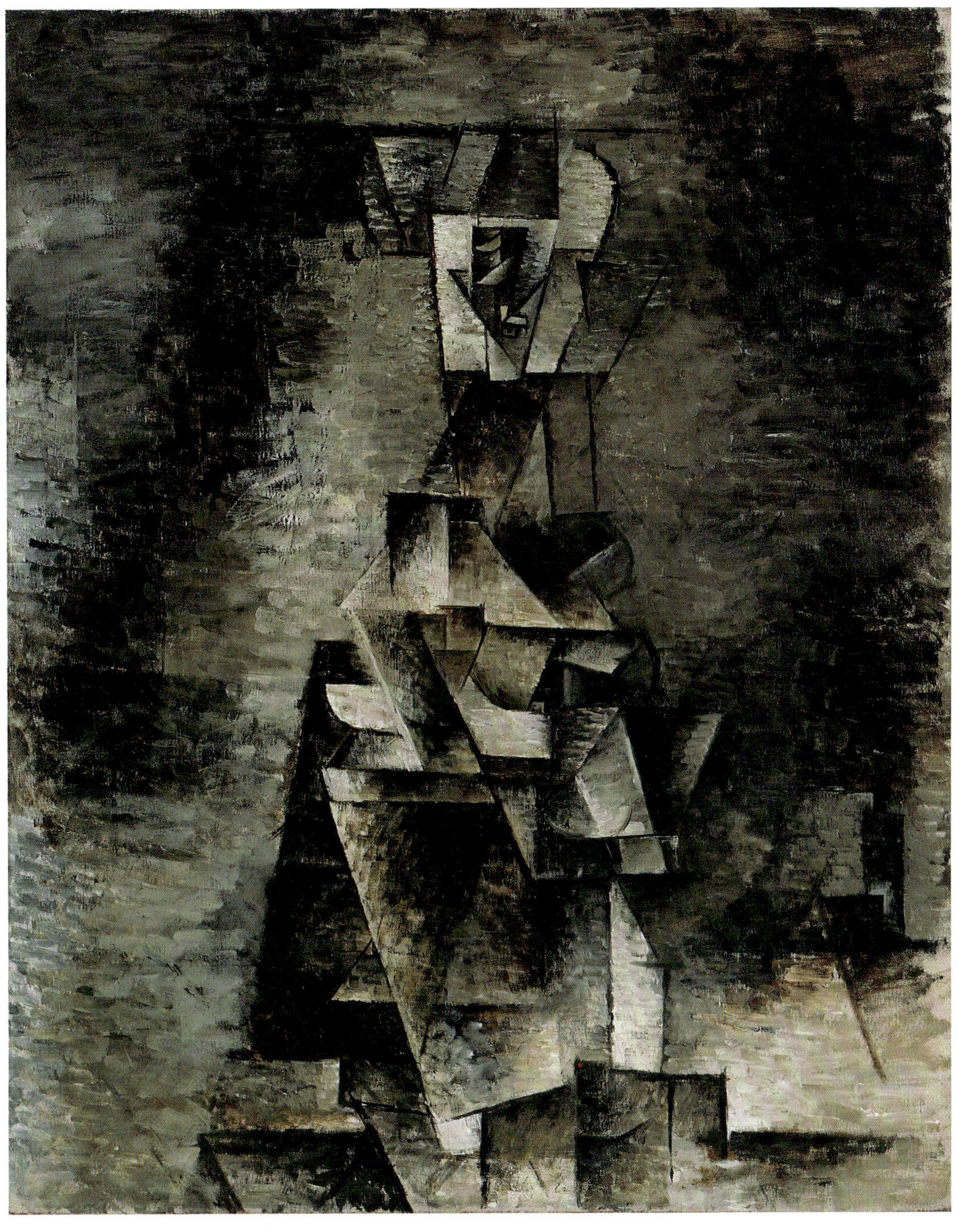

18

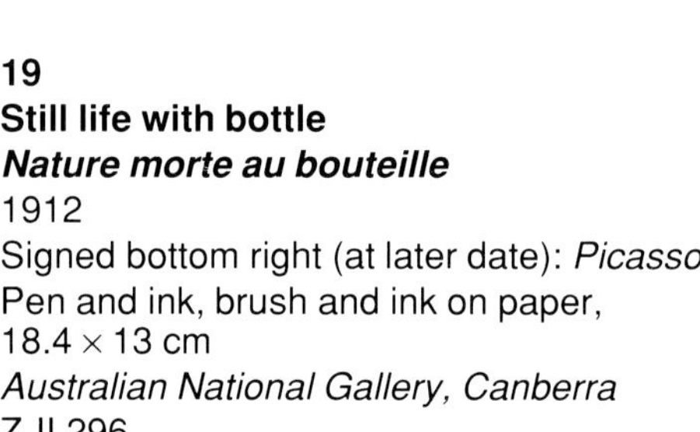

19
Still life with bottle
Nature morte au bouteille
1912
Signed bottom right (at later date): *Picasso*
Pen and ink, brush and ink on paper,
18.4 × 13 cm
Australian National Gallery, Canberra
Z.II.296

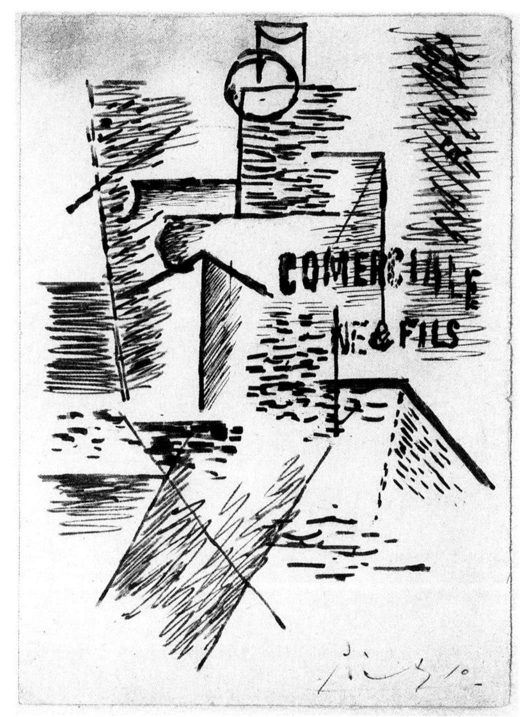

19

20
Head
Tête
Paris or Céret, early 1913
Pasted papers and charcoal on cardboard, 41 × 31.2 cm
Private Collection, England, on loan to Australian National Gallery, Canberra
Z.II**414

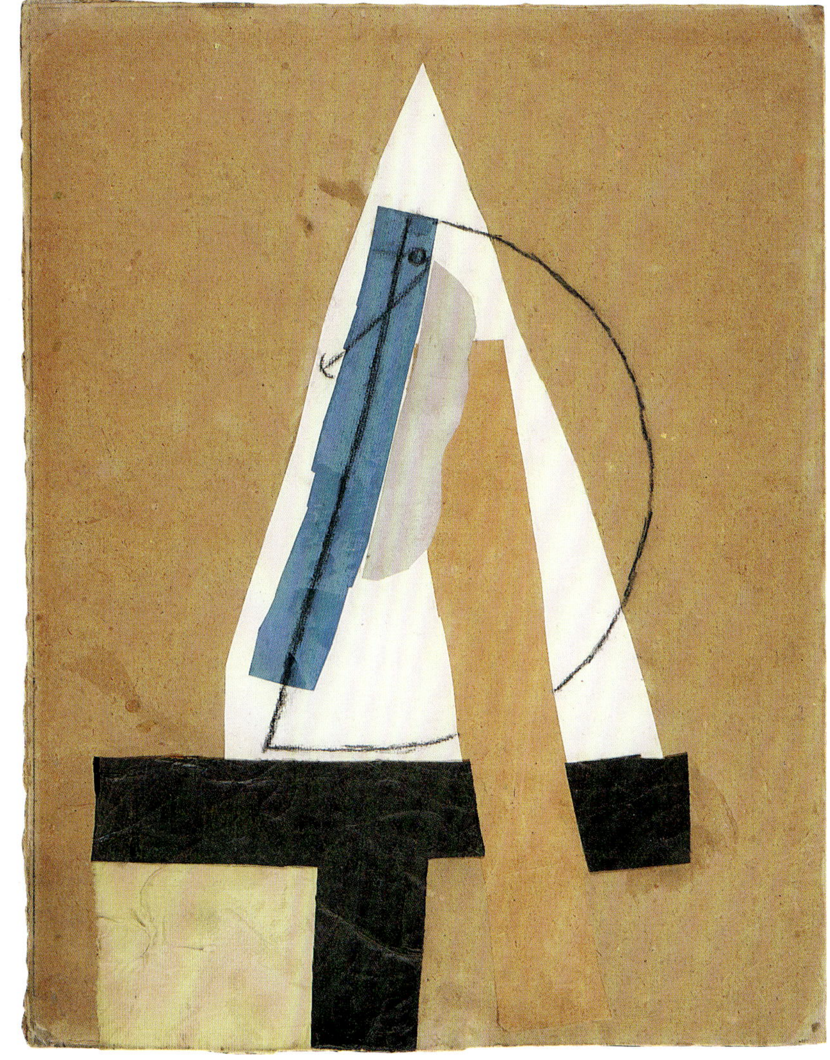

20

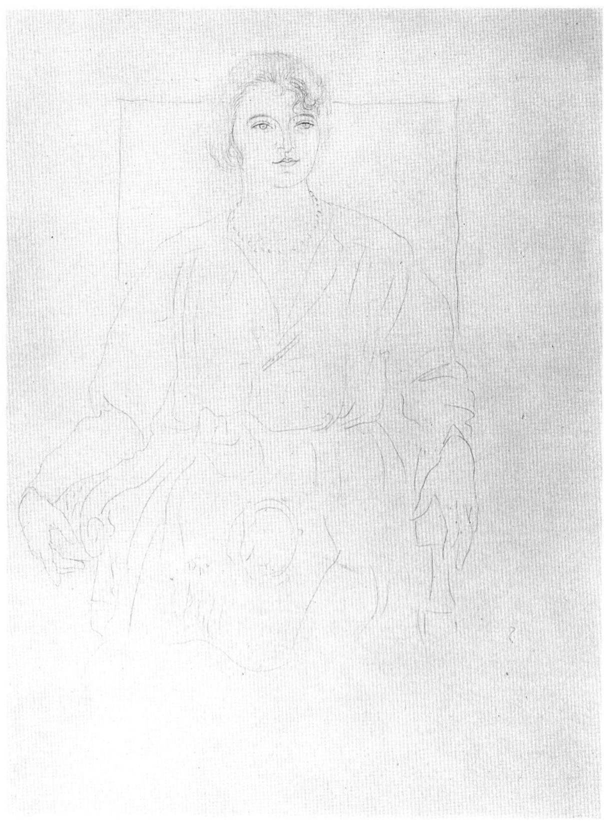

21
Woman with necklace in an armchair
Femme au collier dans un fauteuil
Paris, 1918
Pencil on paper, 36.5 × 27 cm
Private collection, Sydney
Courtesy Rex Irwin Art Dealer, Sydney
Not in Zervos

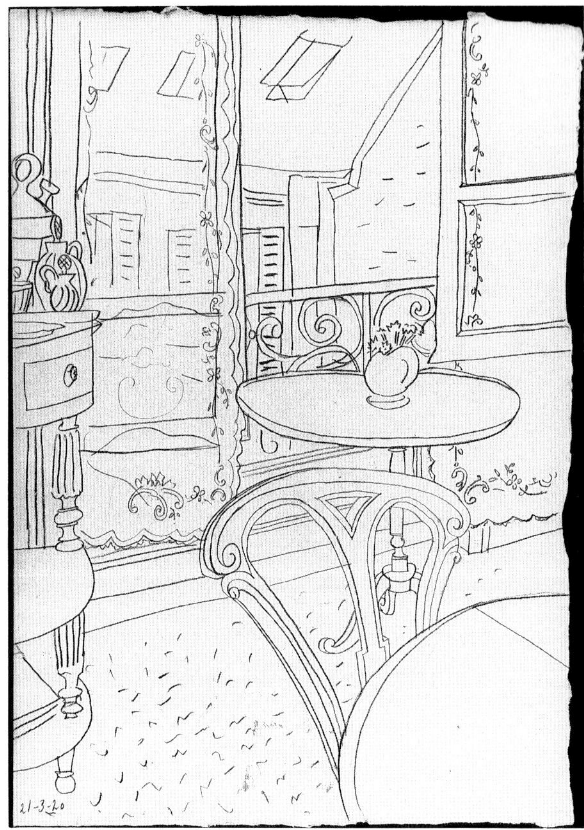

22
Dining-room in the rue La Boëtie
La salle à manger de la rue La Boëtie
Paris, 21 March 1920
Dated bottom left: *21-3-20*
Lead pencil on paper, 34 × 23.3 cm
Musée Picasso, Paris
M.P.898

23
Still life on a table
Nature morte au guéridon
Paris, 1920
Oil on canvas, 119 × 76 cm
Collection Marina Picasso
Galerie Jan Krugier, Geneva
Z.IV.104

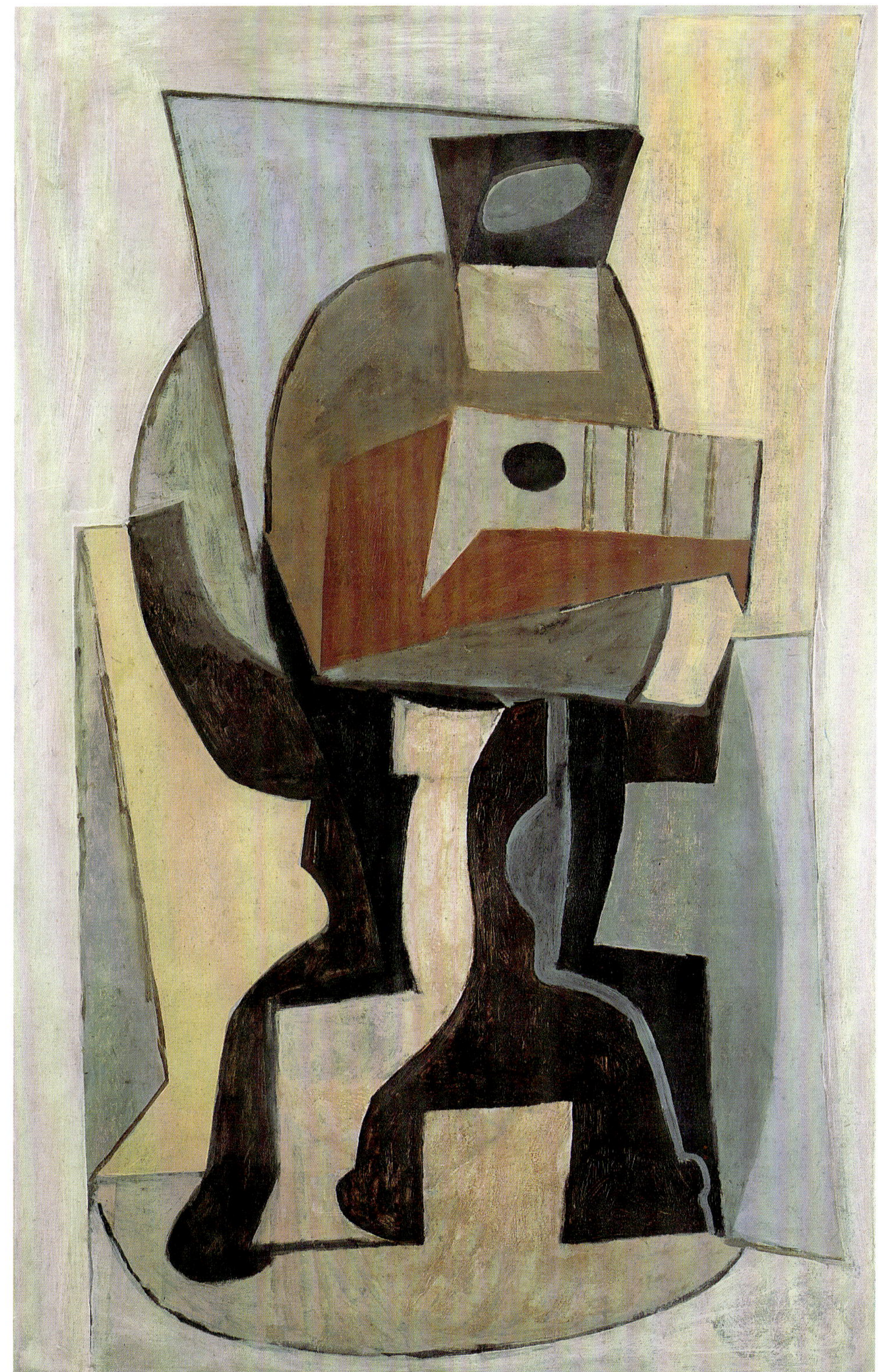

23

24
Seated woman
Femme assise
Paris, 1920
Oil on canvas, 92 × 65 cm
Musée Picasso, Paris
Z.IV.179. M.P.67

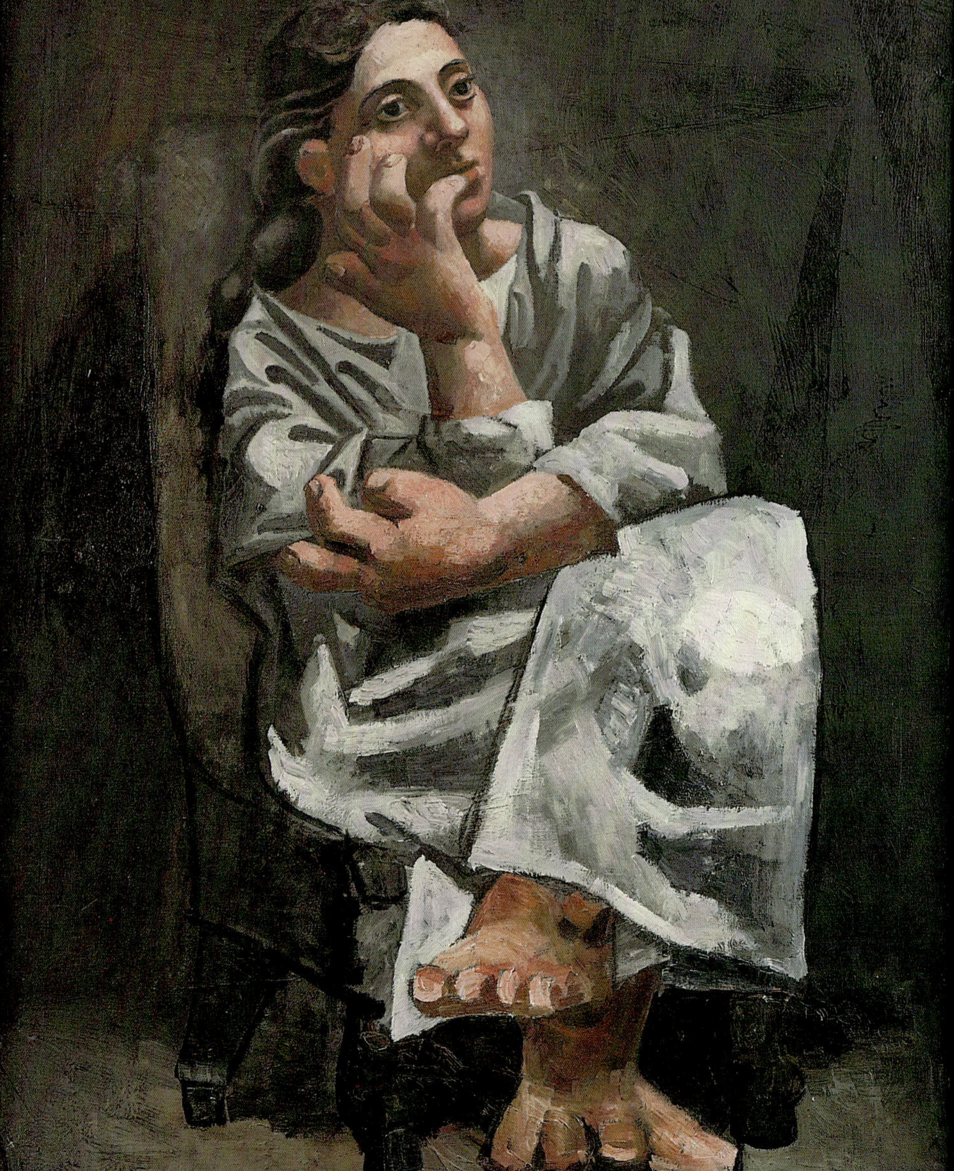

24

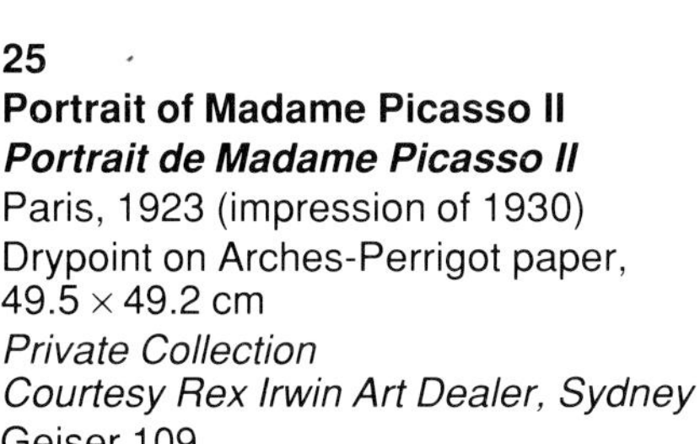

25
Portrait of Madame Picasso II
Portrait de Madame Picasso II
Paris, 1923 (impression of 1930)
Drypoint on Arches-Perrigot paper, 49.5 × 49.2 cm
Private Collection
Courtesy Rex Irwin Art Dealer, Sydney
Geiser 109

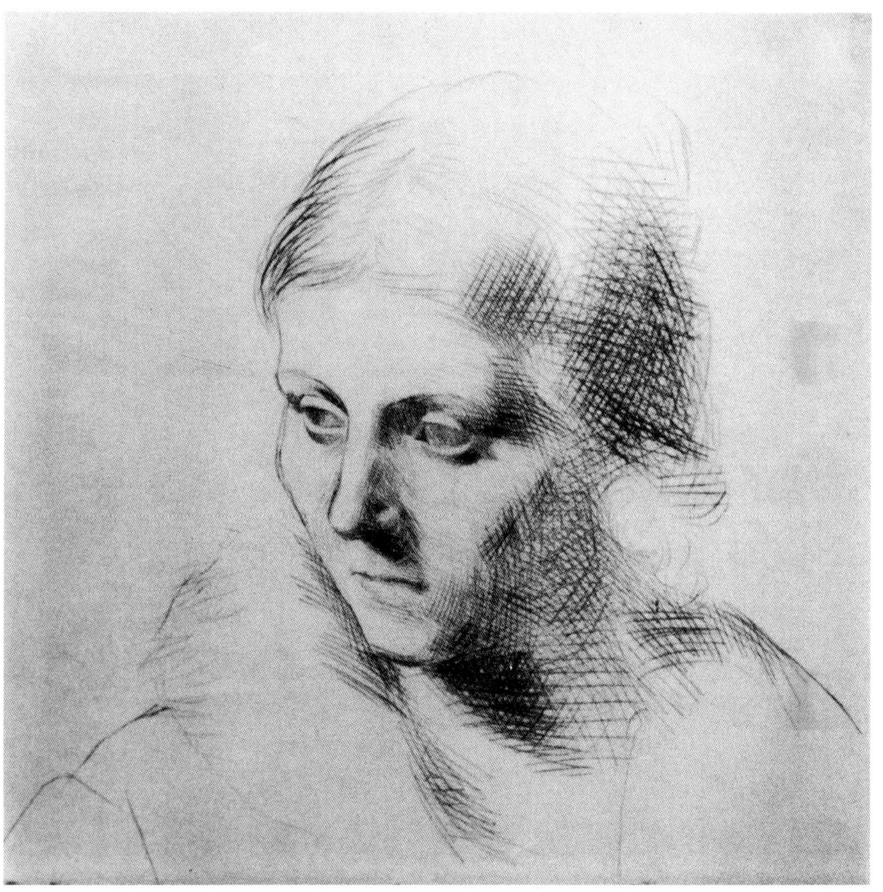

25

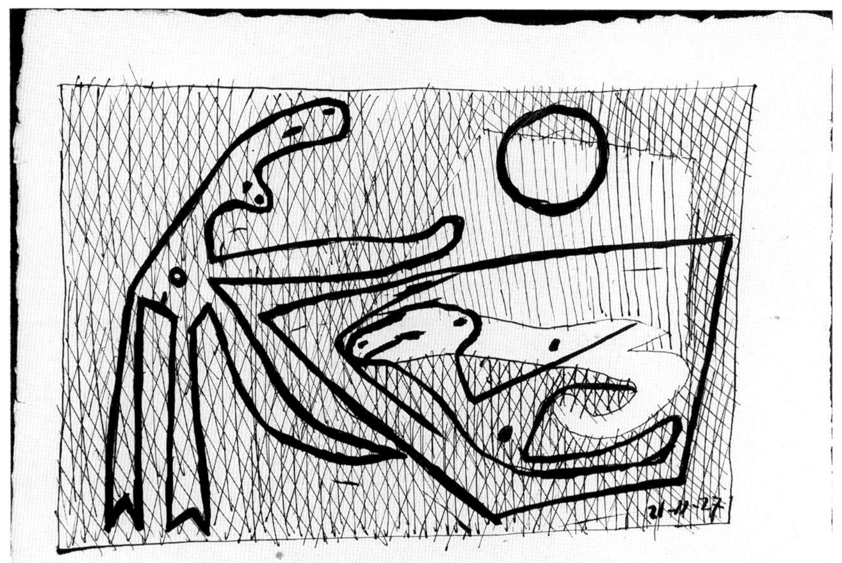

26

26
Ball players
Joueurs de ballon
Paris, 21 November 1927
Dated bottom right: *21-11-27*
Indian ink on paper, 23.5 × 34.2 cm
Musée Picasso, Paris
Z.VII.114. M.P.1019

27
Figure and profile
Figure et profil
Paris, 1928
Oil on canvas, 72 × 60 cm
Musée Picasso, Paris
Z.VII.129. M.P.103

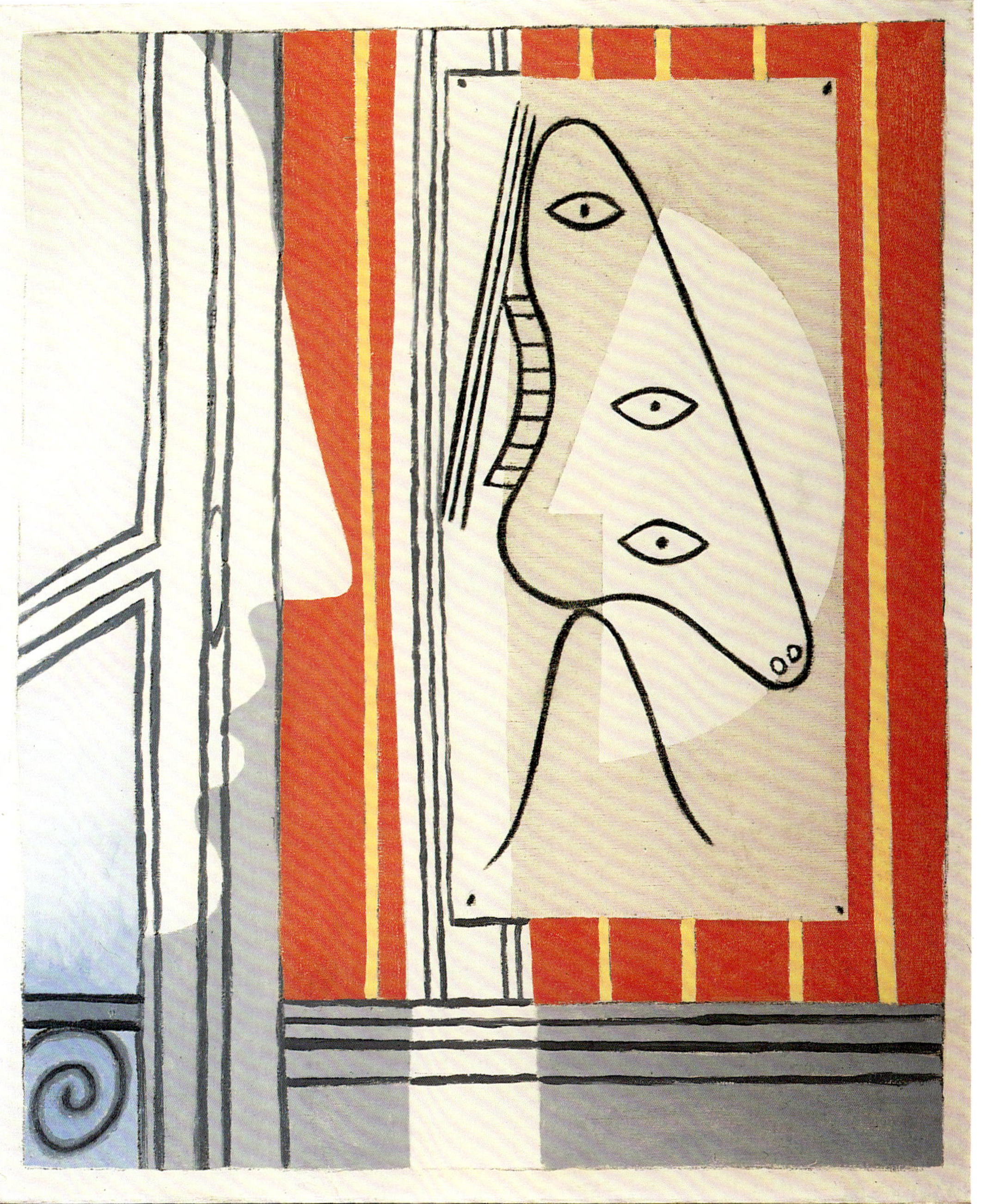

27

28
Study for a sculpture
Etude pour une sculpture
Boisgeloup or Paris, 1932
Signed bottom right: *Picasso*
Charcoal on canvas, 92 × 73 cm
Collection Ernst Beyeler, Basel
Not in Zervos

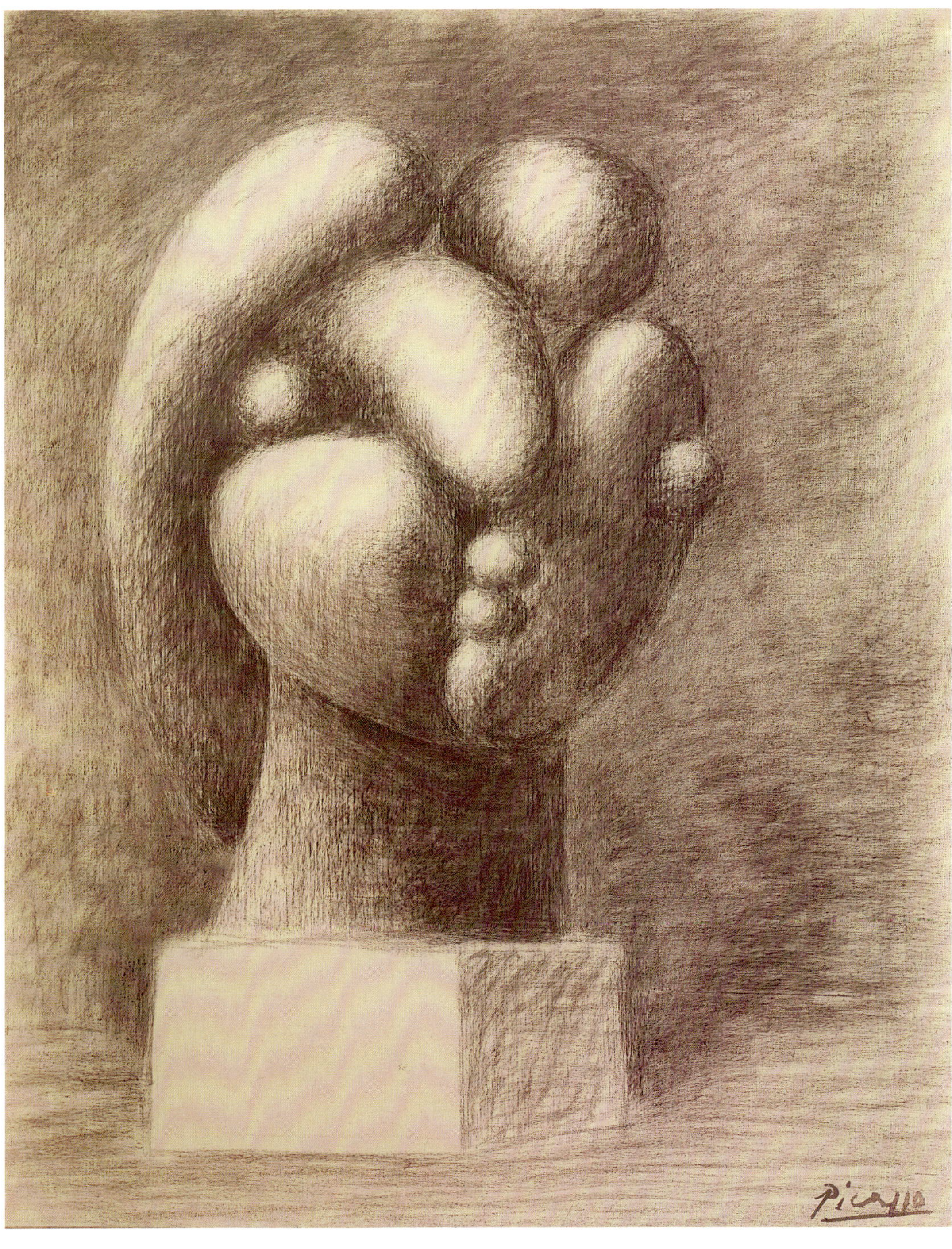

28

29
Reading
La lecture
Boisgeloup, 2 January 1932
Dated (on stretcher): *2 janvier M.CM.XXXII*
Oil on canvas, 130 × 97.5 cm
Musée Picasso, Paris
Z.VII.358. M.P.137

29

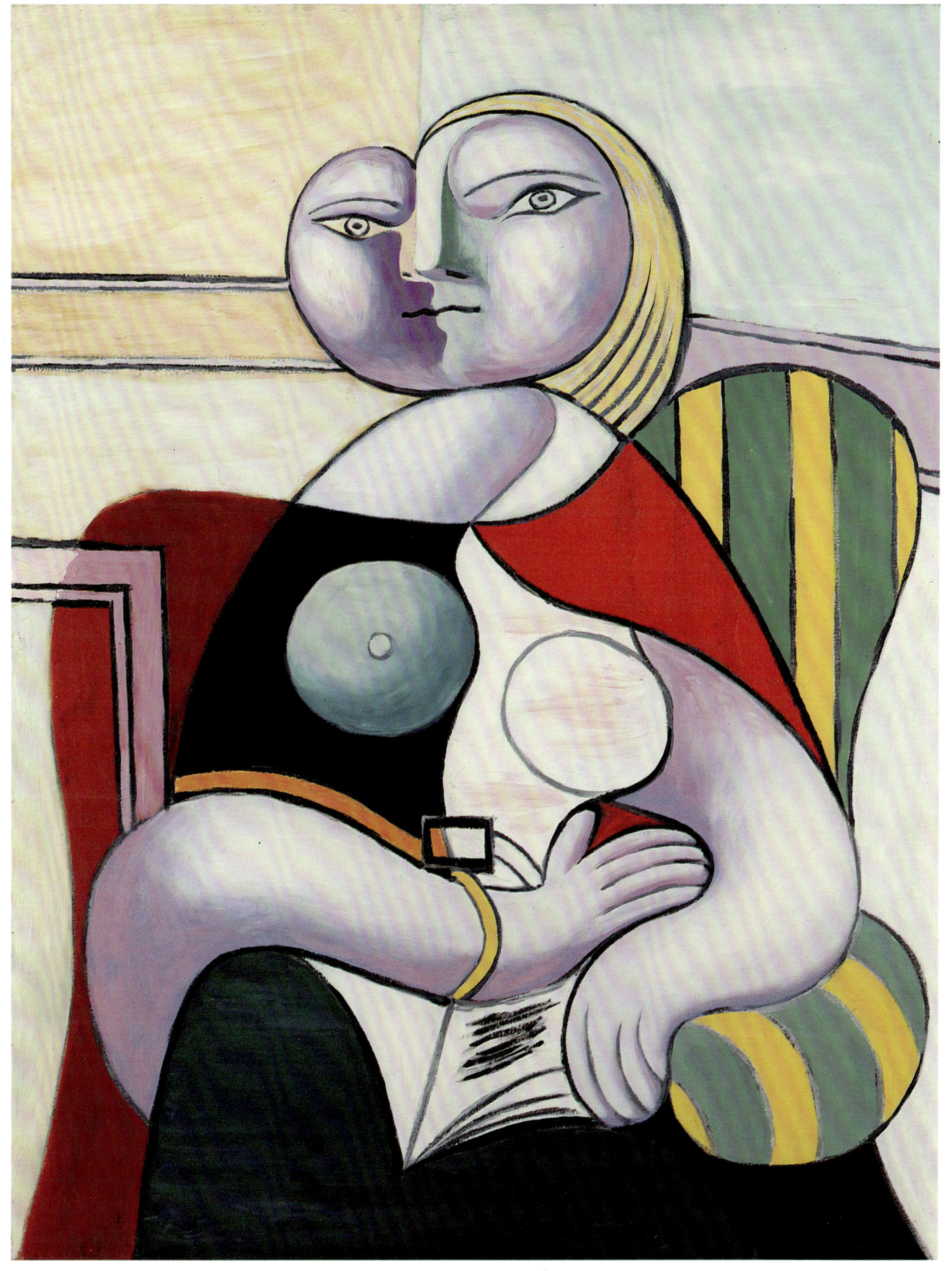

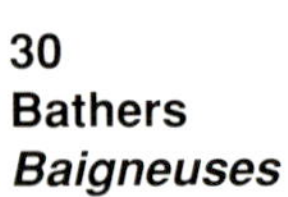

30
Bathers
Baigneuses
Boisgeloup, 6 September 1932
Signed and dated bottom right:
Picasso/ Boisgeloup 6 Septembre XXXII
Oil on canvas, 27 × 41 cm
Staatsgalerie Stuttgart
Z.VIII.61

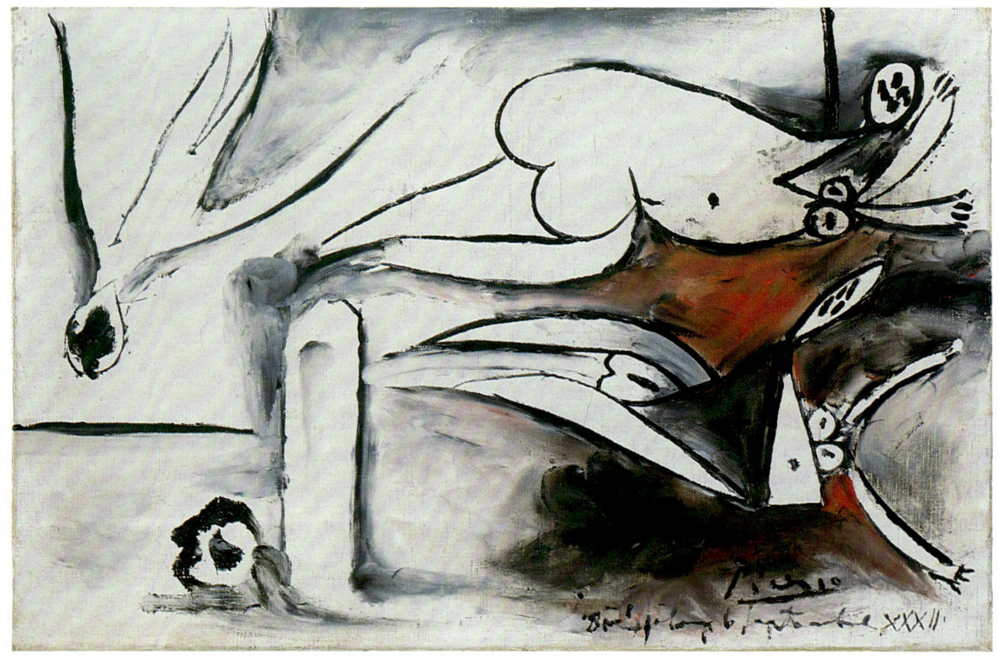

30

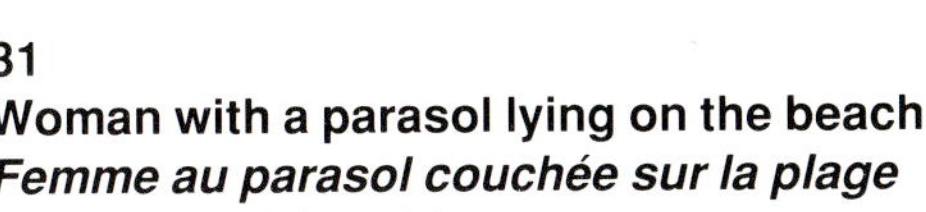

31
Woman with a parasol lying on the beach
Femme au parasol couchée sur la plage
Cannes, 13 July 1933
Signed and dated bottom right:
Picasso/ Cannes 13 Juillet XXXIII
Gouache, wash, pen and Indian ink on paper,
40.3 × 50.6 cm
Queensland Art Gallery
Major Harold de Vahl Rubin Gift
Not in Zervos

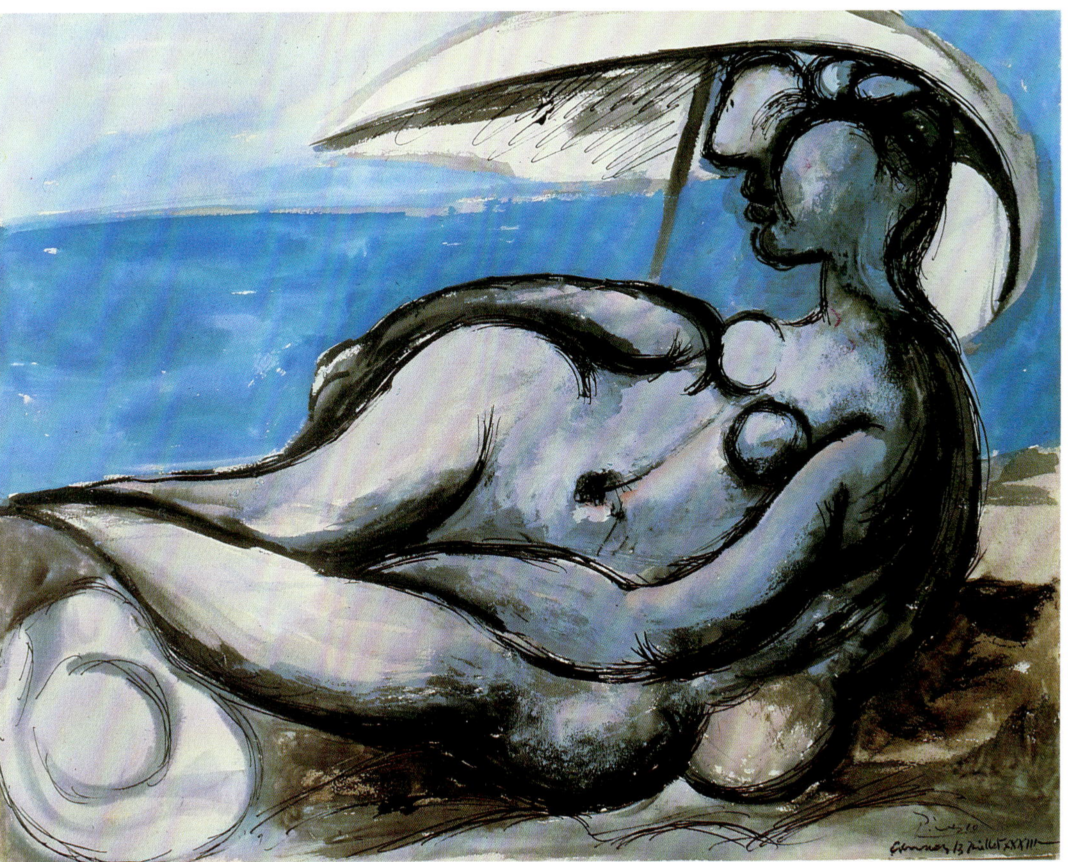

31

32
Scuptor and standing model
Sculpteur et modèle debout
Paris, 7 April 1933
Etching, 36.7 × 29.6 cm
Signed and dated (in reverse) on plate
Art Gallery of New South Wales, 1974
Gift of Sali Herman Fund
Geiser 330/II/b. Bloch 177
Sheet 33 of the series *L'Atelier du Sculpteur*, from the 'Vollard Suite'.

33
Model looking at a sculptural group
Modèle contemplant un groupe sculpté
Paris, 5 April 1933
Signed and dated (in reverse) on plate
Etching, 29.7 × 36.7 cm
Auckland City Art Gallery
Geiser 328/II/b. Bloch 175
Sheet 31 of the series *L'Atelier du Sculpteur*, from the 'Vollard Suite'.

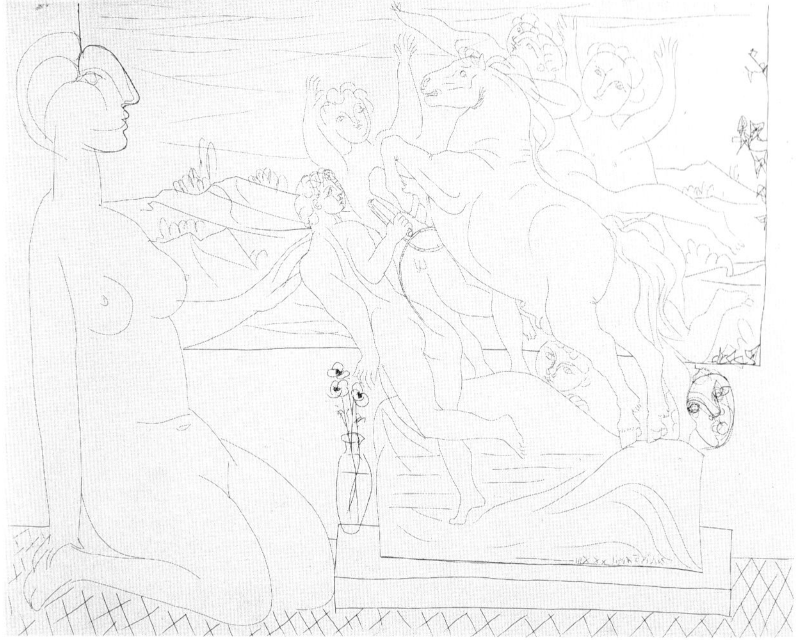

33

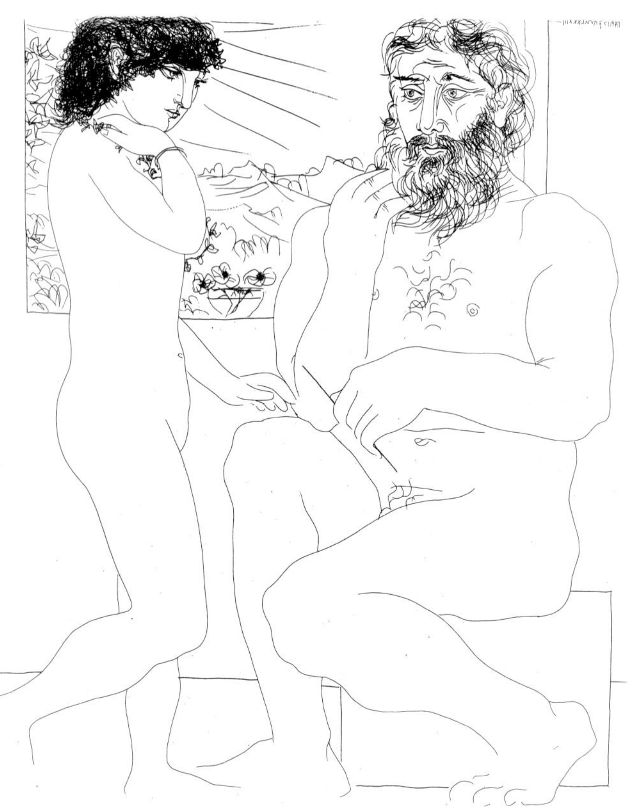

32

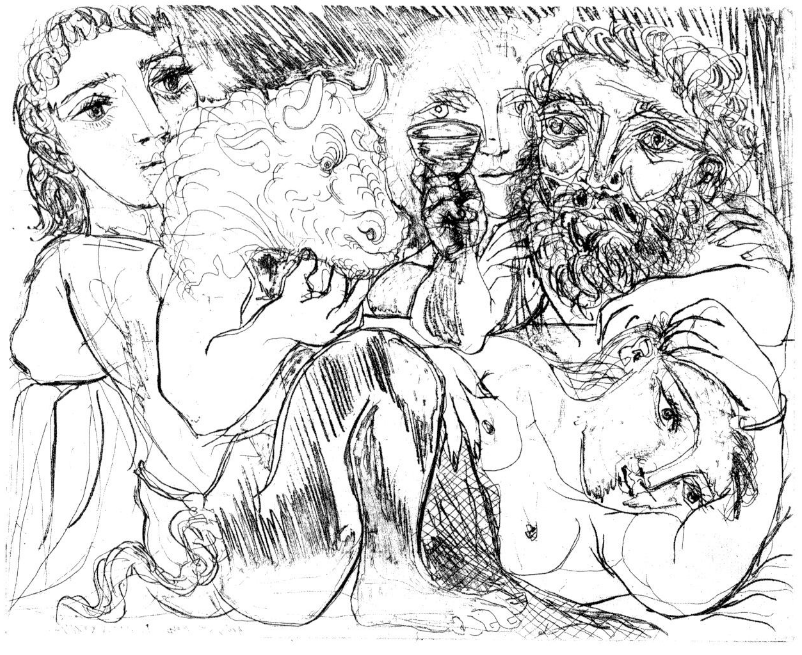

34

34
Minotaur, drinking sculptor and three models
Minotaure, buveur et femmes
Boisgeloup, 18 June 1933
Signed and dated (in reverse) on plate
Etching, 29.8 × 36.5 cm
National Gallery of Victoria, Melbourne
Geiser 368/IV/b. Bloch 200
Sheet 10 of the series *Le Minotaure*, from the 'Vollard Suite'.

35
Two Catalans drinking
Deux buveurs catalans
Paris, 29 November 1934
Etching, 23.8 × 29.8 cm
Auckland City Art Gallery
Mackelvie Collection 1985
Geiser 442/II/b. Bloch 228
Individual sheet from the 'Vollard Suite'

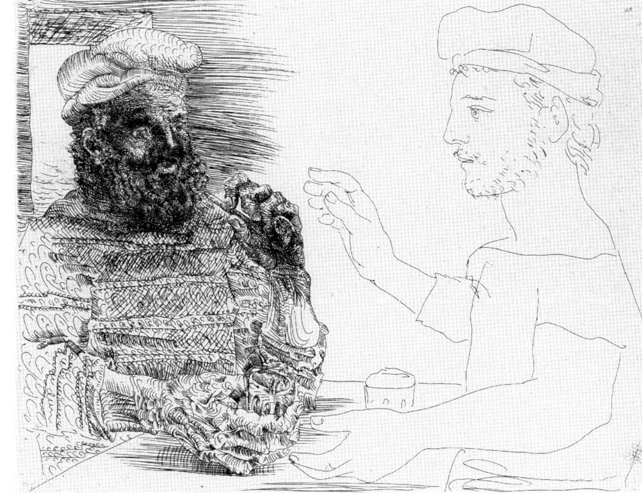

35

36
Faun unveiling a sleeping woman
Faune dévoilant une femme
Paris, 12 June 1936
Etching and aquatint, 31.7 × 41.7 cm
National Gallery of Victoria, Melbourne
Bloch 230
Individual sheet from the 'Vollard Suite'

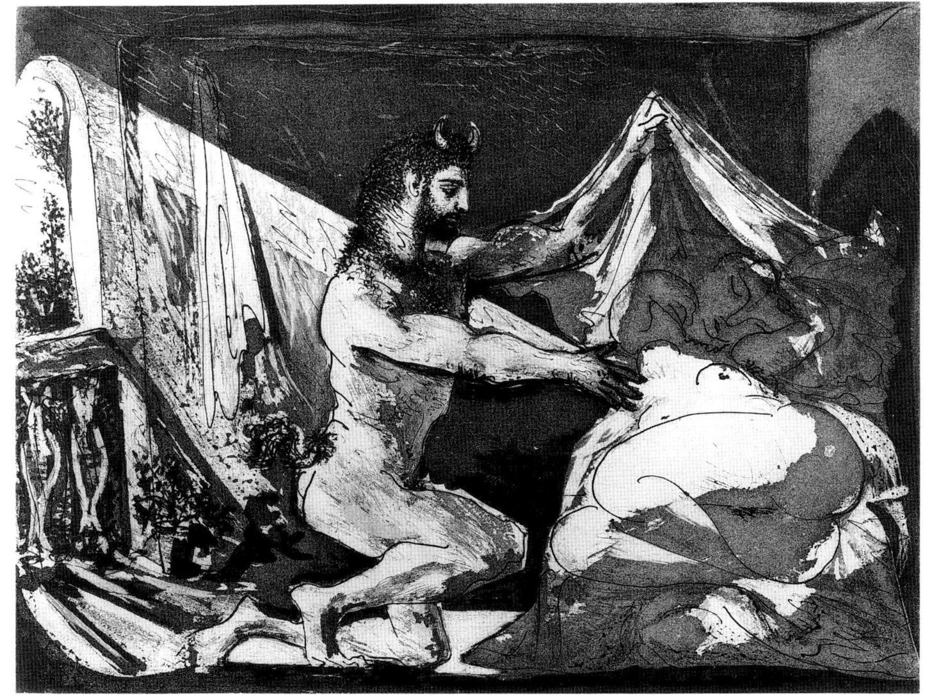

36

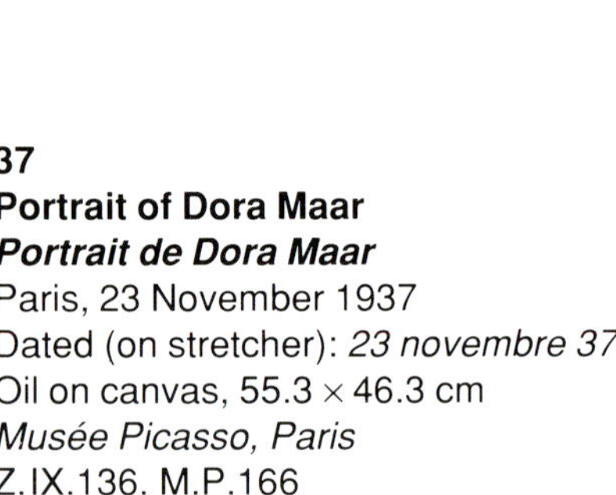

37
Portrait of Dora Maar
Portrait de Dora Maar
Paris, 23 November 1937
Dated (on stretcher): *23 novembre 37.*
Oil on canvas, 55.3 × 46.3 cm
Musée Picasso, Paris
Z.IX.136. M.P.166

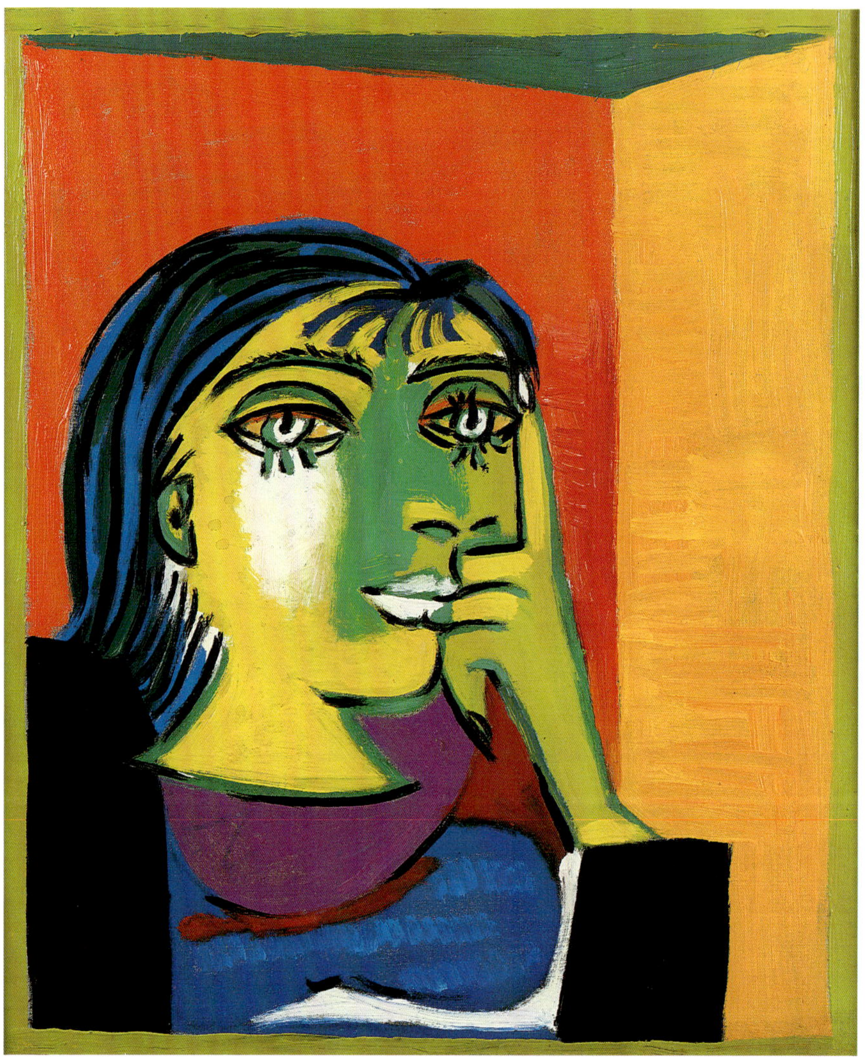

37

38
Weeping woman
Femme qui pleure
Paris, 1937
Oil on canvas, 55 × 46 cm
National Gallery of Victoria, Melbourne
Purchased by The Art Foundation of Victoria with the generous assistance of the Jack and Genia Liberman Family and the donors of The Art Foundation of Victoria, 1986
Z.VII.192

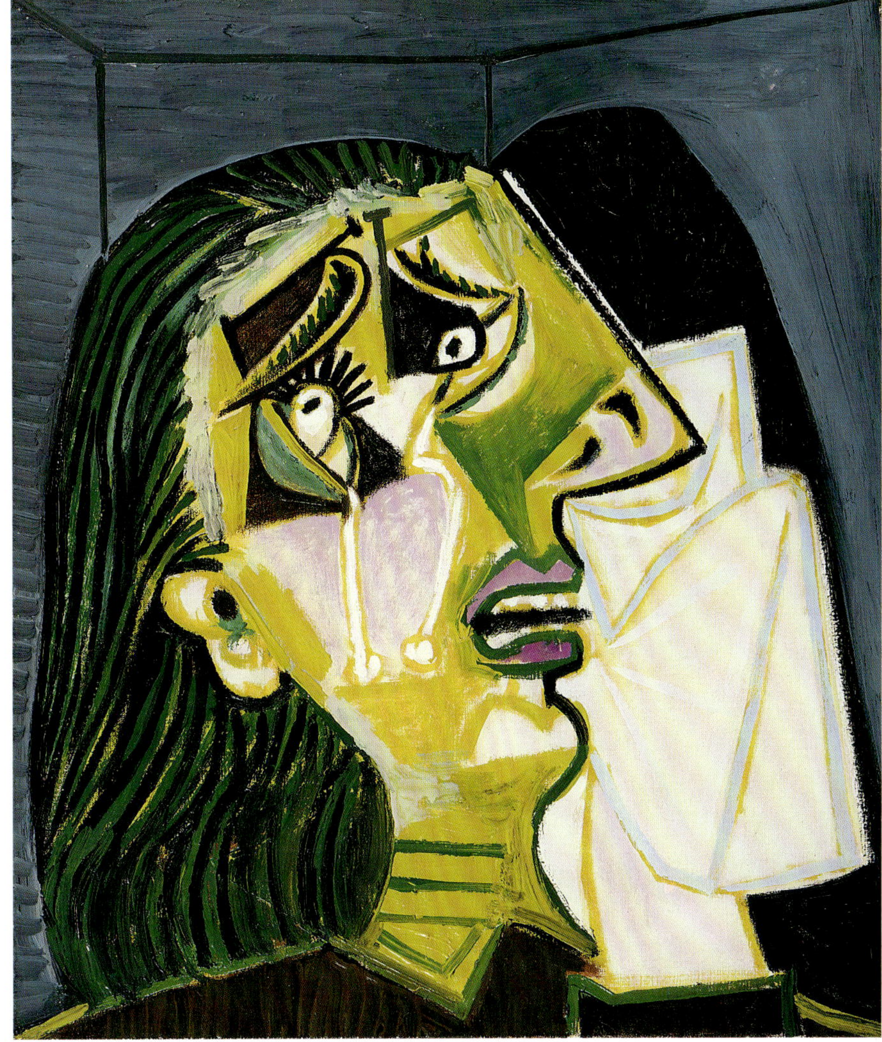

38

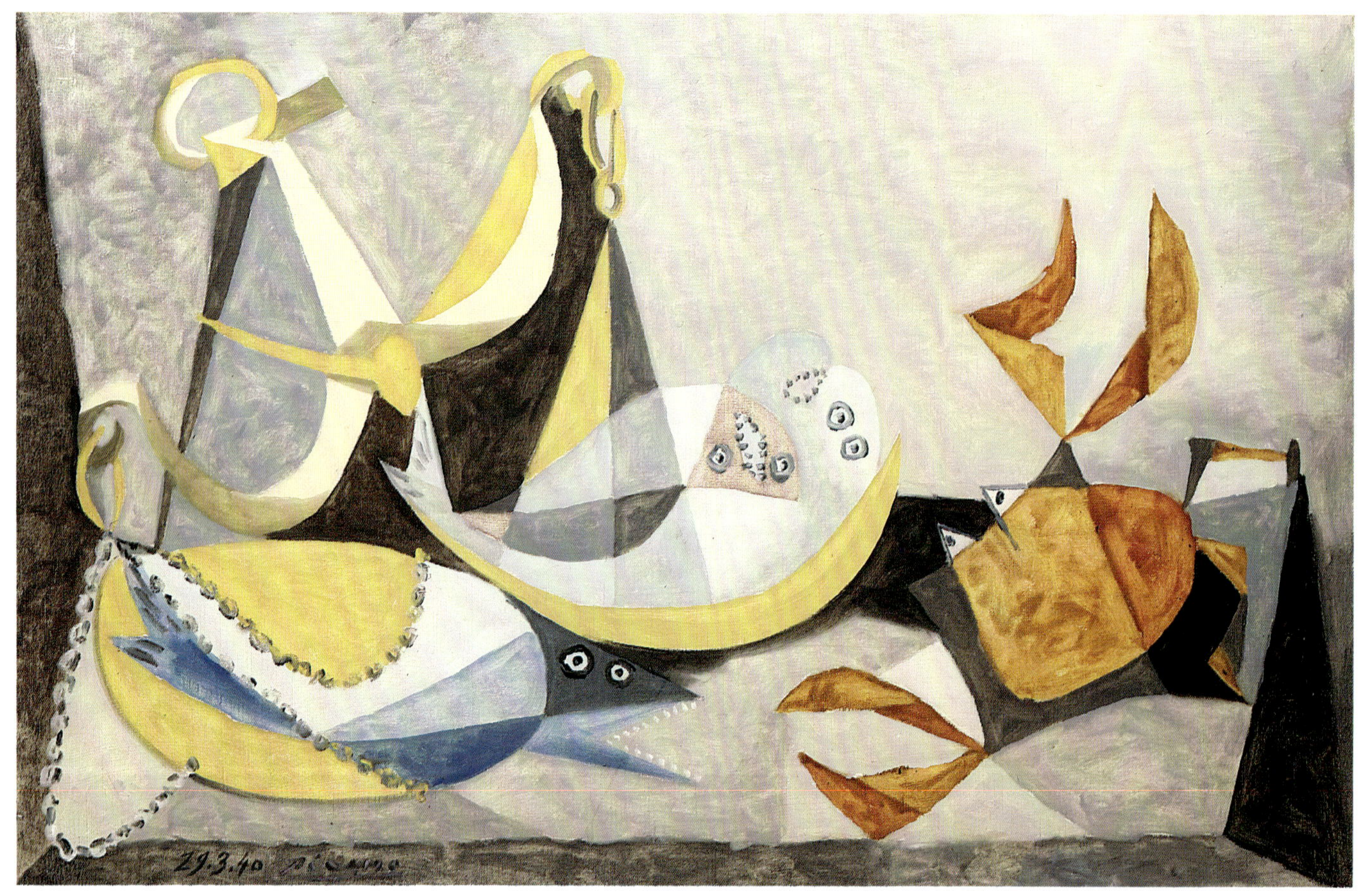

39
The soles
Les soles
Royan or Paris, 29 March 1940
Signed and dated bottom left: *29-3-40 Picasso*
Oil on canvas, 60 × 92 cm
Scottish National Gallery of Modern Art,
National Galleries of Scotland
Z.X.375

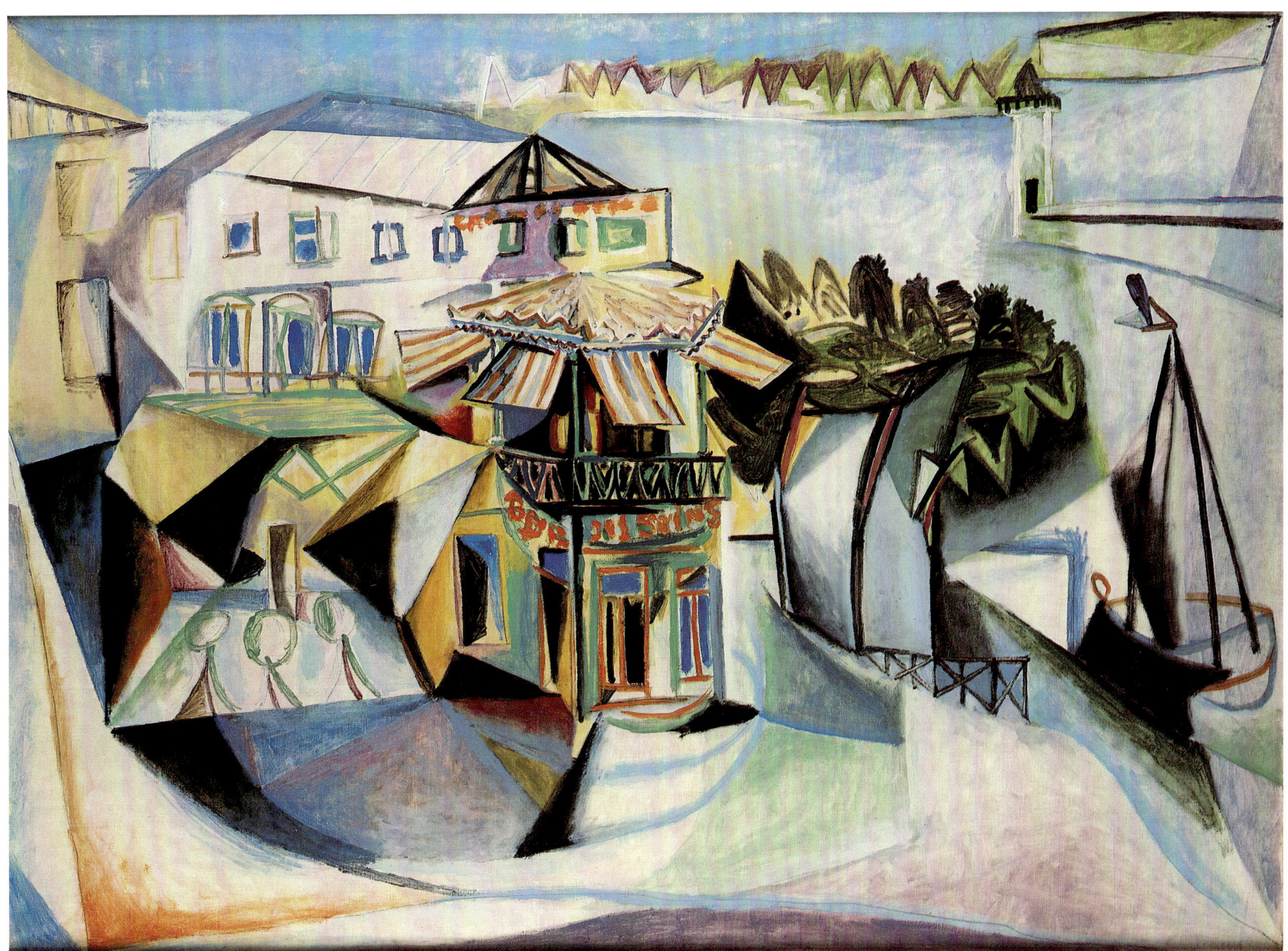

40
Café at Royan
Café à Royan
Royan, 15 August 1940
Dated (verso and stretcher): *Royan/ 15.8.40*
Oil on canvas, 97 × 130
Musée Picasso, Paris
Z.XI.88. M.P.187

41
The rocking chair
Le rocking-chair
Paris, 9 August 1943
Oil on canvas, 161 × 130 cm
Musée National d'Art Moderne,
Centre Georges Pompidou, Paris
Z.XIII.74

41

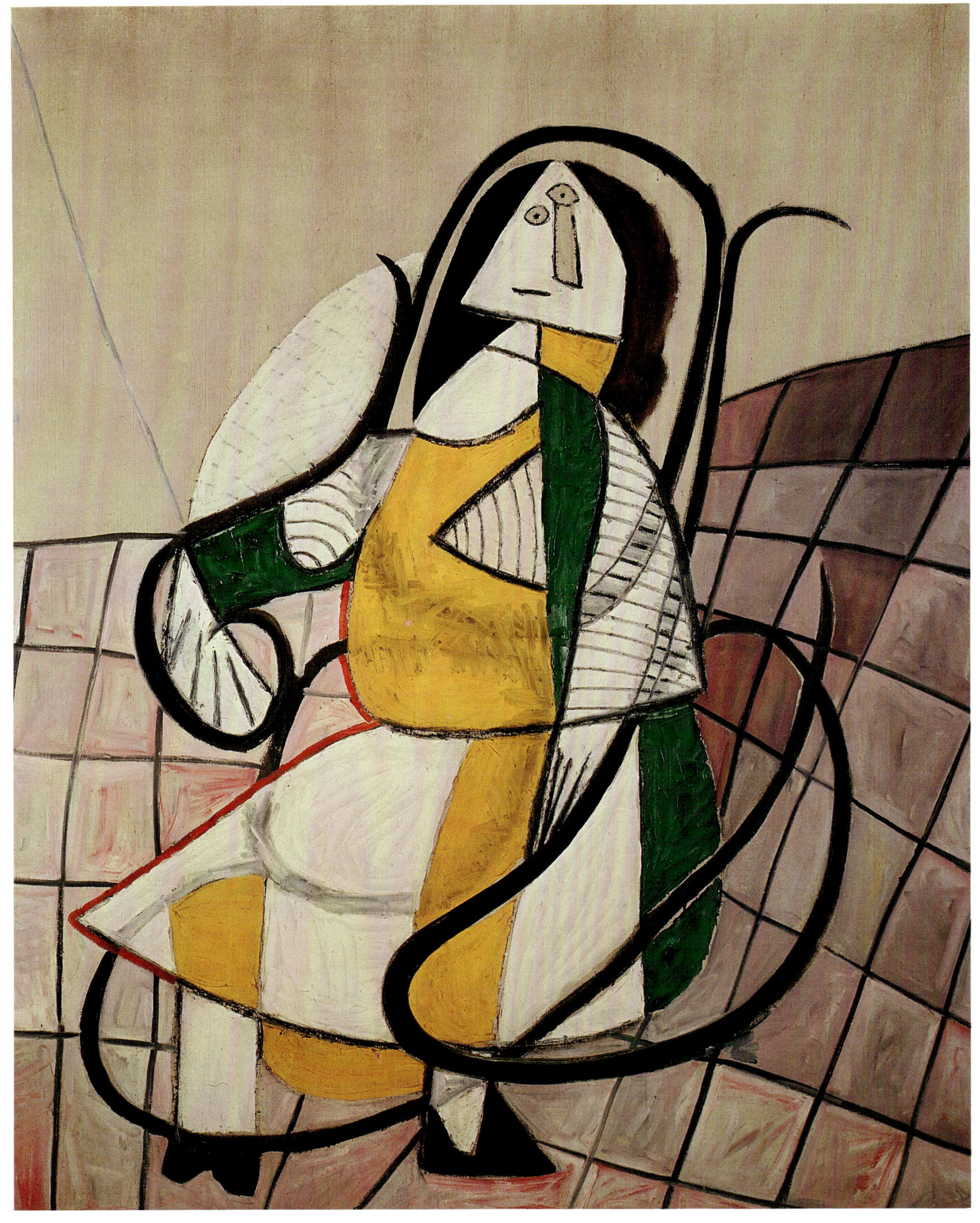

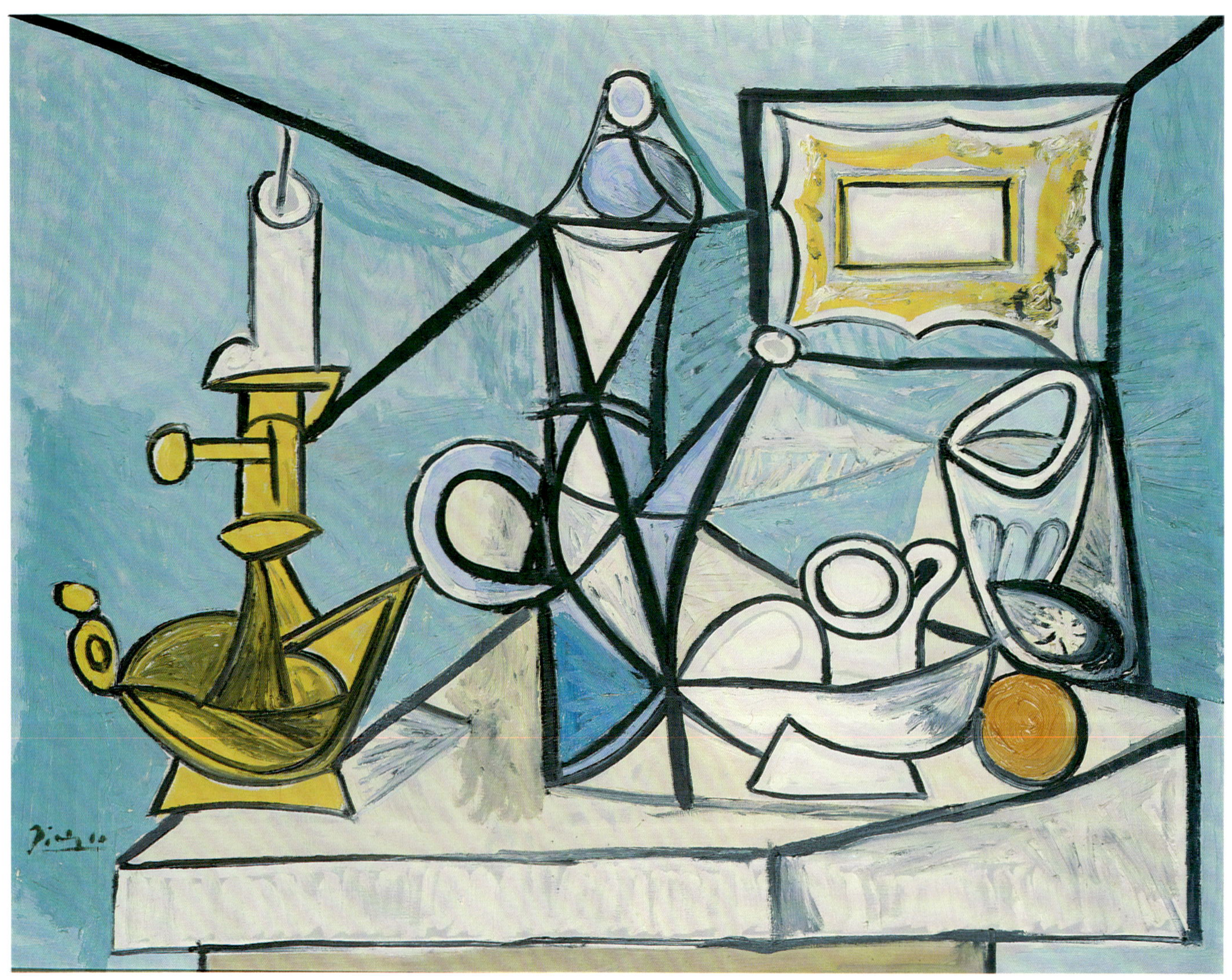

42

42
Still life with candle and coffee-pot
Nature morte au bougeoir
Paris, 8 April 1944
Signed bottom left: *Picasso*
Dated (verso): *8 avril 1944*
Oil on canvas, 73 × 92 cm
Musée National d'Art Moderne, Centre Georges Pompidou, Paris
Bequest of Mme Savary, 1969
Z.XIII.240

43
Woman in blue
Femme en bleue
Paris, 25 April 1944
Dated (verso): *25 avril/ 44*
Oil on canvas, 130 × 97 cm
Musée National d'Art Moderne, Centre Georges Pompidou, Paris
Gift of the artist, 1947
Z.XIII.245

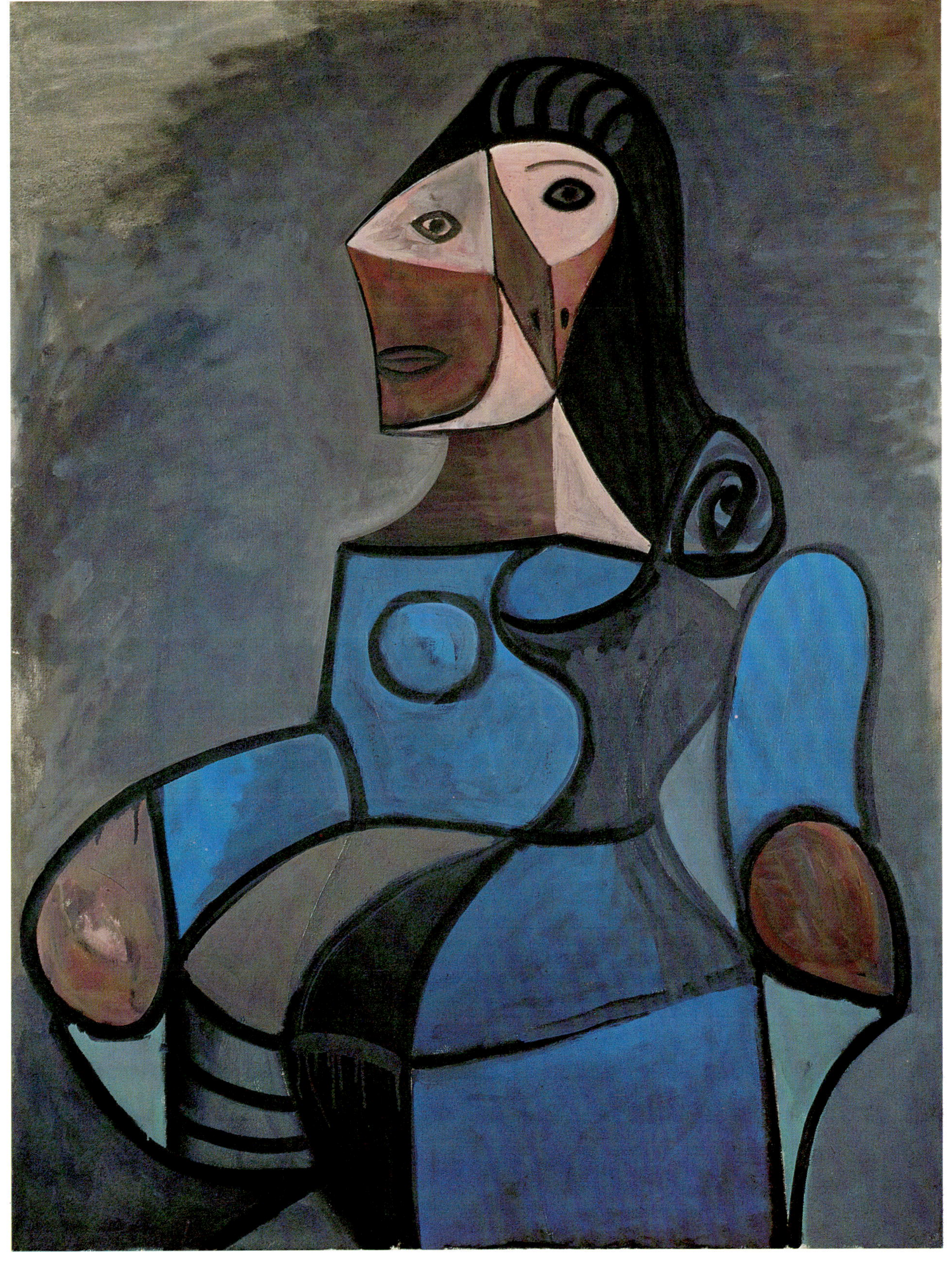

43

44
Still life with skull, lamp and pitcher
Tête de mort, lampe, cruche
Paris, 1945
Oil on canvas, 81 × 100 cm
Collection Marina Picasso
Galerie Jan Krugier, Geneva
Z.XIV.100

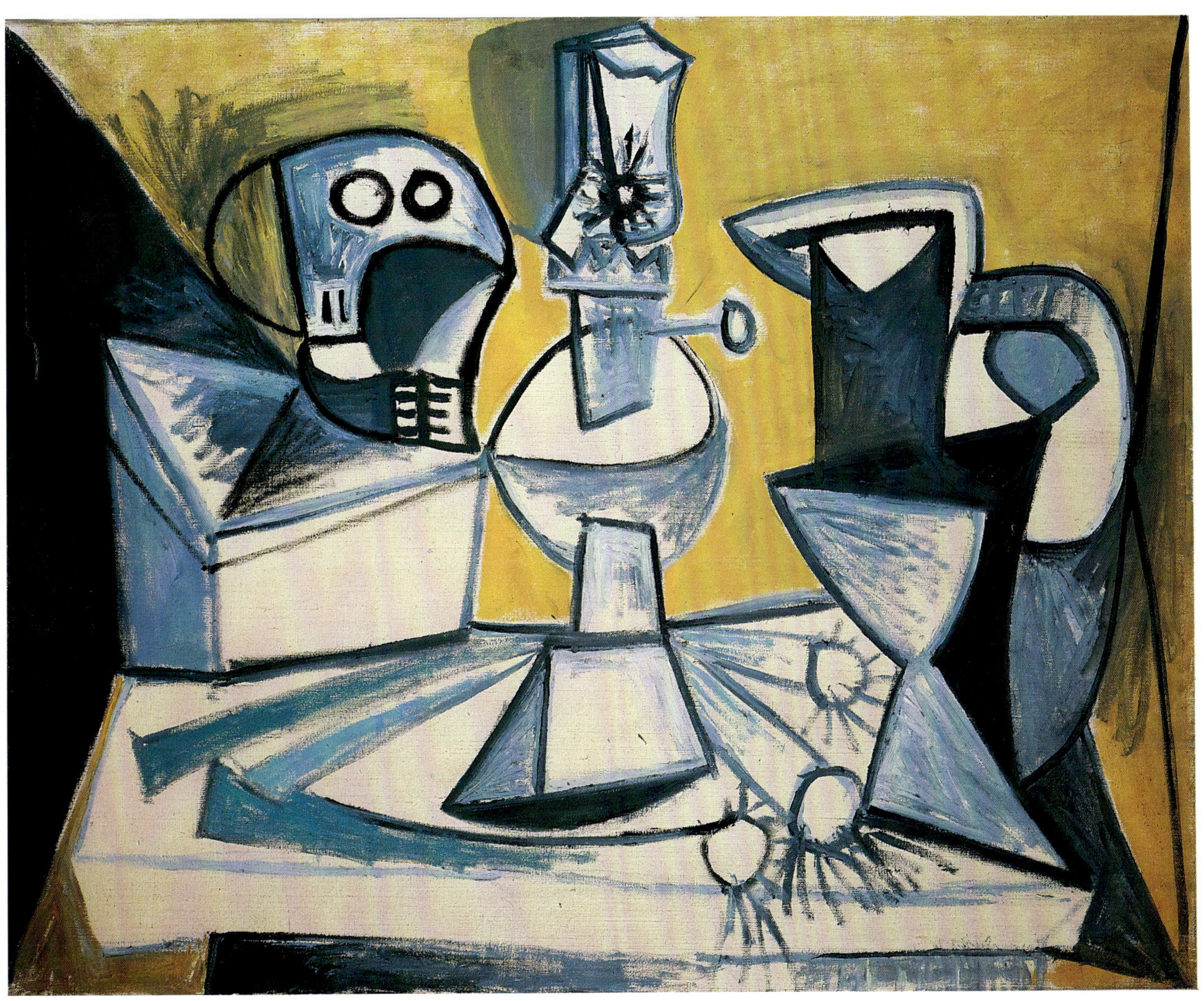

44

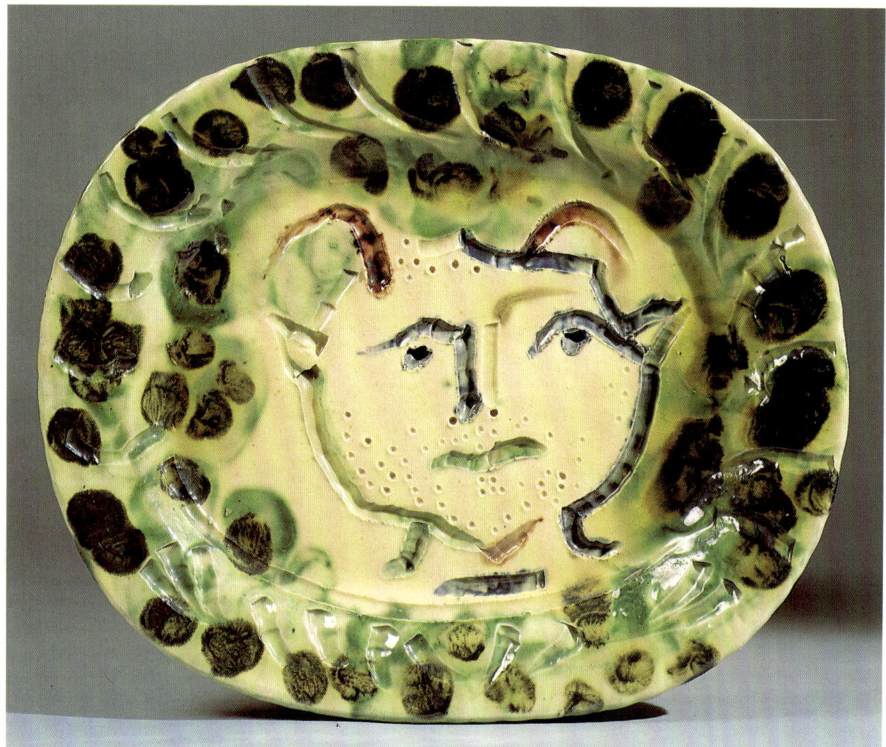

45

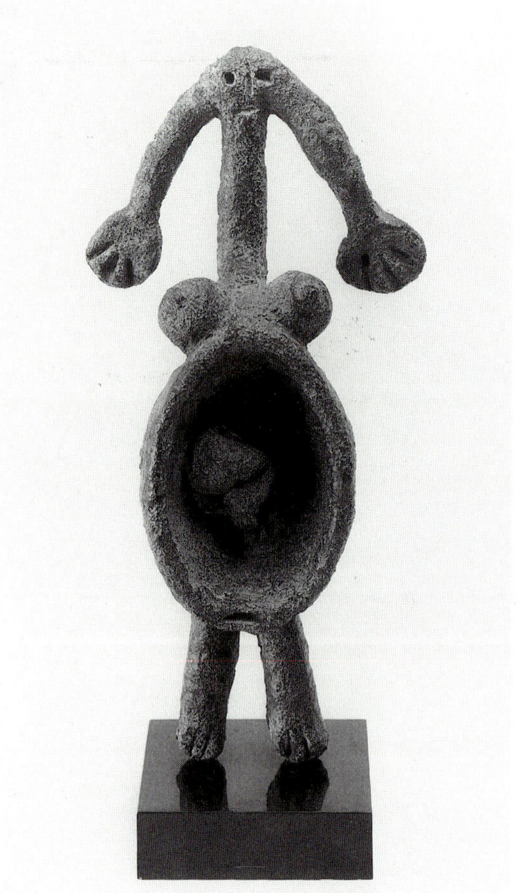

46

45
Head of a faun
Tête de faune
Vallauris, 9 October 1947
Dated (reverse): *9.10.1947*
Glazed ceramic dish, 32 × 38 cm
Private Collection

46
Small pregnant woman
Petite femme enceinte
Vallauris, 1948
Stamped (back of left leg):
E. GODARD CIRE PERDUE
Bronze, 32.5 × 9 × 7 cm
Musée Picasso, Paris
Spies 335 (II). M.P.333

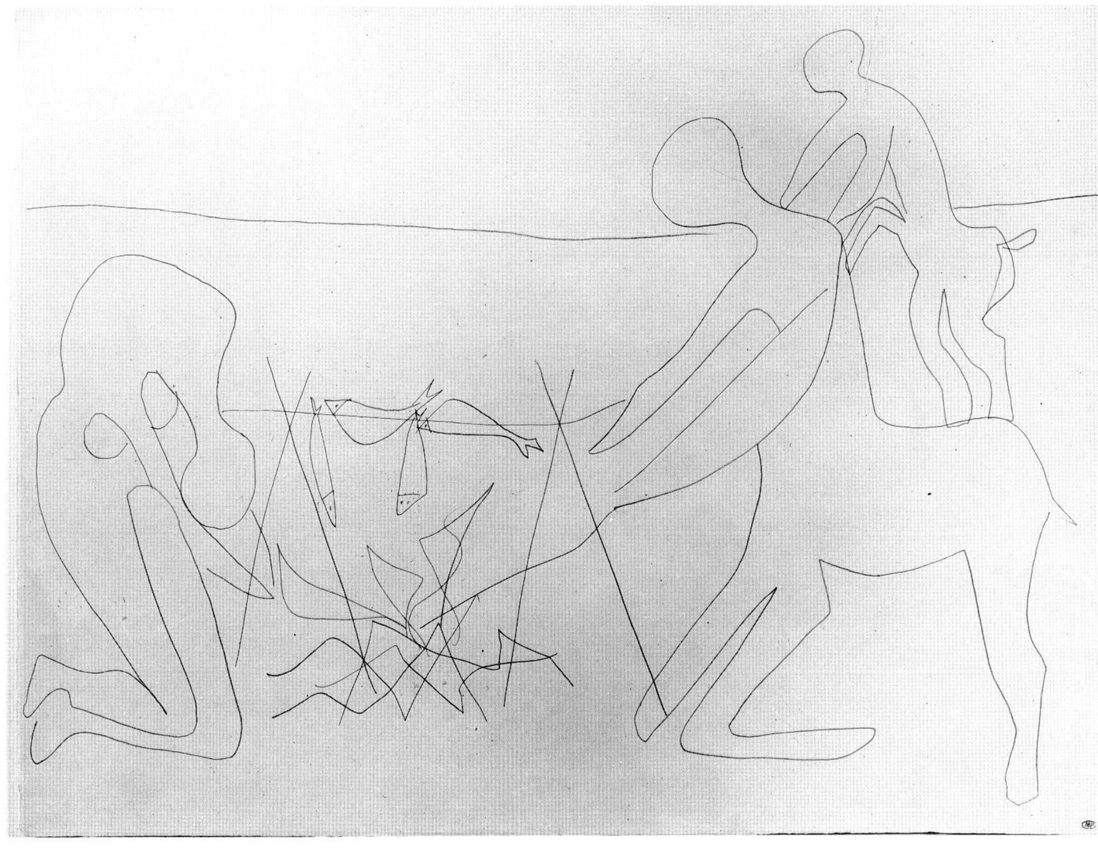

47

47
Centaurs and a woman grilling fish
Centaures et femme faisant griller des poissons
Antibes, 6 November 1946
Dated (verso): *antibes/ 6 novembre/ 46*
Lead pencil on paper, 51 × 66 cm
Musée Picasso, Paris
Z.XIV.280. M.P.1387

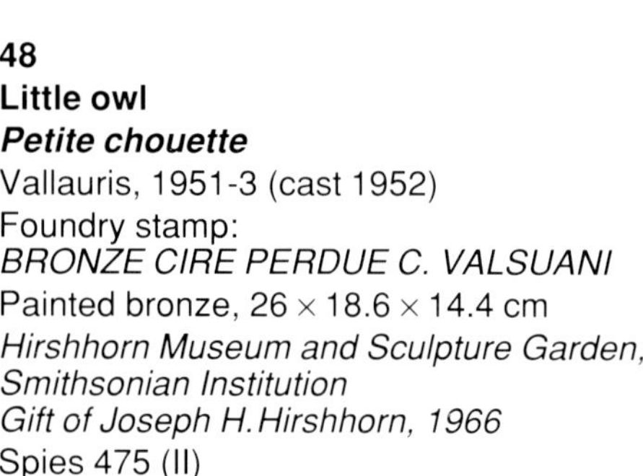

48
Little owl
Petite chouette
Vallauris, 1951-3 (cast 1952)
Foundry stamp:
BRONZE CIRE PERDUE C. VALSUANI
Painted bronze, 26 × 18.6 × 14.4 cm
Hirshhorn Museum and Sculpture Garden, Smithsonian Institution
Gift of Joseph H. Hirshhorn, 1966
Spies 475 (II)

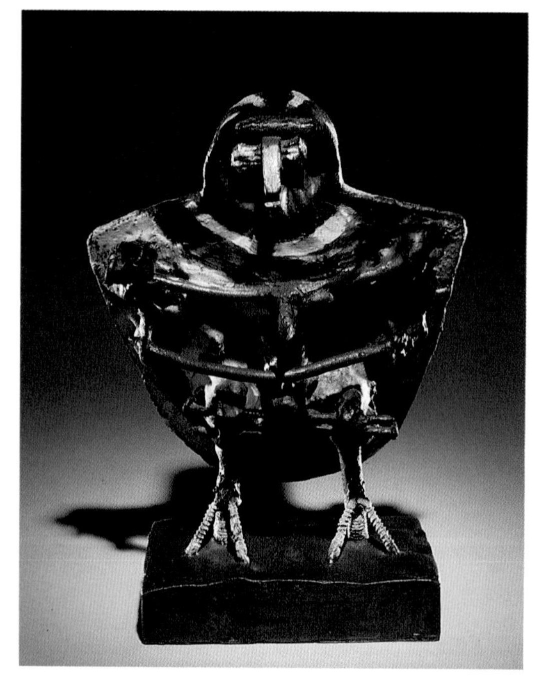

48

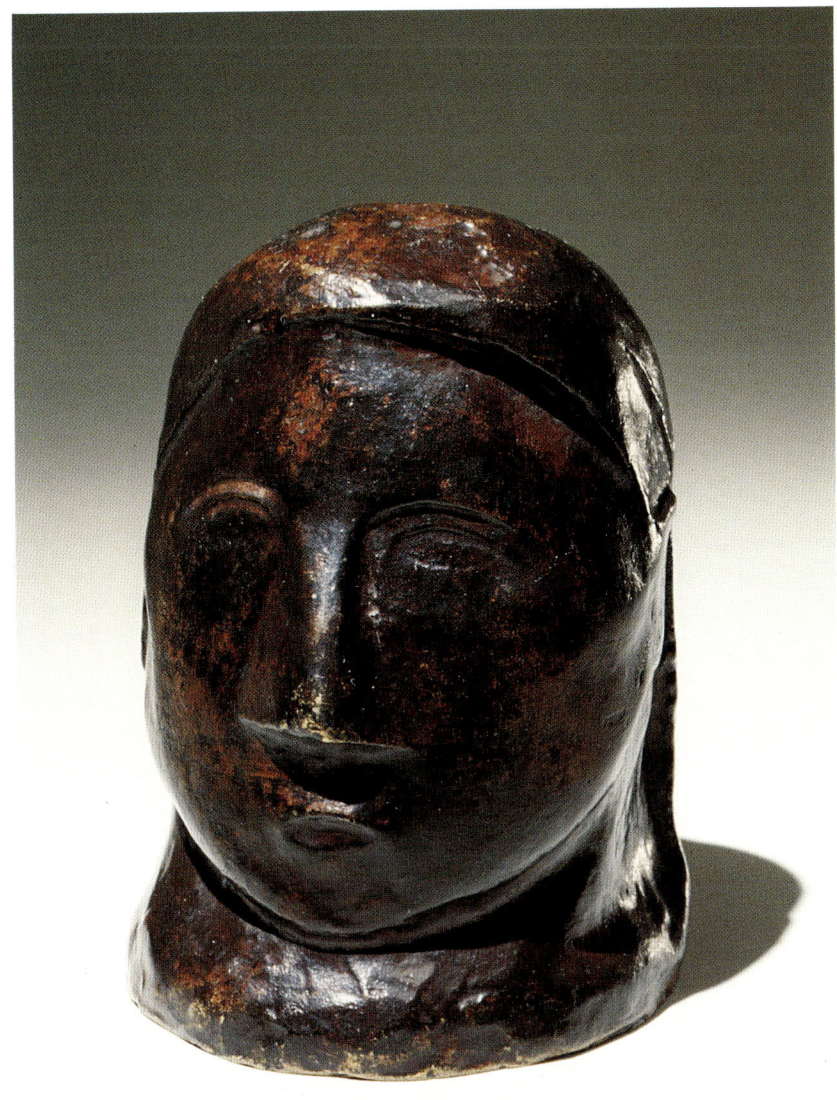

49

49
Head of a woman
Tête de femme
Vallauris, 1951
Bronze, 54.1 × 19 × 35.9
Hirshhorn Museum and Sculpture Garden, Smithsonian Institution
Gift of Joseph H. Hirshhorn, 1966
Spies 411 (II)

50
The cat and the cock
La chatte et le coq
Vallauris, 13 December 1953
Signed top left: *Picasso*
Dated (verso): *13.12.53*
Oil on canvas, 88.5 × 116 cm
Musée National d'Art Moderne,
Centre Georges Pompidou, Paris
Donated by Louise and Michel Leiris, 1984
Z.XVI.55

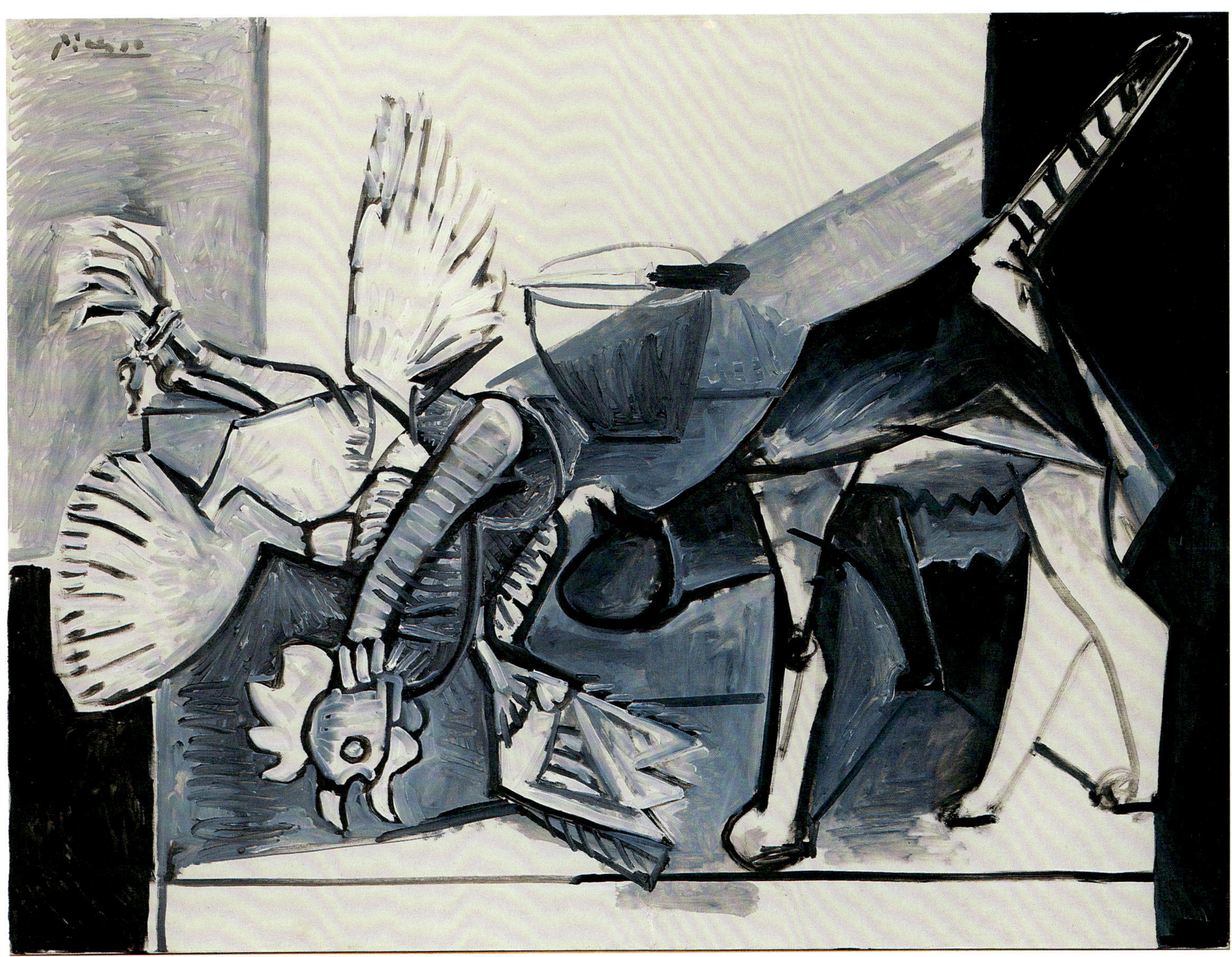

50

51
Crouching woman
Femme nue accroupie
Cannes, 2 January 1956
Signed top right: *Picasso*
Dated (verso): *2.1.56*
Oil on canvas, 130 × 96 cm
Galerie Louise Leiris, Paris
Z.XVII.1

51

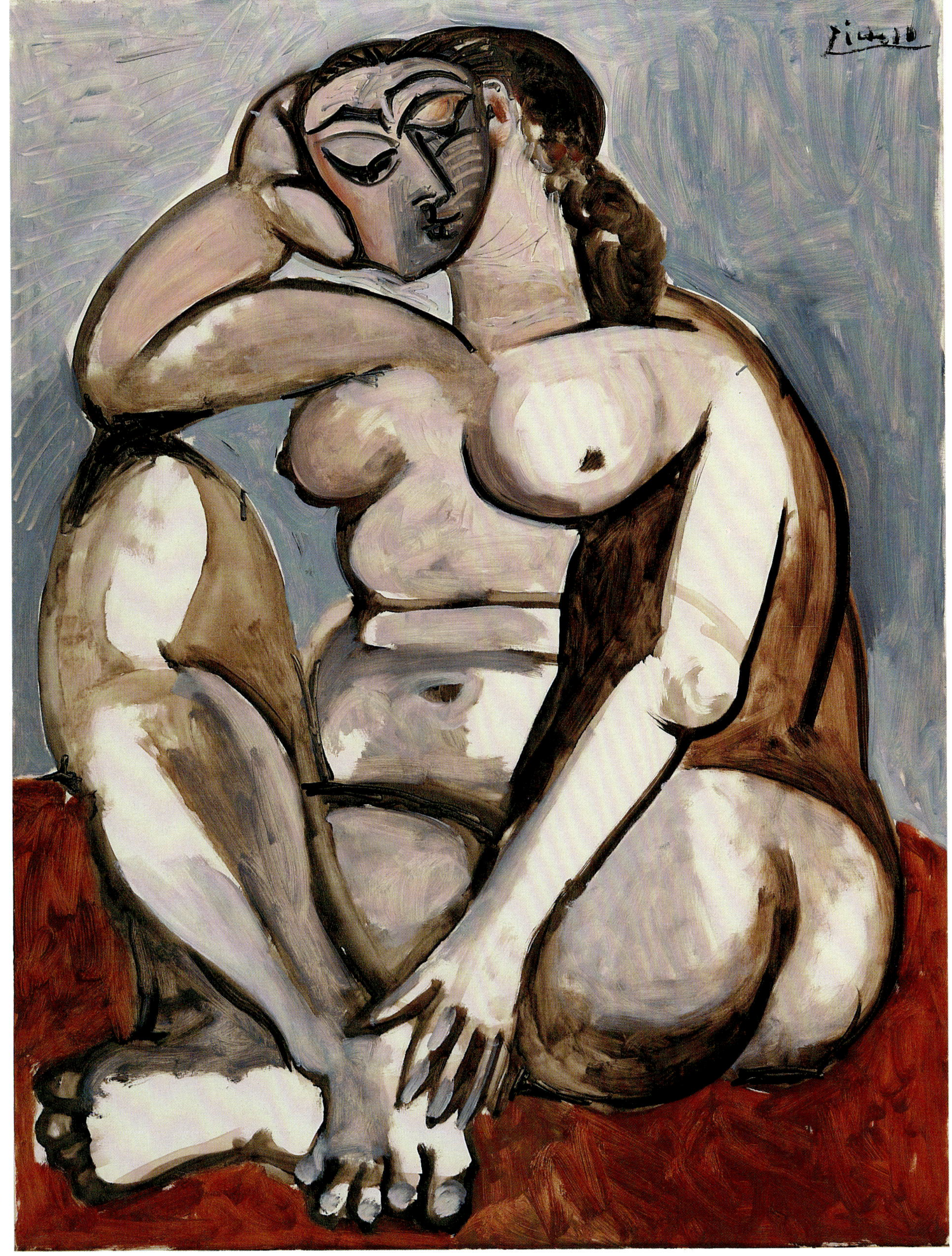

52

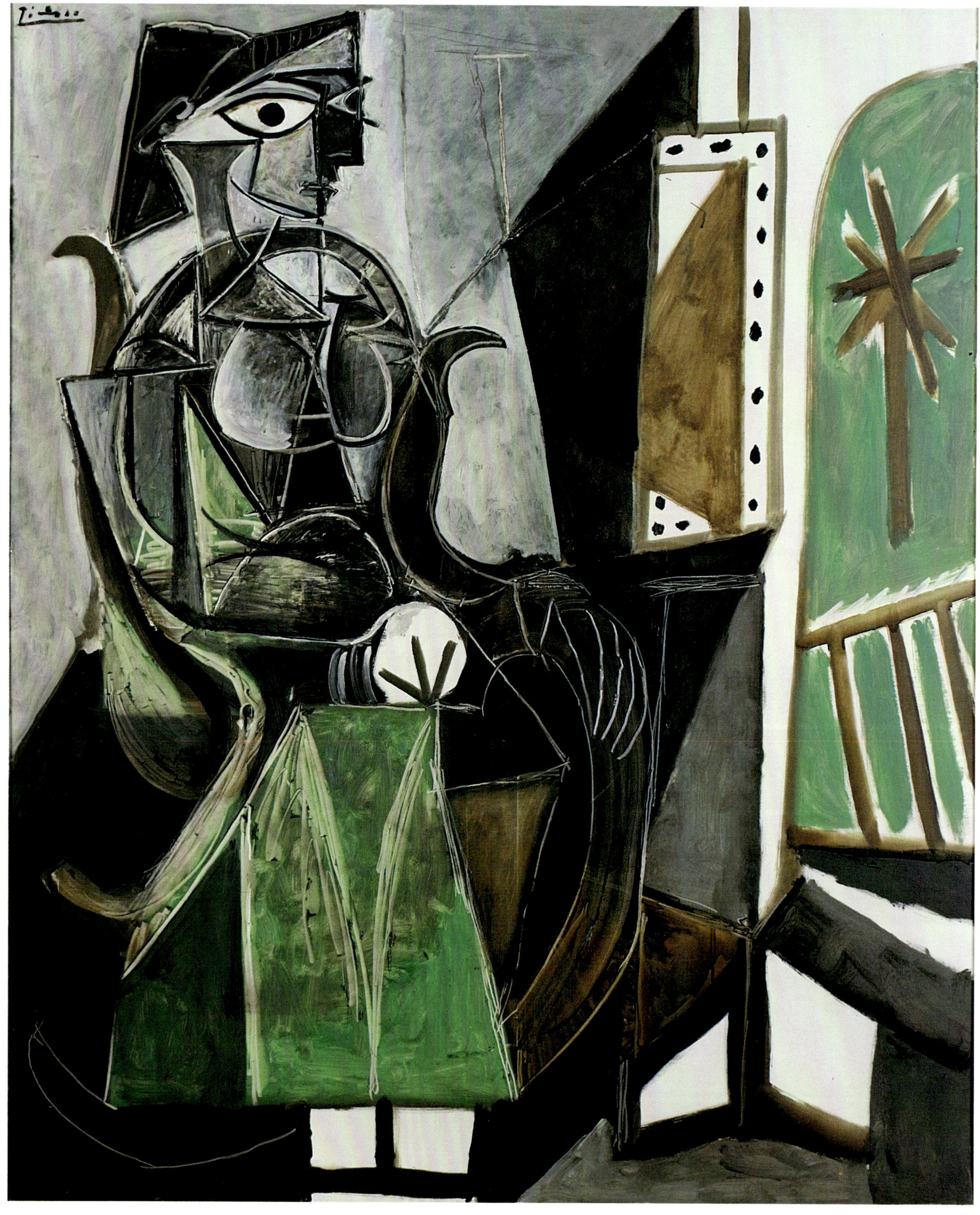

52
Woman by a window
Femme à la fenêtre
Cannes, 11 June 1956
Signed top left: *Picasso*
Oil on canvas, 162 × 130 cm
The Museum of Modern Art, New York
Mrs Simon Guggenheim Fund
Z.XVII.120

53
Portrait of Jacqueline
Portrait de Jacqueline
Cannes, 4 December 1956
Dated on plate
Colour lithograph, 38.5 × 52 cm
National Gallery of Victoria, Melbourne
Felton Bequest 1959
Bloch 827

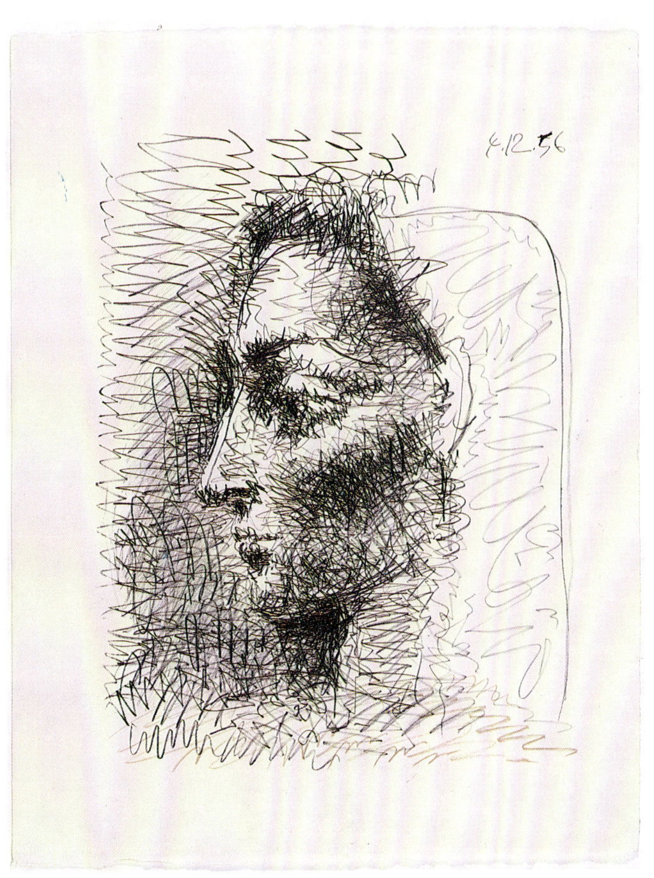

53

54
Reclining nude on a blue divan
Femme couchée sur un divan bleu
Vauvenargues, 20 April 1960
Signed top right: *Picasso*
Dated (verso): *20.4.60*
Oil on canvas, 89 × 115.5 cm
Musée National d'Art Moderne,
Centre Georges Pompidou, Paris
Donated by Louise and Michel Leiris, 1984
Z.XIX.279

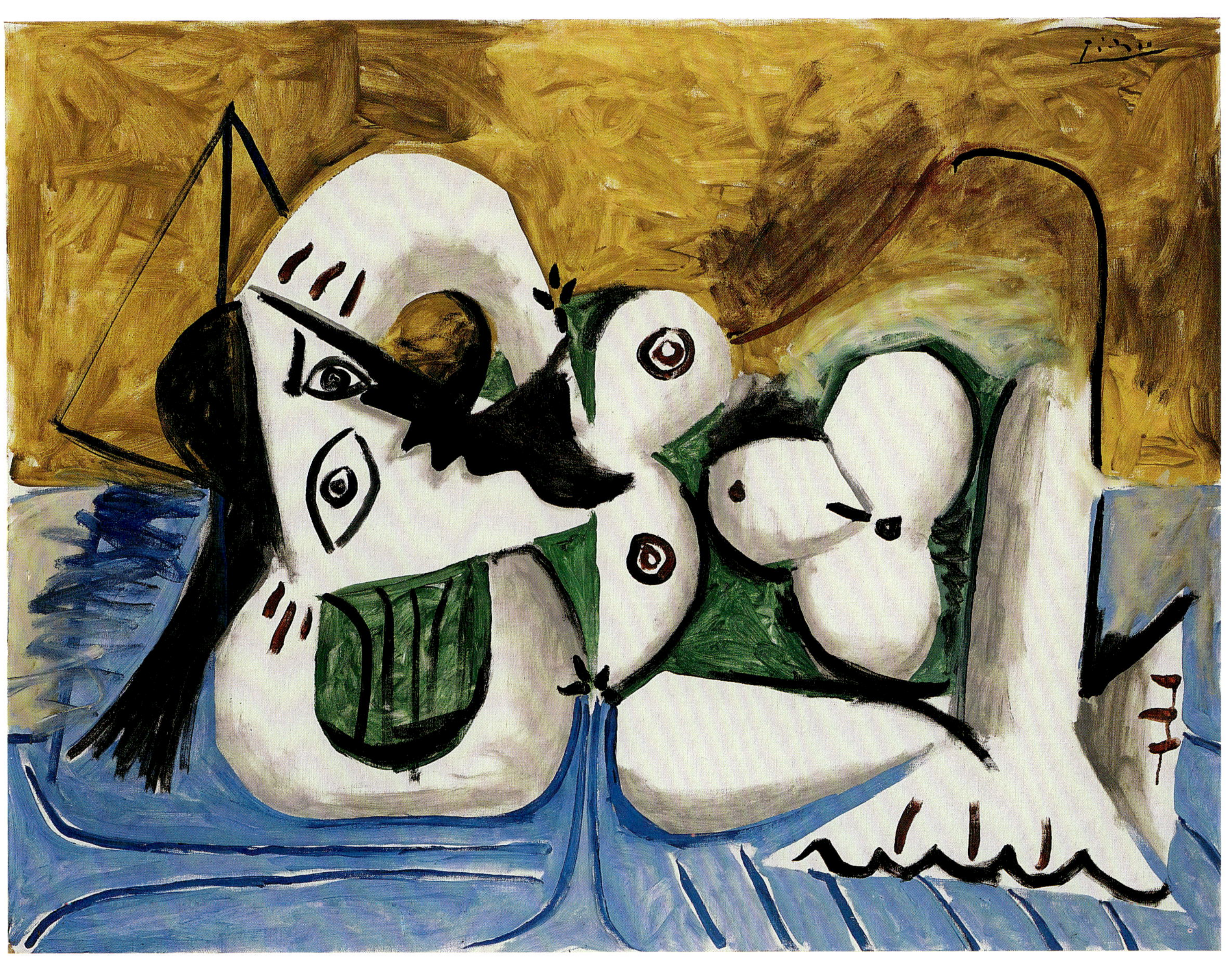

54

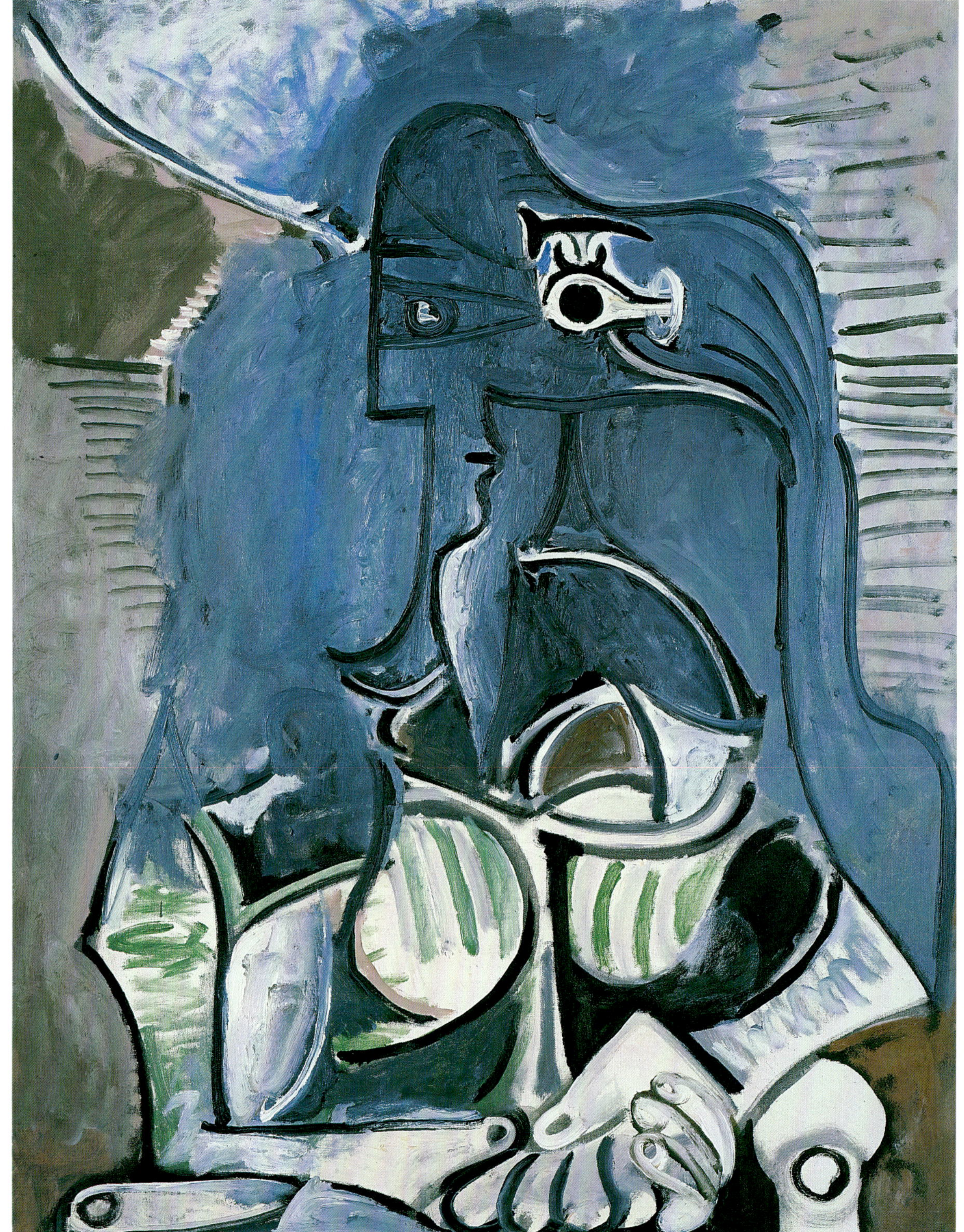

55

55
Woman with crossed hands
Femme aux mains croisées
Mougins, 1961
Oil on canvas, 116 × 89 cm
Collection Marina Picasso
Galerie Jan Krugier, Geneva
Z.XIV.409

56
Head of a woman
Tête de femme
Mougins, 4 June 1962
Signed top right: *Picasso*
Dated (verso): *4.6.62*
Oil on canvas, 73.3 × 55.2
Private Collection, England
Z.XX.250

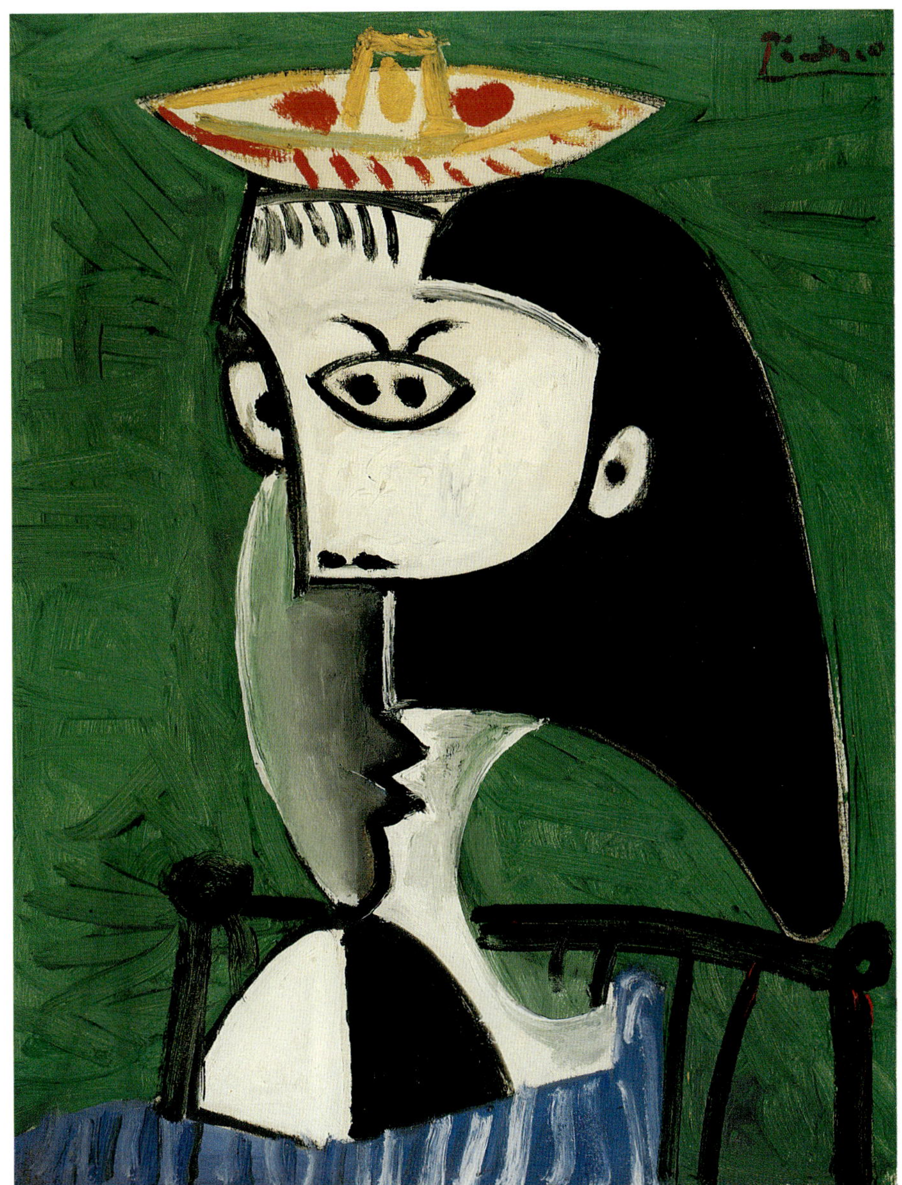

56

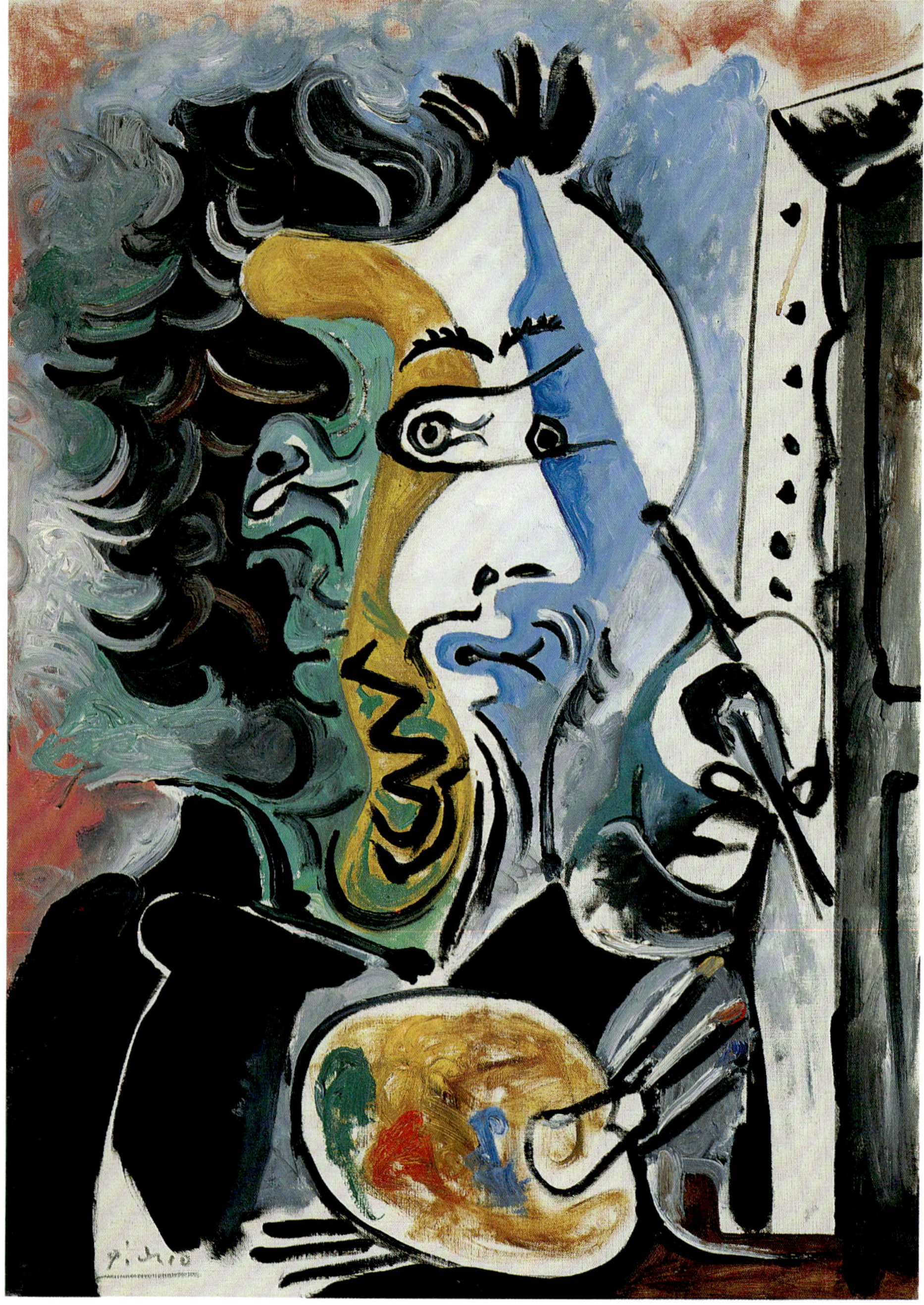

57

57
The painter
Le peintre
Mougins, 16 March 1963
Signed bottom left: *Picasso*
Inscribed (verso): *16/3/1963 II*
Oil on canvas, 92 × 65 cm
Galerie Louise Leiris, Paris
Z.XXIII.179

58
The painter and his model
Peintre et son modèle
Mougins, 1963
Oil on canvas, 81 × 100 cm
Collection Marina Picasso
Galerie Jan Krugier, Geneva
Z.XXIII.159

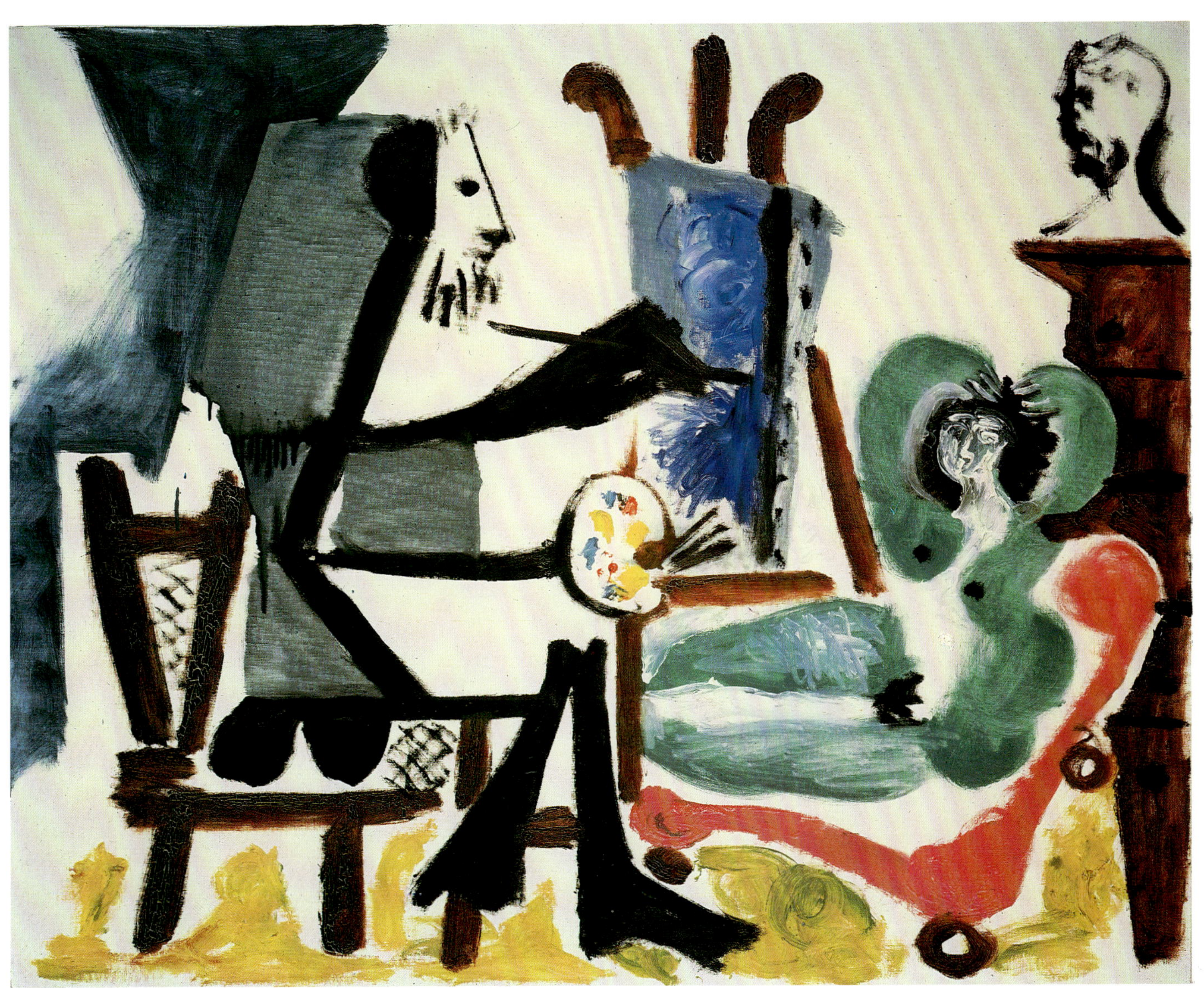
58

59
Lobster and cat on the beach
Homard et chat sur la plage
Mougins, 14 January 1965
Signed top left: *Picasso*
Dated (verso): *14/1/65 I*
Oil on canvas, 89 × 130 cm
Galerie Louise Leiris, Paris
Z.XXV.14

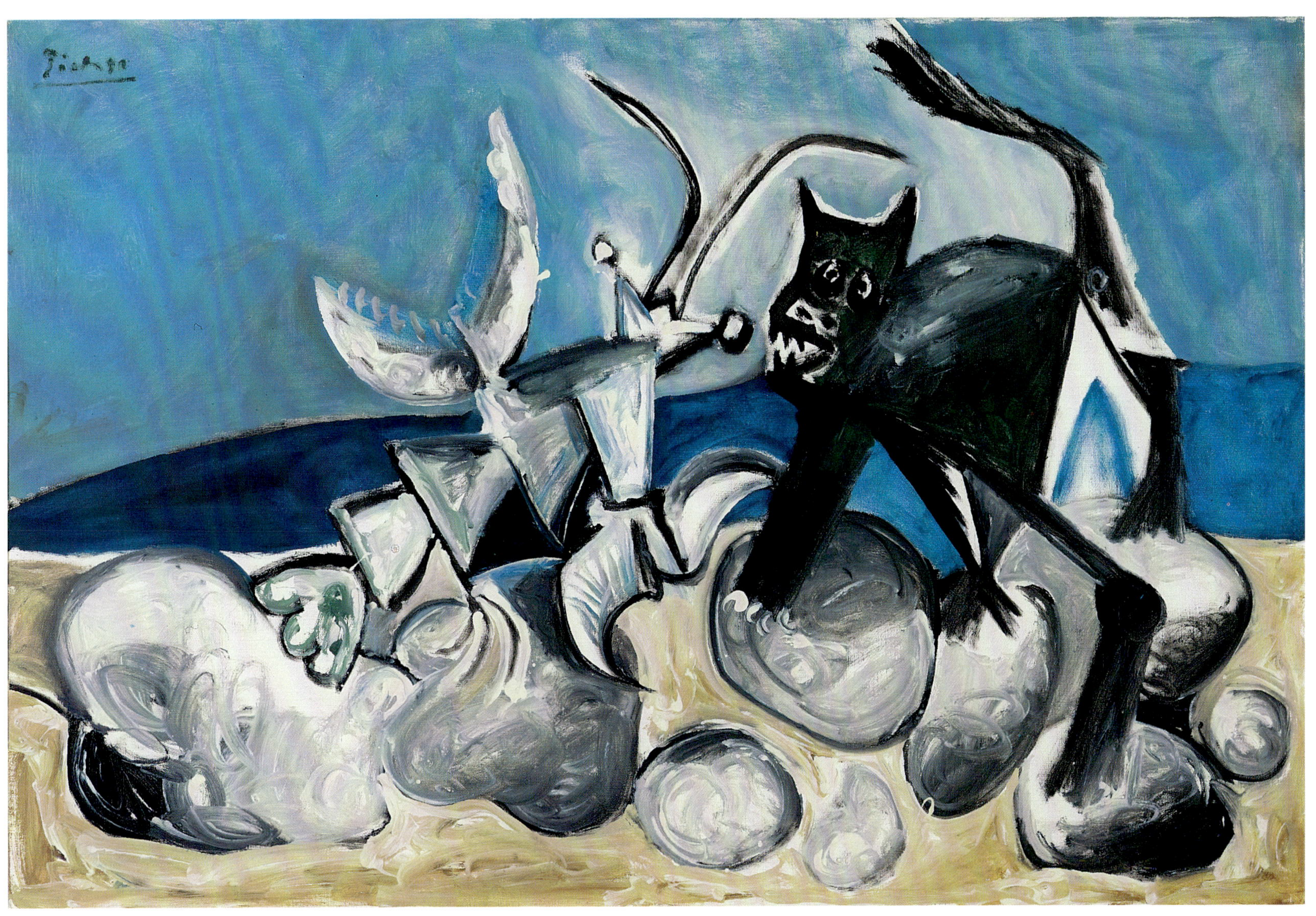

59

60
The aubade
L'aubade
Mougins, 20 February 1965
Signed top right: *Picasso*
Dated (verso): *20/2/65 I*
Oil on canvas, 130 × 195 cm
Didier Imbert, Paris
Z.XXV.42

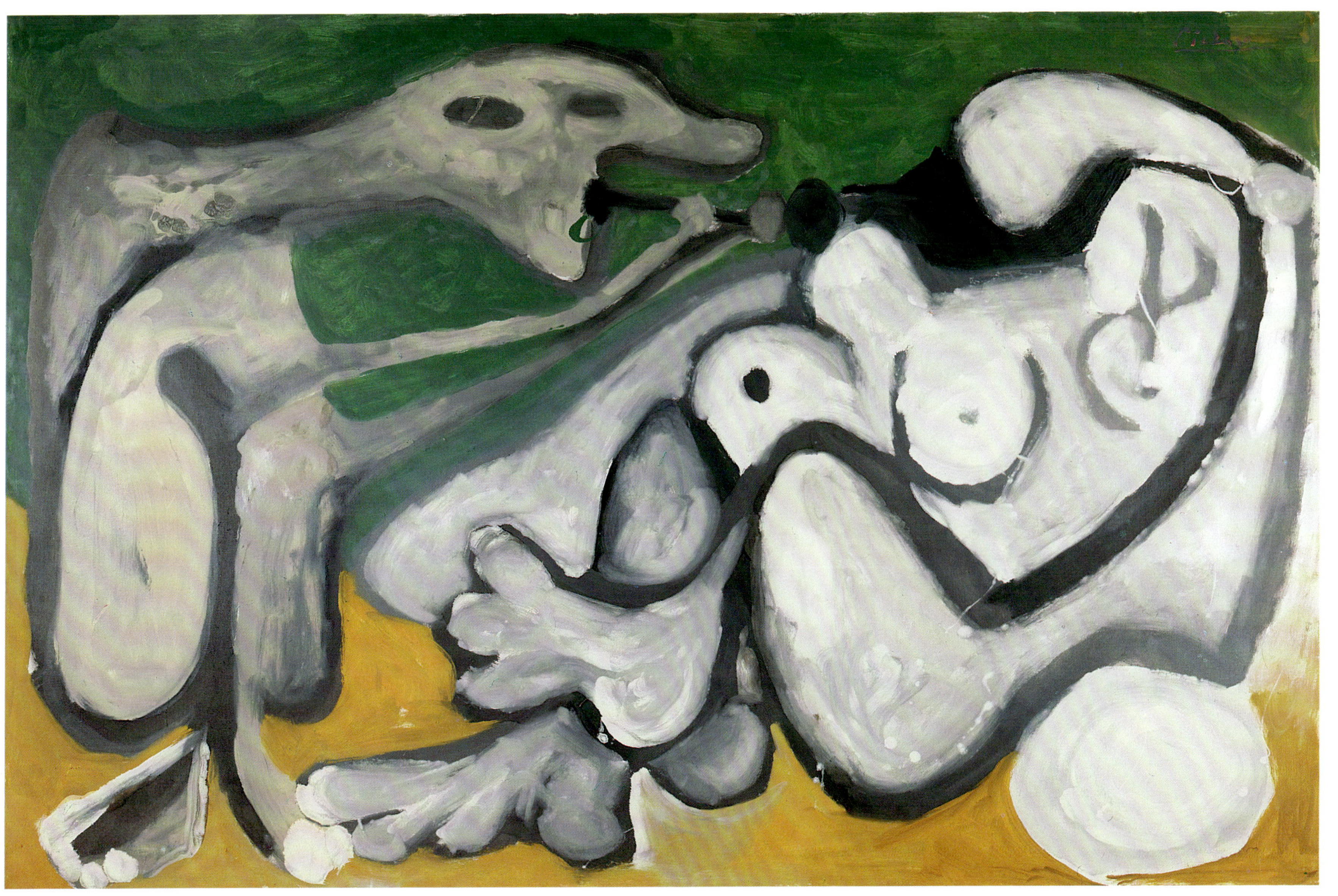

60

61

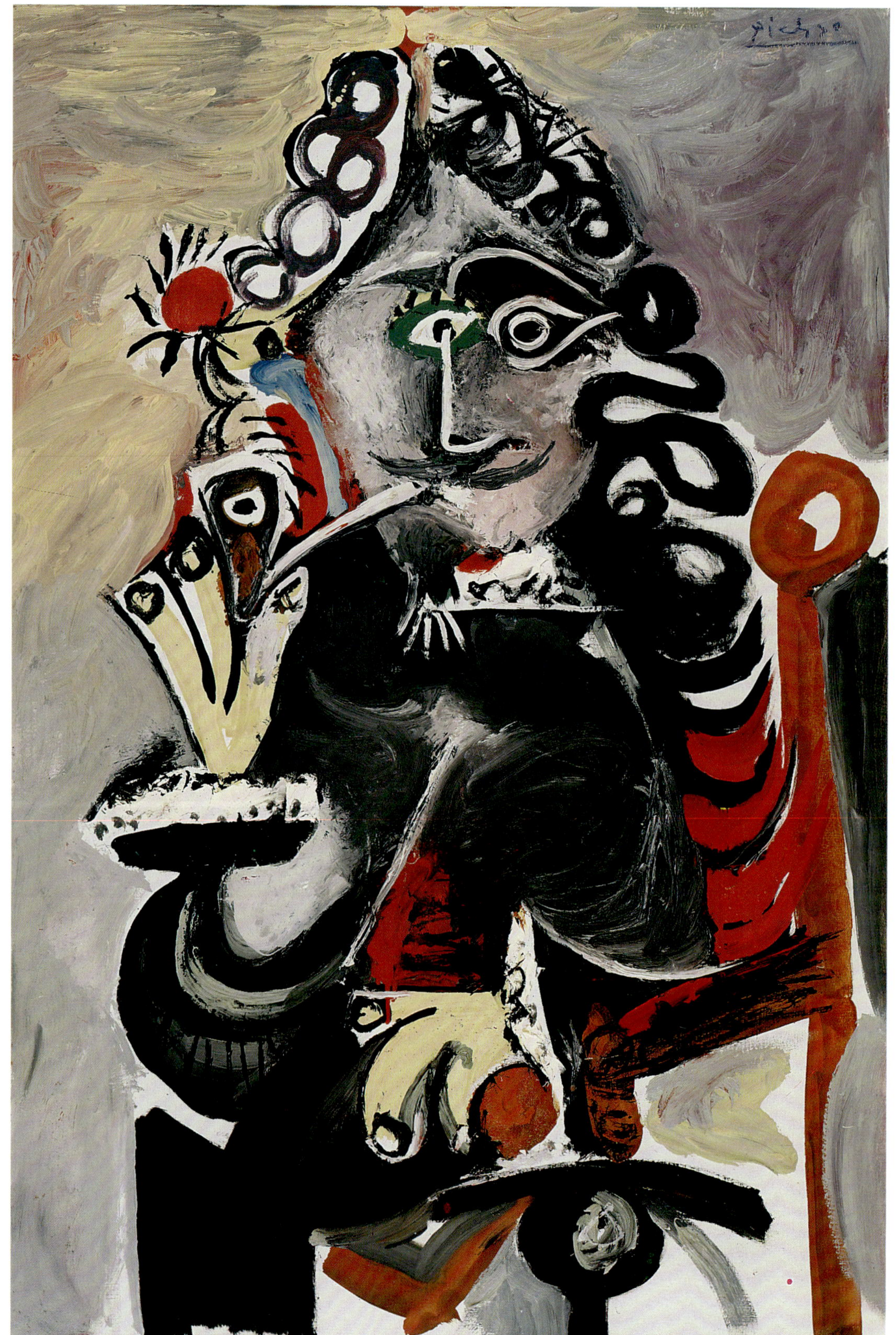

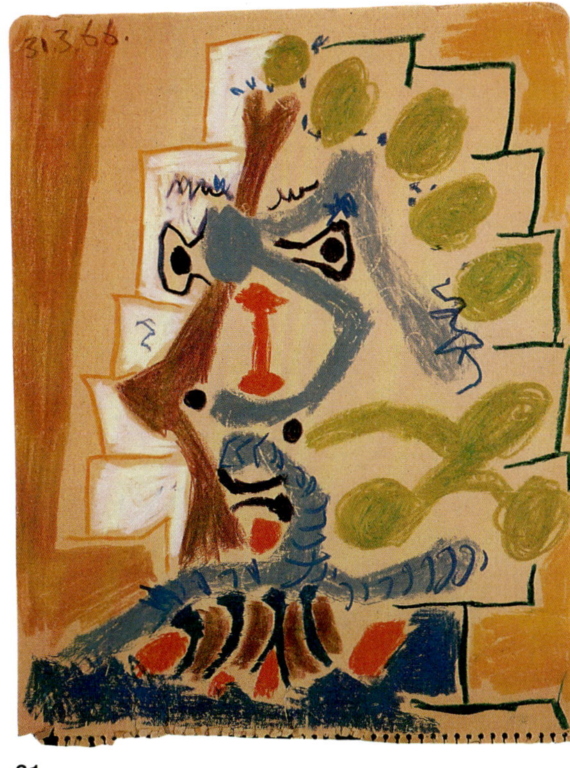

62

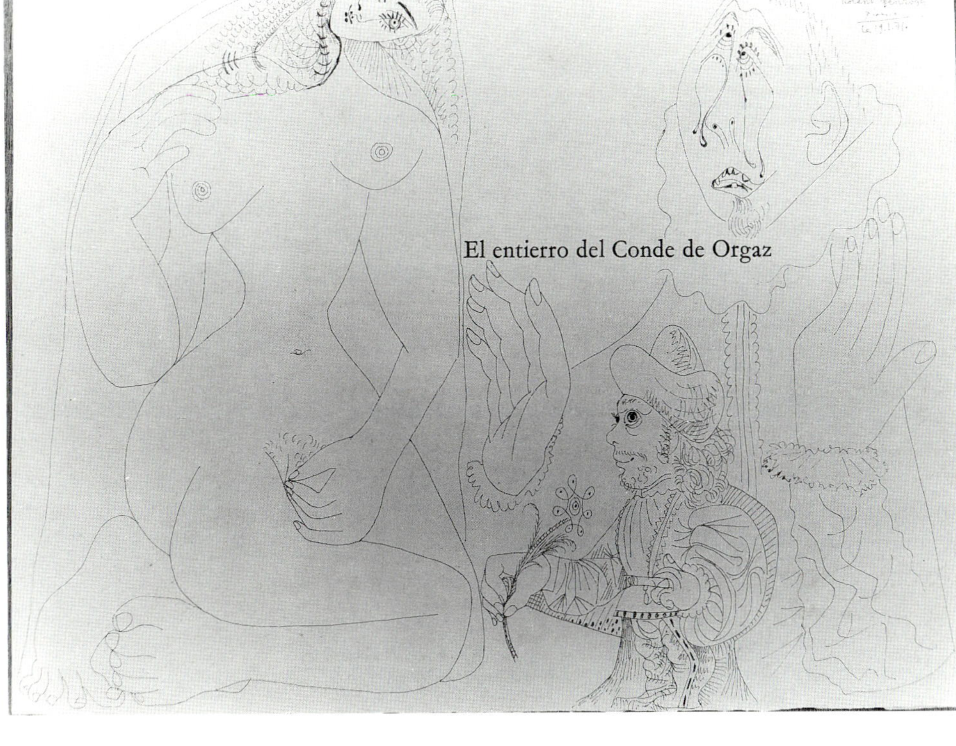

63a

61
Musketeer with a pipe
Mousquetaire à la pipe
Mougins, 13 October 1968
Signed top right: *Picasso*
Dated (verso): *13/10/68 I*
Oil on canvas, 146 × 97 cm
Galerie Louise Leiris, Paris
Z.XXVII.341

62
The painter
Le peintre
Mougins, 31 March 1966
Dated top left: *31.3.66*
Coloured crayon on paper, 31 × 24 cm
Private Collection
Courtesy Rex Irwin Art Dealer, Sydney
Not in Zervos

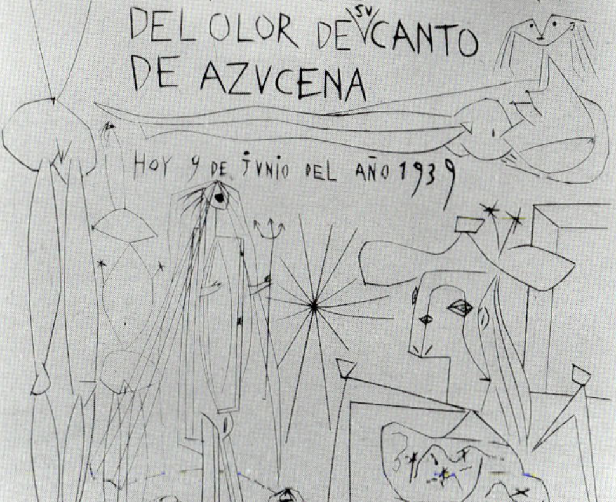

63b

63
The burial of Count Orgaz
El entierro del Conde de Orgaz
Drawing and series of prints accompanying the text of Picasso's play, published by Gustavo Gili, Barcelona, October 1969
Private collection, England
Bloch 1465-1477

a. Half-title of the main text with drawing by Picasso inscribed:
Pour mon ami/ Roland Penrose/ Picasso/ le 19.1.71
Pen and ink on paper, 37.5 × 47 cm

b. 'Trozo de almibar', Paris
Dated on plate: *9 de Junio . . . 1939*
Burin engraving, 34.5 × 24.5 cm

Twelve engravings, 21.8 × 32 cm
Mougins, 1966-7
Dated on plates: c. *15.11.66. III*
d. *11.11.66. VIII* e. *15.4.67. IV*
f. *Dimanche 4.12.66. 5h1/2*
g. *11.12.66. II* h. *17.4.67. II*
i. *3.12.66. II* j. *15.11.66. II*
k. *16.12.66. II* l. *3.12.66. I*
m. *15.11.66. IV* n. *2.12.66. III*

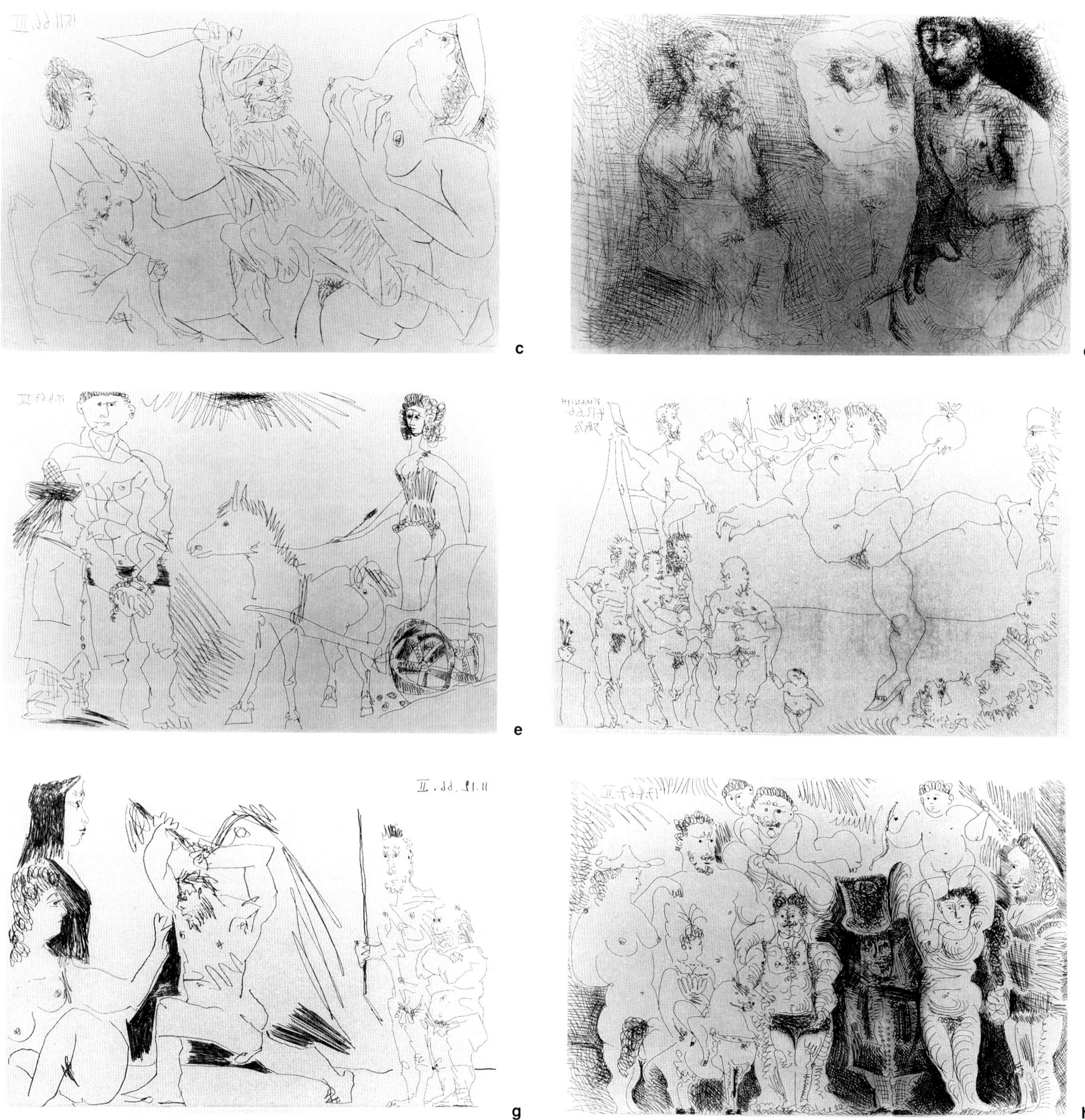

c

d

e

f

g

h

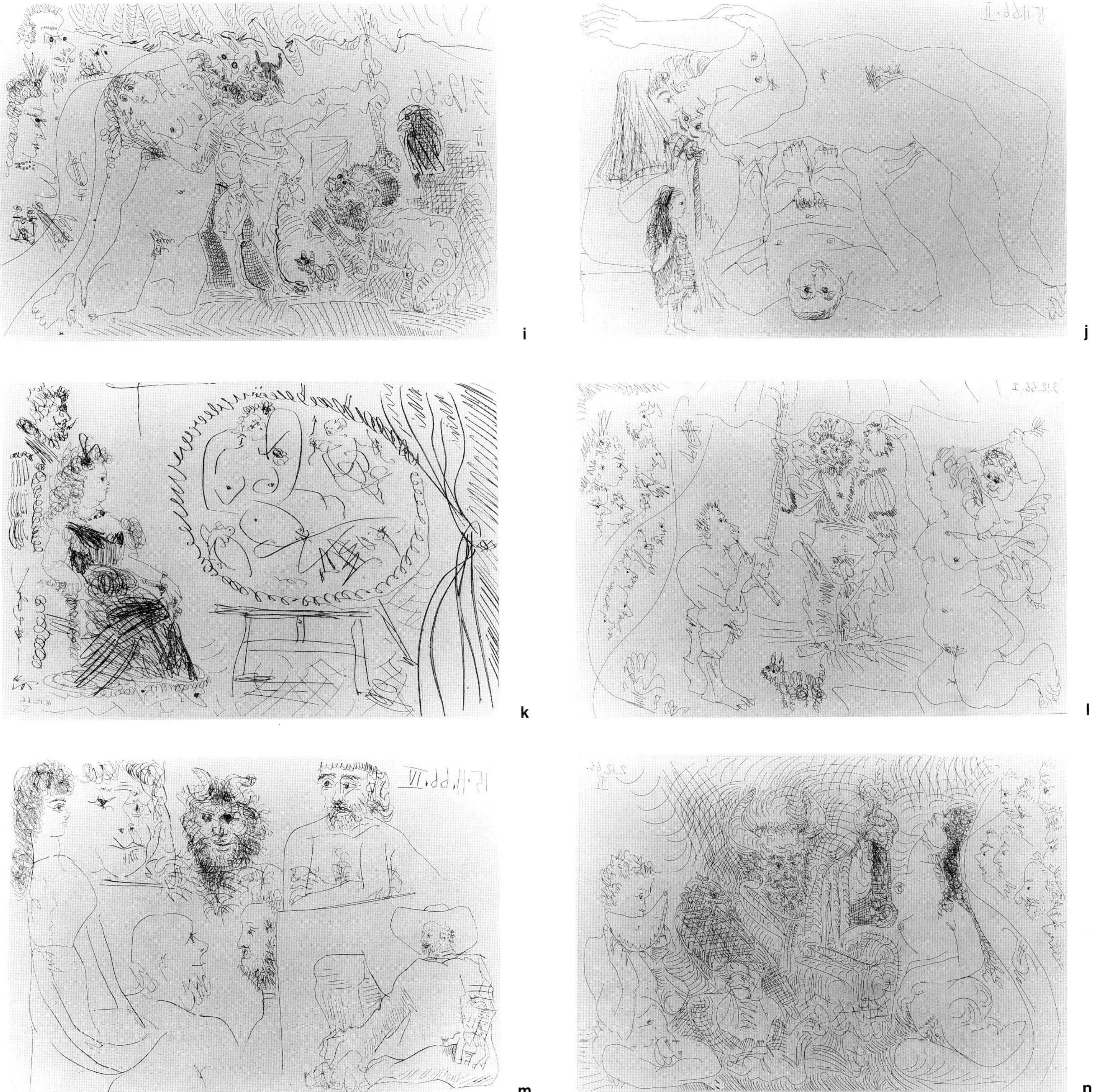

i j k l m n

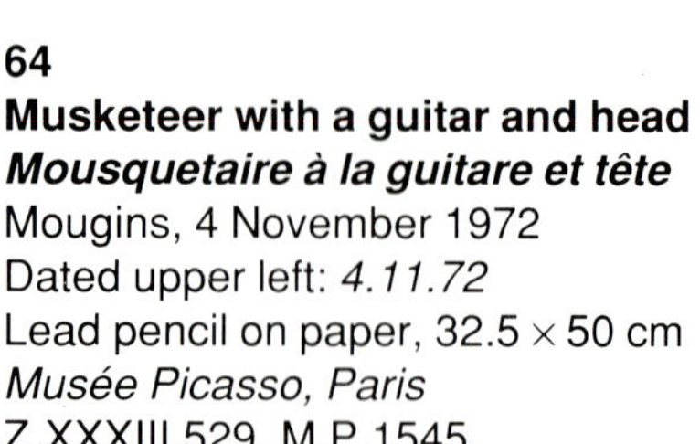

64
Musketeer with a guitar and head
Mousquetaire à la guitare et tête
Mougins, 4 November 1972
Dated upper left: *4.11.72*
Lead pencil on paper, 32.5 × 50 cm
Musée Picasso, Paris
Z.XXXIII.529. M.P.1545

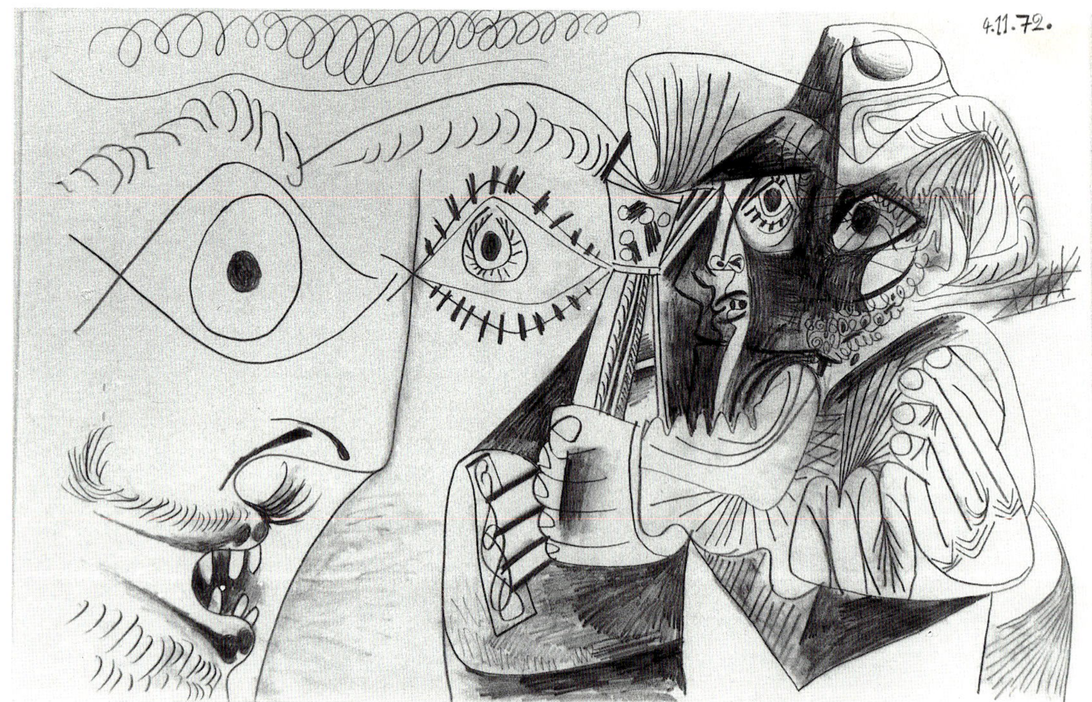

64